FROM ORPHAN
TO
HIGHFLYER

CW01654664

Denis Elliott, Malta, November 1951.
For more photos please visit
www.fromorphantohighflyer.com

FROM ORPHAN TO HIGHFLYER

by Denis Elliott and Philip Martin

Copyright © 2019 by Denis Elliott and Philip Martin.
All rights reserved. This book or any portion thereof
may not be reproduced or used in any manner whatsoever
without the express written permission of the authors
except for the use of brief quotations in a book review.

CONTENTS

INTRODUCTION

Though the idea for this book didn't come to me until April 2018, its roots can be found many years in the past.

I first met Denis at the age of ten when he had decided to bring his decades of driving to a close. Following this decision, he subsequently sold his car to my mother after a mutual friend put the two of them touch, knowing that the specifications of the car that Denis was selling, matched what my mother was looking to acquire.

A friendship between us did not instantly blossom. In fact, my earliest memory of Denis is of him rebuffing my offer to play a game of chess with him. Fortunately, a friendship between my mother and Denis did come about and from that time, whenever a Sunday lunch was cooked, Denis would be one of the invited guests.

As I entered my teenage years, a strong interest in history was born within me and it was then that I began to ask him questions and realise what calibre of a man was sat around our table. A man who has witnessed and experienced so much in his life, who came from, and lived through, an era that is studied by millions around the world yet for the generations of the modern era, is so hard to comprehend. The Second World War defined his generation, it remains the greatest conflict in human history. A conflict that spanned the globe, fought in every condition imaginable. From the Jungles of Burma, the deserts of North Africa, the plains of Russia, across Europe and the oceans of the world. In the towns and cities of multiple continents and in many other fields, both rural and urban, sweltering and freezing, humid and arid. A war in which ideologies clashed, empires died, borders changed, and in which tens of millions died. It was a war that irreversibly changed the world, the like of which we as humans will hopefully never experience again.

To have Denis sat before me, a man who left his adolescent years and entered adulthood as the war progressed and bore witness to German aircraft in the skies of Britain. Someone who experienced the daily life of rationing and blackouts, and a pilot who flew many iconic aircraft in numerous countries around the world. He experienced things that people now read about as taking place in a bygone time with little in common with the modern era. To have him sat before me, answering my questions and telling me about his experiences was worth its weight in gold, to put it mildly.

What really opened the door that exposed me to it all took place when I was seventeen and over the course of a Sunday lunch. Denis asked me if would be willing to help him maintain his rather large garden, as it was beginning to become too much for him. It was an offer I gladly accepted.

From then on, a new world opened up to me. Once work was finished, we would sit and talk, and I would steer the conversation to his RAF service, which he was all too happy to tell me about. It was during this time that I first bore witness to his wonderfully preserved log books, combing through them with awe and fascination, seeing the written entries of the various operations and exercises that he had told me about. It was wonderful, pointing out a specific entry, asking him what happened and then listening to him recount the event with such a high level of detail and eloquence.

As my friendship with Denis reached new heights, so did his with my mother. What started out as the occasional lunch on Sunday soon grew to shopping twice a week and days out, with Sunday becoming a permanent fixture.

Despite all of this, writing a book with Denis about his life never really crossed my mind. Besides, he had informed me a few times during casual conversation that there had been people who wanted to interview him regarding his wartime service, to be used in publications, but that he was just not interested.

The real catalyst for this book was that in April 2018, Denis became very ill which culminated in a fall and a subsequent stay in hospital. I visited Denis every day which resulted in me having a lot of time to think about things during the drive to and from the hospital. It came to my mind that it was a crime that a man who had fought in one of the greatest conflicts humankind has seen, had not recorded his story. It seemed a great shame not to have some record of a man who has lived such an incredible life, whose memory was still unbelievably sharp and who still possessed all his logbooks and other records. These stories needed to be available to the wider public. To me, there has always been huge value in the personal stories of people. While it is always worth studying a battle or an operation in terms of the numbers involved, troop movement, and other similar perspectives, reading or hearing the personal stories of an individual who took part in the battle or event adds another dimension to it. The personal touch of those individual stories adds an emotional and unique depth and value. It takes one right into the heart of whatever battle or event one is reading about. Still, I didn't expect him to say yes to my proposal of writing a book about his life. Denis has never been one to openly talk about his RAF service or to go on parade or attend events. There is always a humble tone whenever he talks about it. To him, it seems to be nothing special. Denis is also quite a private man so I doubted that he would want to share his stories with the world. Still, I had to try, knowing what would be lost if his life story remained locked away within his mind.

One afternoon, Denis was sitting up in his hospital bed and appeared to be in good spirits. After a few minutes of conversing, I told him that I wished to propose something to him. I explained the idea of the book to him; how we could help to further shine a light onto the war in the Far East and on to the flying side of it. I imagined this is something that isn't always thought about. Also, that it would be a nice tribute to the men he fought alongside. I suggested that lessons could be passed on to current and future generations. That it would be a wonderful legacy for him, and that for both of us, 2018 would be quite a symbolic year, being the hundredth anniversary of the RAF and the centenary of the end of the First World War. I then explained my ideas on how the book could be structured and formatted but assured him that these were just suggestions and that he could change all of the ideas if he wanted to. He thought about it and then told me that we should do it, which caught me by surprise. For the rest of Denis' stay in hospital, we discussed chapter ideas, topics to cover, everything that one can talk about in relation to creating a book. Before long, we were both looking forward to getting started.

Once Denis was out of hospital and settled into his new home, we began in the first week of May. Though it was unfamiliar territory for the both of us, we quickly found a rhythm and got into the swing of things, bouncing ideas off one another as we discussed Denis' life from childhood until the fall which resulted in the idea for this book. As we spoke, I really saw how sharp Denis' mind was; how it can work at such a quick pace as he recounted childhood stories in an effortless manner, remembering the smallest detail. Some of which happened over ninety years ago. Fortunately, this rich memory would not only apply to his childhood, but also to every other period of his life. He would speak in an almost soft tone, his emotional state reflecting the story which he was recounting. Denis would always recount the part of his life we would talk about with acute, detailed recollection, though the mood would reflect the topic at hand. A sombre, saddening atmosphere would descend as Denis, sometimes shedding tears, would recount his awful childhood, yet he would spring to life with laughter and quick energy as he recounted tales of flying across the world. To witness this incredible human being delve into the depths of his past with such honesty and energy, while always being very polite and open has been the greatest honour of my life.

Over the course of the summer, we worked most days and were making good progress, but in late August, Denis had another fall, but miraculously, didn't break anything and came away from it unscathed. It was something we hardly spoke about, but from then on, we began working seven days a week, from September until December, when the first draft was finished. Since then, it has been a case of editing, inserting additions and polishing. During this whole process, Denis' enthusiasm and seemingly boundless reserves of energy have been a sight to behold. For hours he recounted stories, or read through what we had written, or suggested new ideas, without seeming to fade at all. There were times when I was tired and Denis would look at me with a twinkle in his eye and ask me if I wanted to continue, which we would.

This book is written in a question and answer format. This was done to ensure that Denis' words were written exactly as he said them, without having to be filtered and adjusted by me or anyone else and in the hope that you, the reader, will feel as though you are sitting here with us, listening to it all.

It is our hope that we have managed to construct this book in such a way that one will be able to read for themselves the incredible life that Denis has lived and will be able to gain value from it. We also hope that this book will help to shine more of a light on the war in the Far East, that we have successfully added to the collective knowledge of human history and that lessons can be learnt from it. Denis never banned any topic from being spoken about during our conversations, so if any questions or topics are missing from this book, it is only due to my shortcomings in formulating and asking the right questions.

Philip Martin

CHAPTER ONE

A BRUTAL CHILDHOOD

Life in the orphanage, foster parents and strict schools.

It is said that the formative years of someone's life have a strong influence on the person that they become. Your formative years were largely spent in an orphanage in West Norwood, London, so it's quite plausible to say that your life could have turned out very differently.

Yes, had I been with my own parents, it would have been different. A prime example of that is when I was a child, I was watching my friends play cricket and one of them called over to ask me if I wanted to join them, I replied that it was best if I didn't, otherwise my mother would scold me and he replied 'She's not your mother, you're only fostered'. It's little things like that which can add up and have a negative effect on a child.

I was born in Croydon and spent most of my childhood being brought up by foster parents, firstly in Orpington, Kent and then in Farnborough, a small village on the outskirts of Orpington.

Under what circumstances did you have to go into an orphanage?

My first memory is of me sitting on my mother's lap, I must have been around two and a half. We were both looking at the fire and I asked what the sparks were, and she told me that the sparks represented people going to church.

But to this day, I am not entirely sure why I went into the orphanage. My best guess is that my mother had an illness like cancer that she knew was going to kill her. I remember her visiting me twice while I was in the orphanage. The first time she brought us pears, the second time, toffees. During her visits, we would converse in the courtyard with my half-brother Harold, who was in the junior house. The orphanage was split into three tiers: infants, juniors and seniors. Infants - until one reached the age of five and started school, then one was transferred to juniors and then if my memory is correct, when one turned twelve or thirteen, they were moved into the seniors. However, I never went into the seniors as I left the orphanage when I was seven.

What about your father?
To this day, I still have no idea who my father was or what happened to him. But when I came across a copy of my birth certificate later in life, I discovered that he had been a milkman.

Growing up in an orphanage, especially in the 1920s, when British society still had similarities and links to the Victorian era, could you describe what memories you have of the orphanage?
My main memories are of how strict and regimented day-to-day life was. I was too young to go to school when I first arrived, which was when I was around three and a half years old and one has to remember, that in those days, one didn't start school until the age of five.

The place was run by females who we had to call 'Sisters' and they were rather cruel people, always ready with a ruler to wrap you over the knuckles if you did anything wrong, which your own parents would never do.

So, it was a very rigid, very disciplinarian type of upbringing. I guess it lacked love, the individual connection that every child needs. In its place, you had this cold, rigid, disciplinarian upbringing.
Very much so. It was a junior version, if you like, of an army regiment, it was run on very strict lines. No affection, love or anything like that was shown to me or any of the other boys. There were quite a few of us, all around the same age with the oldest being around seven, but even so, there was always a lingering fear in the air of being punished for doing something wrong, for committing an infraction of some kind.

As a result of living in such an environment, did you boys band

together and become close? What was the relationship like between you all?
Between us, there was no difficulty at all, we were in it together and it wasn't just the one dormitory, there were two, so there was a fair number of us all in it together. We all got on quite well.

A few of us started school at the same time; I still remember that school. I was five years old so it was after the summer of 1929. It had a very tiny playground and there was only one master (teacher). The philosophy of education there was learning by rote, in other words, by repetition. I remember that we were given a frame inlaid with slate and a piece of chalk, with which I learnt how to write the alphabet, my name, birthday, various words and things like that. I was in that school for two years, until I was seven. At that point, I moved in with the first foster parents and that included a change of schools.

I remember that a group of us were walking home from school one day during the winter and we were scraping ice out of the gutter by the road and eating it. It was on this occasion that one of the boys was killed. He was trying to scrape ice out of the gutter when he was hit by a car. His head smashed against the corner of the curb which split his head open exposing his brain, which was grey. Being five years old, I didn't know what colour a brain was, at the time I didn't even realise it was a brain. Five years old and having to witness something like that, I can still picture the incident now.

While we're on the subject of winter, I remember my first Christmas at the orphanage, I was about three and a half. The boys and girls were all seated in the dining hall at a big table, the girls at one end, then the senior boys, then junior boys and then us infants at the other end. We had all been told that Father Christmas was coming to see us so we were all quite excited. Then he came out of the kitchen and started walking down my side of the table giving every child an apple while saying 'Ho ho ho!'. When I saw him, such a big man, with a big beard and red robe, it terrified me. So when it was my turn to receive an apple, I dived under the table screaming ‘go away!’ I remember that. All the other children, who had seen Father Christmas before couldn’t understand what was going on. The House mother came over saying that he had an apple for me, but I just screamed that I didn’t want it, that he was a horrible man. Eventually he worked his way through the room, handing out apples and exited once he had finished.

So, the people who ran the orphanage did make sure that Christmas was celebrated.
Oh yes, they put on a Christmas lunch, which was when Father Christmas came to visit, resulting in my reaction. Also, the house mothers would tell us to put a sock at the end of our beds. In the morning, everyone had a little mouse made out of sugar in their sock and a tangerine, all of us except for the oldest boy at the end of the dormitory who was seven. He would often misbehave so he received a bar of soap. He was so upset by this that he burst into tears, it was the only time I saw him cry.

What sort of things would be deserving of a punishment in the orphanage?
One example was at the end of each room were chamber pots that we would use to urinate in overnight, we were only allowed to urinate in it though, nothing else. Well one morning, a number two was found in one of the pots. We were marched downstairs in our pyjamas, the ‘Sisters’ then proceeded to put us over their laps, took our trousers down and proceeded to examine our bottoms for evidence. It turned out to be the oldest boy, so he was dragged away for punishment. I never found out what punishment he received. This was the same boy who had a bar of soap put in his sock at Christmas.

Another example that sticks in my mind is when I was being taught how to put on boots for the first time, as opposed to the shoes I was used to. Boots of course, required lacing up, which one of the ‘Sisters’ was showing me how to do, but whenever I made a mistake, she would whack me over the knuckles with a ruler. There are two examples.

So, what did you do at the orphanage on a day-to-day basis. What did they try to teach you?
The day began with us all getting up together at the same time, then downstairs to have a shower or strip wash, then back upstairs to get into our ordinary clothes. After breakfast, we would go to school if it was a school day, and if not, then the day was spent playing games inside or out in the school yard.

On one occasion, I was playing tag with another boy out in the yard, he tripped over, broke his leg and began howling. He was carried inside and I was called in soon after, where I was told that I had been a wicked boy for breaking his leg despite the fact that I was nowhere near him. But even so, I was still caned over the knuckles for being such a naughty boy.

So you entered the orphanage at three-and-a-half-years-old and left at the age of seven?
I arrived when I was around three-and-half-years-old and was there for roughly three-and-a-half to four years, until I was seven.

It's always hard to try and get someone to analyse themselves and the effects that spending their first years in a place like that can have, but did being raised in such an environment and experiencing what you did have an effect on you as a person growing up?
Very much so, not only in my myself, but I noticed a lack of confidence in anything I tried to do that was a bit out of the ordinary. It was a very unusual beginning to life and I would notice that older boys, say twelve or thirteen were partaking in activities, mainly sports, and I would say to myself, 'there is no way that I will ever be able to do that!' Even then, I had no confidence in my own ability.

It seems as though that living in an orphanage resulted in you not being allowed to explore, to form your own personality and as a result, you were quite limited in self-esteem and belief in what you could achieve.
Yes, exactly. Life was spent either in the orphanage, school or in

the grounds of the orphanage. The only time we went out of the grounds was across the road to church on Sundays, and even that was regimented. We had to march there. It wasn't a natural life like I saw the other boys having with their own parents.

So, when you had the option in school to take part in a sport, be part of a sports team, I assume that these things never came naturally to you.
What stood out in my mind was when teams were being assembled to play football, or something like that, I was never picked in any team or if I was, it would be last, as the captains knew that I wasn't any good. In cricket for example, there were two or three occasions when the batsman hit the ball straight at me and I turned around and ran away rather than try and catch it.

Eventually, you left the orphanage. What was it like to step into a slightly more normal environment, going from the orphanage to a foster family?
Well from the age of around seven right until I was called up by the RAF, I was brought up by foster parents. One day, the Welfare Officer of the orphanage collected Harold and myself. The three of us were taken by bus to Victoria bus station, from there we walked to Victoria railway station and taken by train to Orpington railway station. Once there, we were met by a couple who were to be our first foster parents. To my surprise, the man was wheeling a pram with a toddler inside. I tumbled over and was asked by my new foster faster if I was tired to which I replied that I was. So he took the toddler out of the pram and put me inside, and I feel asleep. Once there, we were bedded in a box bedroom, with myself in the bottom bunk and Harold in the top one.

But overall, despite monthly visits by the Welfare Officer to check up on us, living with them was a terrible experience. At first it was Harold and I. But after a few weeks he left. The reason I was given was that 'he was a bad example to you'. One occasion that comes to mind is when the foster father asked me to fetch a tool from the shed, I remembered that I had done this obediently on another occasion and Harold had told me that I was a timid mouse and that I should stand up for myself and next time, to tell him 'to get the bloody thing himself'. So the next time he asked me to get a tool from the shed, I said to him 'get the bloody thing yourself' in a raised voice. He was furious and asked me to repeat myself, so I did. He then downed his tools, I ran into the kitchen but he caught up with me, bent me over his knee and gave me a really hard smacking. The foster father was a violent, nasty man, in my opinion. I have memories of him beating his wife and beating myself.

One particular memory which shows how horrible a man he could be, was when I witnessed him violently attacking his wife whilst he was drunk. He had her on her back on the sofa in the living room, and she was screaming and trying to fight him off, I tried to drag him off and he simply picked me up with one arm and hurled me across the room. Luckily I landed in an arm chair, but he threw me with such force that if I had hit the wall, it probably would have killed me. I was only eight years old when it happened. Fortunately, the postman, who lived next door knew I was being mistreated and reported it to the council, he told me this later when I ran into him when I was twelve.

Was your first foster mother any different than your first foster father?

Yes, she was a nice person, but the trouble was that she couldn't go against her husband. One thing about my first foster mother is that she would sometimes bake cupcakes in the morning and they would be cooling in the tray as I left for school so I would take one so I would have something to eat. I thought that she never noticed until I ran into her after the war and she told me that she had known every time but had never mentioned it to her husband or he would have beaten me.

Anyway, it was while I was living with the first foster parents that I saw the sea for the first time. I was eight years old. All the parents in our road organised a trip for the children to visit the sea. For this, we went to Margate. There was a girl of around twelve in charge of the small group of children that I was a part of. She said: 'Look, there's the sea'. There was a road with a roundabout with a fountain in the middle which ran next to the sea and I thought she was referring to the fountain, so I came out with something like 'is that it?' 'No,' she said, and directed my eyes to the sea. Upon seeing it I was absolutely transfixed, it was love at first sight. We went on the beach and the other children who had been to the beach were taking off their shoes and socks, so I followed their lead. Once I was paddling, the girl told me to dip my finger in the sea and taste it. It was then that I learnt that the sea was salty. I remember that we then went for fish and chips. I have always remembered seeing the sea for the first time. I still love it, even now.

On one occasion my first foster parents went to the circus. I was left in the house on my own. The house was lit by gas lamps and I was warned not to try and light them. They hid the matches anyway. This was during the winter as it got dark quite early. I was in a pitch black house on my own and was scared, so I went and sat on the front step and started sobbing. Mr Davidson and his wife who lived over the road heard me so came and comforted me and invited me into his house, where he poured me a glass of milk and gave me some cake, which cheered me up. Eventually my foster parents returned and me being not there, started calling my name which caused Mr Davidson to go out and give my foster father a piece of his mind, which caused quite a row. Once it was over, my foster father ordered me to bed.

Not long after that event, my first foster father brought home a goldfish that he had won at a fairground. This inspired me to write a story for a contest at my school. I was still in infants' school but it was a new one that I had transferred to when I moved in with the first foster parents. I wrote a story about how goldfish breathe without lungs and won first prize, which was a book about Robin Hood.

Later on when I was still in junior school, I believe that the headmaster also raised concerns with the council about my foster father. Basically, if you arrived after the school bell was sounded by the prefect, a mark was noted in their book. If you received three marks in one week, you were caned. I usually went without any sort of breakfast and I was made to wash all the dishes that were covered in cold grease before leaving for school. If I was lucky, I received a strip of bacon or something. Anyway, all this caused me to be late more often than not, which resulted in weekly canings. One day I just broke down and started sobbing. The headmaster asked me what the problem was and I told him everything. A few weeks later, I was sent to live with the second pair of foster parents in Farnborough and transferred to another school there.

Were the second pair any better than the first?

When I arrived at their house for the first time, my new foster mother opened the door and said the following, these were her exact words 'Oh good, a darkie, perhaps he will bring us some luck'. I have never forgotten that. She was always quite a superstitious woman.

But yes, living with them was much better, I was given some freedom and a deal of responsibility that I wasn't given in the orphanage or with the first foster parents. For example we had a canary named Mickey, a cat named Peter, and a dog named Max. I was allowed to take Max out for walks on my own and I could go on shopping trips for my foster mother by myself. However, that's only one of a few examples where I can say that I had any freedom. I wasn't allowed out to play with other children, for example. But I will say that I wasn't alone there. I had been with my foster parents for about a year when I was joined by a boy named Billy who was four years younger than me. Though he was younger, it still provided us both with a partnership as we were both in the same situation. There was also an older boy named Tom who was there before I arrived.

What were the second set of foster parents like?

The foster mother was very strict and was fifty four when I went to live with them in 1933, I was nine. She was born in 1880, so as you can imagine, she practically embodied the Victorian era. She never showed any affection or love towards me or anyone, not even when I returned from overseas after the war. She viewed herself as of a higher class than she actually was. Once, when I was twelve, word had got around that one of the female members of the Royal Family had injured her leg so was walking with a limp, so my foster mother started to limp too, even though she was fine. I brought it up at the time, why she was walking that way, and it made her really angry. In her mind, walking with a limp brought her closer to the level of the Royal Family. She also had two ways of speaking, one to the welfare officers, neighbours, people like that, to make her seem better educated than she actually was, and then her actual way of talking which was littered with grammar and pronunciation mistakes. She hated it if you tried to correct her. These things made her feel special, as though she was of a higher class.

A good example of her strictness was when she gave me a block of jelly marked out in cubes which she told me to break up and put in hot water, which I did. As I was breaking the cubes, I started to say a rhyme of 'jelly belly, jelly belly' to myself. She yelled at me to stop and told me that she would not tolerate language like that in her house.

My second foster father was a lovely man, he could only walk with great difficulty. He was officially disabled due to an accident involving his back that he had suffered before my time that left him bent over. He was quite an understanding man. I only ever saw him lose his temper once. I can say that we really were good friends. He taught me many things, like how to repair punctures on bicycles, look after the chain and re-connect the links if they came apart and practical things in the house and out in the garden too. I would have liked him to have been my own true father; he was that kind of man. He was very good at woodwork and also enjoyed gardening. He used to grow his own vegetables and even used to cut the back lawn with hand shears.

Did you ever see Harold again?

Yes, but unfortunately it wasn't to last long. After he left the first foster family, he went to a village named St Mary Cray which was a couple of miles away from Orpington and Farnborough. After that I didn't see him for a few years until I was in secondary school. I must have been eleven, he was well into his teens by then. He waited for me outside the school gates and said that he wanted to talk to me, to have a proper conversation about the past. I had to be home straight after school so didn't stick around, otherwise I would be in trouble. I told my foster mother what Harold had told me and she warned me that he was 'a very wicked boy' and that I was never to speak to him under any circumstances.

So when I ran into him for the second time at Farnborough bus terminal, I just ran away. I never saw him again. I later learnt that during the war, he joined the Merchant Navy and was on the cargo ship, MV Nottingham when it was torpedoed in the North Atlantic. There were no survivors. How I wish I had spoken to him. I would have learnt so much and filled in so many gaps regarding my background and what happened. His name is on the Merchant Navy Memorial in London.

I remember you telling me that you also had a half-sister, whose brother was Harold.
Yes, she was eleven years older than me having been born in 1913. I can't say much about her as my memories of her are quite vague and I didn't find out that she was my half-sister until after the war, when the second foster parents' adopted daughter, Daisy, informed me that we were related. I never did see my half-sister following the war. I don't know what happened to her. To me, she was known as the 'egg lady' because she looked after chickens and sold eggs.

Not long after joining the second pair of foster parents, you broke your neck.
I must have been around nine when this happened. I was playing in the playground and tripped over and banged my head on the ground, a very hard surface. The result was vertebrates five and six in the neck were broken. I was taken home. I didn't go to hospital. I was placed in a position with pillows around my neck so I couldn't move. The family doctor was called, who was quite elderly, and he

said that I had a sore throat and gave me something called 'Friars Balsam' to treat it. It was disgusting, a very bitter taste, so my foster mother used to pour it on to a sugar cube to mask the taste. It didn't really work, I could still taste it, I can still taste it now.

Eventually, the two vertebrates fused together. I would not find out about it until 1956 when I was in Malta and suffered another neck injury which resulted in a hospital visit.

When people think of the 1920s or the pre-war period, many tend to think of a more strict society, where among other things, public behaviour and expectations were clearly set. Is this portrayal true in your opinion?
I found that life changed considerably at the outbreak of war which coincided with the time I left school at the age of fifteen and started work. The way it most noticeably changed for me was that the men I had been working with were called up and I suddenly had more responsibilities. I found that I thrived on those responsibilities, and not just at work, but after work at night school where I went to study accountancy.

When the night school had to close because of the wartime blackouts, I joined the Air Training Corps and really expanded my abilities there. I passed exams and gained certificates and was finally able to tell myself that I was just as good as everyone else. For me, life changed in that way.

If we go back a bit, I recall you telling me once how your Secondary School was quite modern in its design for the time, but that the style of education, shall we say, stuck to the older methods. What was the school itself like?
Well, it was very large. There were around five hundred boys in the boys' school and a similar number in the attached girls' school. I first went there in September 1935, just after I had turned eleven and had passed the equivalent of the eleven plus. The school was named Orpington Central School.

The headmaster was a very strict man, very strict indeed and he would not only impose his strictness onto us boys but also onto the masters. In class, we weren't even allowed to whisper let alone make any other noise without the risk of punishment, as indeed I once discovered when all I did was whisper to the boy next to me 'I can't find my pen' and he replied 'well look in your desk' to which I replied that it wasn't in there. The master heard this, so I had to go to him and was promptly caned across both hands, three times in total. He was the sort of man who really caned you. It wasn't a tap, he would raise his arm above his head and put everything into it, to cause maximum pain. These canes were only thin bamboo canes so they really hurt. Caned three times just for saying that I couldn't find my pen, it was that sort of discipline.

On another occasion, I had received a fountain pen as a Christmas present from the sister of my second foster father. The problem with it was that it constantly leaked. Once, I was using it to complete some geography homework when it started to leak everywhere. I tried to clean it up with blotting paper but it wouldn't soak it all up, so there were still stains on the paper.. So when I was back at school, I handed in this homework. The geography master was quite angry and gave me a big lecture on the standards he expected for the homework he gave out and that mine was the most disgusting he had ever seen. I was then told to put out my hand and was then caned twice, but I disliked this master so much that I refused to let him see me cry. So I took it, and then just left the empty classroom. He was a big fat man, I can picture him now.

Punishments did not always lead to caning though. On one occasion, I was eating an apple, trying my best not to get caught when the boy sitting behind me put up his hand and told the master that I was eating. The master asked me if I was eating and I tried to hide the contents of my mouth under my tongue and tried to give an answer. I was told to spit the contents into the bin and not to do it again. The boy who told on me was then called up in front of the class and the master asked him how it felt to be a sneak, which was quite an insult.

As he made his way back to his seat, I whispered to him that I was going to sort him out at playtime. The master heard this and said in a quiet voice that nothing will happen at playtime. However, I was so angry with the boy that I would have half killed him if given the chance but by the end of the class, it was mostly forgotten about.

Looking back at your time in this school, do you feel as though the standard of education was good?
This school, which was a secondary modern, had a whole range of classes. It was on two levels, had around ten classrooms, plus a full-size gym with a range of sports equipment and every subject had its own master. The assistant headmaster taught maths. Then there were separate masters for Science, Woodwork, Gardening, Geography, History and English.

But the environment you were taught in, judging by the story that you told of being caned for whispering about your pen, it seems like that you were taught in an environment of fear and strict discipline.
Again, I go back to the word discipline, it was very, very disciplined. For example, when we went from class to class, we would have to walk in silence, in single file. The headmaster would patrol the corridors with his cane tapping against his heels, looking for anyone to step out of line. A prefect was appointed for each of the two levels of classrooms and they were responsible for reporting any boy who was caught running down the corridor, or breaking any other rules. The prefect would then have to report it to the headmaster and if they didn't, then the prefect himself would be in trouble, it was that kind of discipline.

What sort of things could get you in trouble, what sort of things were the prefects expected to report?
Well I have just given one example, anyone caught running through the corridor, or any boys caught speaking to each other, that was against the rules. We had to concentrate on going from wherever we had left to getting to wherever we were supposed to be going.

But I do have one story to tell you that shows how extreme discipline in schools could be.

What happened?
Well as I have mentioned, the school had two wings, one for the boys and the other for the girls, who were completely separated from us boys, even in the playground. On the occasion of this episode, a boy from a very poor family, who didn't have a father, was caught red handed stealing from boys' coats in the cloakroom. He must have been around thirteen at the time. He was immediately taken to the headmaster. The headmaster informed him that he would be caned in front of the school.

All of us boys were assembled in the hall. This boy was brought out on to the stage, stretched out face down on a table by masters and then caned across the backside by another master until he was screaming for mercy. It went on for several minutes in which the boy must have been caned around twelve times. The master caning him started with the cane above his head and really put a lot of force into it. It was such a cruel event that half of the boys in the hall were in tears at witnessing this cruel spectacle. The headmaster eventually called a halt to it and the boy himself was expelled. It left such a strong impression.

That is a truly horrific story. Do you know what became of that boy?
Sometime later, after the war had started, I heard that he had gone into the army and had reached the rank of sergeant.

Was this discipline evident in society at large or was it just limited to a few institutions like schools?
Oh, it was quite evident in day-to-day life. If a child was running around in the street, making too much noise then adults who knew the family, even if it was more as acquaintances, would often go and report it to the child's parents. That was quite common.

A classic example was 'scrumping' for apples in an orchard, which we had in our rural village. Before the war, that was definitely frowned upon and would land you in trouble with your parents. After the war, people didn't care so much.

Fortunately, things seemed to change after the war, incidents like the one I spoke about, with the boy being caned for stealing, that sort of brutality wasn't allowed to happen.

So, when you were growing up, would you say that there was a certain way that men, women and children were supposed to behave and that the people and society would enforce it?
Yes, certainly before the war, it was very Victorian, shall we say, the opinion that children should be seen but not heard being an example. My foster parents were typical examples of people who had been brought up during the Victorian era, my foster mother especially who had very strict rules and regulations over what could and couldn't be done.

You have spoken about how the girls were educated in a different wing of your school to the boys. Were boys and girls generally kept apart outside of school too?
Yes they were, especially in my case. I remember once, when I was about ten years old, a group of us boys were in the playground talking about girls we liked. When it was my turn to speak, I told everyone that I liked a girl named Joan. Everyone else thought that Joan was ugly because she wore a black eye patch but to me, she was beautiful. Anyway, one of my friends told me that if I liked Joan so much, I should write her a note telling her, so that's exactly what I did. My friend gave it to her one day and in it, I wrote 'Dear Joan, I love you very much and one day I want to marry you. Love Denis'.

One day I came back from school and my foster mother ordered me into the front room, which meant I was in trouble. Standing there was Joan's guardian. It transpired that Joan had put the note under her pillow and it had been discovered by her guardian. So, I was asked what this note was and if I had written it. When I confirmed that I had written it, I was chastised. Then my foster mother said the most unbelievable thing. She asked me if I loved the cat and when I said yes, she said something like 'see, that's love, what you wrote in this note isn't love'.

Joan's guardian did everything to keep us apart; she would even keep watch outside their front gate after school. However, over the next few years, we did meet up a few times - I would pretend to my foster mother that I was going to the ATC, but I have no idea what Joan told her guardian. Once, we went to a play about Latin American dancing, another time we went to the circus. I was posted out to Malta a few years after the war had finished and she asked me for an address to write to. I wrote to her three times without response and when I arrived home on leave, I noticed that their house had been boarded up. My foster mother told me that they had vanished in the middle of the night. To this day I believe that my letters were intercepted and my foster mother knew where they went.

How did things change for you as you got older?
Well for the first few years, I still lacked self-confidence and wouldn't stand up for myself but that changed as I got older, especially when I started work at fifteen once I left school.

In the first three years that I was with the second set of foster parents, there was an older boy who lived there named Tom, who I have already mentioned. I didn't really like him or get on with him too well. He was three years older than me and had quite a big build for his age. Because he was older and bigger than me, I looked up to him in the beginning, but despite this he used to bully me and bend me to his will. But on the other hand he would also act like a protector and ensure that no harm came to me. For example, he would force me to act as lookout for the police when he wanted to steal things like bicycles; anything that could be sold. I didn't want to but wished to avoid conflict so went along with it. Though as I said, he would often protect me.

Once we went to visit a friend of his who had a sister who must have been around sixteen. I was around twelve. She was a natural bully and started slapping me for no reason. Tom quickly saw what was going on and put a stop to it.

Tom had to leave the house when he was fifteen over a disagreement regarding his pay packet once he started work. What happened was that once a foster child started work, the council would stop paying the allowance that they gave to foster parents. Our foster mother expected him to hand over his pay packet for her to keep to make up for this financial loss, with him keeping the rest of it. But when she asked for his pay packet he absolutely lost it and a blazing row took place, a screaming match between the two of them. In his eyes, he had done the work, so he deserved to keep every penny of it. In the end, he stormed upstairs, grabbed a suitcase, packed all of his belongings in it, and stormed out.

Our foster father, in the only time that I had seen him angry, had tried to whack him with his stick and had accidently caught me. At that point, he lost all of his anger, and his immediate concern was me, and he kept asking me if I was alright. So Tom went to live with his best friend, who had the sister who slapped me, but that didn't work out too well as his friend's mother began demanding money as well, to cover his upkeep. In the end he intercepted me walking home from school one day and asked me to tell my foster mother that he wanted to come back. When I told her about this conversation that Tom and I had, she asked me if I wanted him to come back. I informed her that I didn't, and her reply was to state that in that case, he wasn't coming back.

So, there was Tom, and their adopted daughter Daisy who you mentioned earlier. Did they have any children of their own or look after any others?

They had a biological son of their own named Bert who when I went to live them, was already twenty-seven. Daisy was adopted by them when she was two and was around ten years older than me when I joined the family. Then there was Tom and myself, and then later on, just before Tom left, Billy joined us, I was eleven at the time and he was four years younger than myself. So including my foster parents, seven of us lived in the house at one time.

1929 to the early 1930s are synonymous with the Great Depression. Though you were young, do you remember the effects it had on Britain and to your two foster families?
I remember realising at the time that life was becoming more austere. But we lived in a tiny rural village, life generally seemed to carry on, the horrific conditions that the industrial parts of Britain went through didn't seem to affect us to such an extent. Our milk was still delivered by horse and cart in glass bottles. Everyone would watch the horse to see if it would have a poo in the road and if it did, it was quickly scooped up and put on allotments or on flower beds.

But I remember throughout the thirties, if we had toast, we would be allowed to have either butter or jam on it but not both. Despite both Bert and Daisy working, and money coming in from the council, money was still very tight. There were also a lot of men, many First World War veterans, out on the streets begging, or selling matches or some other items in an attempt to earn some money. Many of them had a limb or two missing and all of them on the street suffered from a shortage of money. There was no welfare state back them.

Aside from school and being at home, what other activities did you partake in, in your rural setting before the war started?
My main activity was being a member of the church choir. The first choir I joined was at All Saints Church when I was with the first set of foster parents in Orpington, the second choir was with St Giles Church when I lived with the second set of foster parents in Farnborough until January 1939. The commitment to the choir included mid week practice as well as Sunday services.

I remember that I used to take my own Bible into church services so I would have something to read. One day, one of the other boys stole it and I know that because I saw him holding it. When I asked him to give it back, he told me that he wasn't going to, which resulted in one of the older boys stating that there was going to be a fight for it at the back of the church. We all went there after choir practice where the other boys formed a rough circle. I threw a punch that landed on the boy's nose, causing it to bleed, and he started crying. By this point, the fight had been broken up and I got my Bible back.

Another thing that really sticks out is when I was out with the dog. I heard the distant rumble of thunder, and decided that it was best that I make my way home. Unfortunately, the storm moved faster than I did and before long I was caught in torrential rain. To get home, I had to cross a lane, which was bordered by thick hedging. I went through a gap in the hedge and pulled Max the dog close to me, giving him more shelter than I was getting myself. But eventually the rain eased enough for us to make a run for it. Once we were inside, my foster mother told me, 'You're soaking wet, get everything off'. I was eleven years old.

CHAPTER TWO

WAR IS DECLARED

Entering the workforce, the Air Training Corps, Biggin Hill and witnessing the Battle of Britain.

On September 3rd 1939, Britain declared war on Germany. Where were you at the time of this announcement?
I was in church listening to the vicar's sermon when a warden walked in and handed the vicar a piece of paper. It was read out and informed us that Britain was now at war with Germany and that we should all go home and listen to our radios. On the way home, an air raid siren suddenly went off but it turned out to be a false alarm, but at least everyone got to know what it sounded like as no one had heard one before.

When I arrived home, the atmosphere was one of apprehension, one couldn't help but talk about anything else. I asked my foster father how long he thought the war would last for, he looked at me and said 'Oh you'll never be involved'.

How did day-to-day life and society change?
Society quickly changed. Overnight, all the men who were fit and of military age were called up and children were soon sent off into the countryside which affected almost all families. Rationing was quickly introduced on the essentials like petrol, sugar and butter, but it soon expanded to include things like meat, eggs, cheese and children's sweets. Eventually, clothing became rationed too. Britain's entire industrial output was soon geared towards the war, so a factory that made cars was soon making tanks.

People were quickly encouraged to do more, so scouts were told to find things like metal gates which they were told would be melted down and turned into tanks and Spitfires. Women were encouraged to knit more, things like scarves and balaclavas and they were soon encouraged to join the labour force, mainly being sent into factories to make up for the number of men being called up.

But despite the apprehension, many people didn't believe that the war would last too long. It was the view that 'Oh it will soon be over'. It wasn't until Dunkirk happened that people really realised the significance of the situation and that the outcome wasn't so secure.

You had left school in the summer of 1939. What were you doing during those first war years?
Immediately after I left school, I started working in a town named Hayes as an assistant in an electrical showroom which itself was part of a chain. But there was a problem which resulted in my last name being changed. When I began working there, they required proof of age, so they contacted the authorities - I assume Kent County Council - to get a copy of my birth certificate, but they were unable to find one. The result was that my birth certificate was found but that my name was 'Denis Elliott' and not 'Denis Kimber'.

Why did you have the last name of 'Kimber' for first fifteen years of your life?
The reason I had been given the last name 'Kimber' was because I went into the orphanage with my half-brother, whose last name was 'Kimber', so they just gave me his last name. I had it until the truth came out when my actual birth certificate was found. It's fortunate that my biological father had registered a birth certificate with my actual name on it.

What was it like working in the showroom?
Very quickly, I was given a lot of responsibility and before long I could quote the items that we stocked, and could basically run the shop myself. The reason for this is that a lot of my superiors were called up to the Armed Forces so I had the opportunity to advance quite quickly. I remember that the superintendent of the shop smoked so much that he was deemed medically unfit for Army service and another supervisor was called up to the RAF. Years later I would run into that supervisor on an island just off the Burma coast, by which

time I was a pilot.

A lot of women were brought out of retirement to fill in the posts that the men had left empty which eventually resulted in me being the only male working in the shop until a week before I was called up. That is when I began to train another male to take over from me. During this time, the Luftwaffe were conducting air raids and I remember on one occasion, the high pitch noise of a falling bomb sounded. I was outside watching these planes fly over with the female cashier who was taken out of retirement to do the cashier job. We heard a bomb falling, both ran inside and I yelled at everyone to get down. The cashier dived onto her hands and knees and I did the same and landed not far behind her. The supervisor, who was only in her twenties had not heard the bombs falling and didn't know what to make of the two of us on our hands and knees so close together.

Despite most people's purse strings having to be tightened, we sold a surprising amount of goods, especially electrical. People were starting to buy electrical goods in much greater numbers. One way to purchase things was through something called a 'Hire Purchase', which for many, was the only way to buy goods like this at the time. With a 'Hire Purchase', the customer would fill in a form where they would agree to pay back the cost of the item in instalments.

The popular items were electrical kettles, irons, fridges and cookers. Though basic, they were becoming very popular. However, the wiring was very basic; no earthing wires in those days. I remember having to connect lamps in the showroom to the mains, which involved putting a positive and negative wire to the mains. If you mistimed it, you would receive a shock, like a kick.

The responsibility I was given increased to the point that I became 'Assistant Cashier' and was put in charge of the store room where things like cables and bulbs were kept, among many other things. Once, the supervisor instructed me to lock up the store. The other staff member had gone home and the supervisor was running late for her bus due to a late customer so I was given the keys.

So I locked up but then began to worry about having the keys because if the place was hit by bombs, questions would be asked as to why I had been left with the keys. So I cycled after her bus, it was the 119 bus which ran from Sidcup, to a place called Wallington which was the name of a district on the other side of Croydon. I caught up with the bus. She was the last passenger and once she got off, the look on her face was quite a sight when she saw me. I gave her the keys and she admitted that she had also been worried about me having them.

But in December 1939, I had to have my appendix removed. Before Christmas, the two male staff at the electric showrooms where I worked had been called up and in their place, a retired lady had been brought in who became the cashier and a much younger lady who became the supervisor, I have already mentioned them.

I'm sure it was on the 3rd of December. I had to clean the floors of the showrooms. I was sweeping the floor behind the counter where the cashier worked when I heard a customer say to the cashier 'is that boy alright?' In the next instant, I dropped the broom and fell to the floor with intense stomach pains. It was decided that I should go home and the person in charge of the clerical office above the showrooms had a car and kindly took me home. At this point I was still in pain, so my foster mother decided that the best place for me would be my bed. Once I lay down, the pain eased off somewhat and I went to sleep. During the afternoon, my foster mother brought up a bowl of porridge. She was a great believer in porridge being the cure of all ills, but on this occasion, I couldn't touch it. I decided to go downstairs, and I had hardly got downstairs when the intense pain returned and I just collapsed to the floor moaning that I wanted a doctor.

My younger foster brother Billy was sent to the doctor's house to ask for him to make an emergency call, which he did and after examining me, told my foster mother that I had 'appendicitis' and that he would immediately phone for an ambulance to take me to hospital.

At the hospital, they inserted an enema and put me to bed. Not long after, I was put on a trolley and wheeled to the operating theatre. Unfortunately, the surgical team were not ready. The nurse who was with me kept on trying to reassure me that I had nothing to worry about and that everything would be fine, when in reality, I was a bundle of nerves. Before long, I was wheeled in, pyjamas removed at which point I noticed that there was an anaesthetist by my side holding a mask which immediately caused me to remember that at the age of eight, I had seen the same mask when I was having my tonsils removed. The memory of the awful smell came to mind when the mask was clamped to my face and the ether administered. I immediately jumped up and made a run for it, but I was grabbed and dragged back by the staff who clamped the mask on and then the operation went ahead. What made it worse was that this was a theatre where students would sit and watch from above. It was after five in the afternoon that I came around and became aware that my foster mother was sitting by the side of my bed along with a neighbour who I had no liking for. In total, I was in hospital for three weeks, but made it home for Christmas.

After being discharged from hospital, not much changed for me until the late summer of 1940 when I volunteered with the fire fighters. It was expected that able-bodied people, even those too old or too young to go into the Armed Forces, volunteer to help the nation, so joining the fire fighter fighters was my way of doing that.

The team I was in covered a very small area so fortunately, during my time there, we never had to tackle any fires so my time was mainly spent playing cards. They taught me some new games too.

But I was only there for a few weeks as in October 1940, I joined the Air Defence Cadet Corps with a friend of mine named Cyril Goldsack, who lived on the same road as I did. In January 1941 the ADCC was renamed the Air Training Corps and we were given new uniforms. Originally, I wanted to go into the Navy Cadets due to my love of the sea but my foster mother vetoed that. Her reason was that the Air Training Corps was further away from London than the

Navy Cadets. She felt I would be in more danger in the Navy Cadets which was closer to London. The capital was being bombed quite badly, especially in area of the docks.

At first I went once a week after work but that quickly became five times a week, plus a social event on Saturday night. By the way, I was in 173 Squadron.

What sort of things did you do and study with the ATC?
The lectures in the ATC covered a wide variety of aeronautical subjects, these were: Airmanship, Meteorology, Navigation, Aircraft Recognition and Morse Code, which in turn served to help us through the necessary exams to be passed when joining the RAF proper.

We also took the 'Air Training Corps Proficiency Exam' which covered English, Maths and Navigation. If you passed, which I did, it allowed you to skip a few exams during the pilots' ground course. I also passed a test for Morse Code, I reached twenty-five words a minute.

Basically, after work, I would cycle home, grab whatever I could to eat, usually something on toast, then cycle down into Orpington to attend the ATC lectures which took place in two flats that had been rented for this purpose. Sometimes we even had lectures in the stairwell between the two flats.

First, it would be decided what the lecture would be, then it would take place in the main room, though there would sometimes be more than one subject lectured on per night. As this was going on, a different lecture would be going on in the other flat. If you were lucky, you got a chair though most of the time you would end up sitting on the floor.

Lectures would generally finish around 9pm and invariably we would head outside and hear all the noise, which was mainly anti-aircraft guns. Shutters would block out most of the noise when we were inside. Most of us had to cycle around two or three miles to get home in pitch darkness, no streetlighting or anything like that. It was a full blackout at the time.

While cycling in this eerie darkness, I would often be accompanied by the sound of wave after wave of aircraft going overhead to or from London. You have to understand that in 1941, air raids on London were a common occurrence. This rather gruelling existence, that went on for week after week eventually became too much for me to the extent that one night I arrived home exhausted and refused to go into the shelter but went straight to bed. Quite a rebellious act for the time. I nearly paid the price one night when a bomb caught our house in its blast which buckled our front door and broke plaster off the ceiling, which then covered my bed clothes. Yet somehow, I slept through it and didn't hear a thing. My foster mother quickly came rushing in, and ordered me down into the shelter, claiming that 'bombs were dropping all around'. Those were her exact words. Ironically, there was only one. But I was so exhausted after dealing with this sort of thing for so long, that I just grunted, rolled over and went back to sleep.

However, the ATC wasn't just lectures; there were many practical things as well. For example, we had to learn how to fire and take apart rifles, which could vary in sizes from .22 to 303. We had to do the same with Vickers machine guns. For a sixteen-year-old boy, it was good fun.

There were also days where flying was the main objective. These took place during the two occasions when our squadron were allowed to camp for two weeks at Biggin Hill airfield. On our first occasion, I was taken up in a Blenheim Bomber aircraft and ironically, I hated every minute of it. This plane had four seats in various positions for the crew. We all drew lots as to who would sit where, the most sought-after seat being that of the co-pilot. I drew the co-pilot seat but quickly traded it for the seat of the rear gunner after discovering that the previous person seated in the co-pilot's seat had vomited everywhere. What I hated about sitting in the rear gunner's seat was the view and G forces imposed on me when the pilot went into steep turns. This caused me to swear to myself that I would never go up in an aircraft again.

There was also a big emphasis on lectures while we were there, but on one occasion we went to the camp cinema to see a film about aircrew training. One scene showed a formation of aircraft and how disciplined they were in maintaining that formation and all the while, gentle music was playing as a backing to the film, and it appealed to me as the music was so pleasant, I wondered what it was called. I had seen the film with B flight but when A flight went to see it, I tagged along to see it again, just so I could hear the music. The surprising thing is that it took many years before I learned the name of the song.

About ten years later while sitting in my own room, while still in the RAF, that same song wafted through the air. I quickly found the source of it and asked the guy what it was called; it was called 'Magic Fire' by the German composer Wagner. That piece has always stirred something deep inside me. I can picture the film now, the aircraft flying in formation to that track.

Biggin Hill is such an iconic airfield in Britain. It played a major role in the Battle of Britain and was very important for the RAF. What memories do you have of it?
Our first time at Biggin Hill was soon after the Battle of Britain ended. We were billeted in Nissen Huts and had our meals at the same time as the ground crew had theirs. On one occasion a group of us were surrounding a Spitfire and the pilot asked me if I would like to sit inside it, to which I gave an enthusiastic 'Yes please'. Once inside, he asked me if I would like to start the engine. Once again I happily said 'Yes'. So he told me to pull the appropriate toggle and the engine roared into life. Then he said 'push the throttle a little way forward', but my push was more like a shove, and the engine roared even higher and nearly jumped the chocks preventing the wheels from moving forward. The pilot had to reach in and pull the throttle back to the closed position otherwise who knows what

would have happened.

What was the atmosphere and day-to-day life at Biggin Hill?
The impression I got while I was there was the cheerfulness of the place. The aircrew and groundcrew all seemed to be a happy bunch. Biggin Hill had no runway in those days, there was a field nicknamed 'the bump' due to a slight hillock in the centre. It also struck me as quite a large airfield.

Cyril and I used to cycle there when we were sixteen and both in the ATC. We would bike up a lane named Cudenham Lane which leads through a village named Downe. Eventually we would reach a hedge just outside of the perimeter of Biggin Hill.

On another occasion when we cycled there, again, both in the ATC at the time, we asked the sergeant in charge of air traffic control if we could have some training on the Link Trainer. This was a ground model of a machine that has the same controls as a plane. It would lift up on bellows and you could 'fly' it like a regular plane. On entering air traffic control - I was ahead of Cyril - we went through the door and saluted, then immediately apologised to the sergeant there as I thought he was an Officer. To which he replied, 'No son, you did the right thing, you salute the office of an Officer, whether he is there or not'.

When we asked about the Link Trainer, he informed us that the instructor wasn't there, but said that we looked sensible enough so asked us to promise that we wouldn't be too rough with it if he gave us the keys. There were two Link Trainers, I got in one and Cyril in the other. We switched them on, and then we had a pretend dogfight which meant manoeuvring them for about an hour in quite a violent fashion until we got bored. Once we had finished, we switched them both off and returned the keys.

Back at control, the sergeant thanked us both and asked if we would like a real flight if it could be arranged, to which we agreed. He phoned around the different dispersal areas which resulted in a

Belgian pilot offering to fly us, and another dispersal had a Tiger Moth available. So, we had to make our way over to that dispersal. We arrived. I won the toss to go up first and got into the cockpit.

Once we were in the air, the pilot asked me if I had flown before and at the same time, pushed the stick forward into a steep dive, then pulled it back and did a loop which thrilled me into hoping that he would do it again, but he didn't. A bit more flying around and then he landed. I got out, Cyril got in and I watched him and quickly reached a state of jealousy when the pilot did not one loop, but two. But I got compensation when Cyril got out and I saw that he had been sick and proceeded to swear that he would never fly again. Later on, we were reprimanded by the ATC Adjutant for going up on a flight that he had not authorised. But it was much different from my first flight, I thoroughly enjoyed this one.

Living in Kent at the time, and being so close to London, what are your memories of the Battle of Britain and the Blitz?
During the Battle of Britain and the Blitz, the entire area was on tender hooks. Life carried on as normal as possible but if people were out and heard a plane overhead, it was natural to duck into a doorway or somewhere to take cover. But overall, not a lot changed, the buses still ran, people went to work, milk was delivered when available. People seemed to socialise more. However, all windows had to be blacked out and there were 'Air Raid Wardens' whose job it was to enforce it. The propaganda was also very strong. This was designed to keep morale up, you know, 'Dig for victory' and all that. But one cannot underestimate the influence that Winston Churchill had personally in keeping morale up. His speeches had a quite an effect on people.

On one occasion when the Battle of Britain was being fought, Billy and I were returning home from a church service when suddenly the air was filled with noise as Spitfires and Hurricanes engaged German Messerschmitts in the skies above us, probably half a dozen in total. We saw a parachute open, which we later learnt was a Hurricane pilot bailing out of his plane. He landed in an allotment and the

Hurricane crashed in a field.

We started running for a woodland area when a man called out to us to come over into their shelter, which was a converted double garage. Once we reached the wall of the man's house, Billy, who was crying due to the noise and the odd bullet casing hitting the ground, was hoisted over and I scrambled over it myself. The shelter was well stocked, it had a 'kitchen' at one end and the rest of it was made up of beds, chairs and sofas.

On another occasion, I was with Cyril, and we decided to cycle to Biggin Hill. We reached the boundary fence at the end of airfield and before long, witnessed ten Spitfires take off in a loose formation. Due to our position, the left flank of these Spitfires flew right over our heads. But not long after taking off, the Spitfire at the head of the ten started to slowly drop out of the sky. It disappeared out of sight but I later learnt that it had crashed due to a hydraulic failure. Fortunately, the pilot was ok. To witness ten Spitfires take off in such a fashion and to hear the noise coming from their engines, it was really impressive.

During the summer of 1940, it was quite common to see Spitfires, Hurricanes and Messerschmitts in the skies. Even when it wasn't possible to see them, one could hear them.

During the Blitz, any family who had an air raid shelter spent night after night in them but even they weren't guaranteed to keep you safe. At a house quite close to where I lived, about a quarter of a mile away, the Anderson shelter of a family there was directly hit by a bomb that was believed to have been jettisoned, which killed everyone inside.

On another occasion, the church tower was set on fire by incendiary bombs. The beams holding the bells in the tower were destroyed causing the bells to fall to the ground. They weren't replaced until after the war so a recording would be broadcast via loudspeaker to take their place.

Another family I knew, who lived on the next road to me. They took a taxi into London to attend a wedding and were directly hit, killing everyone. There were quite a few casualties for such a small village.

There were several occasions during this period where after attending the ATC, I had to cycle just over a mile to get home, and would be caught out in a raid such as the time that a bomb fell so close to me, falling on a field, that it blew me off of my bicycle which resulted in a torn left trouser leg and an injured left knee. The most ironic thing of all is that my foster mother was more concerned about the trouser leg than she was about myself, due to the cost it would be in clothing coupons to replace a pair of trousers.

An unbelievable story is that of the Adjutant of my ATC unit. One night, him and his wife were at home during an air raid and were sheltering under the stairs as they didn't have an Anderson shelter. Their house was directly hit and by sheer luck they survived as the staircase that they were underneath was left standing, everything else having been destroyed.

Looking back over those first war years, which occurred and affected me during such an impressionable age, there were so many incidences that all roll together in my memory and are crowded together like a film, lasting several years. It was a period which served the average adolescent well in that we respected authority but at the same time, we had free hands in other ways. This gave us more time to enjoy life rather than be under the restrictions of the authoritarian rules of the older people in charge. People themselves became more open and would crack jokes. For example, if it got to nine or ten at night and no German aircraft had appeared, people would start joking that they were late and not on time. When they would approach, there was a psychological effect in that many of them would purposefully not have their engines synchronised, the sound of which had quite an effect on many people, it was done to instil fear.

Fortunately, there were occurrences during the war which, as fate would have it, I was to miss due to being overseas. The first ones were the V1 rockets which were commonly nicknamed 'Doodlebugs'. They were essentially engines with wings and explosives attached with no navigation system, the result being that they would fall out the sky once their fuel ran out and explode on contact with the ground. The public had an advanced warning of its impending crash because its engine had quite a distinct sound and once the sound of the engine cut out, you knew it would be a matter of moments before it crashed.

But over a period of time RAF fighter pilots learnt the trick of flying alongside the Doodlebug long enough until they were wingtip to wingtip at which point the pilot would bank left or right, thus tilting the Doodlebug off balance causing it to crash, ideally away from built-up areas.

The other was the V2 Rocket. The V2 was a straight forward rocket packed with explosives that were fired at an angle straight up into the sky towards England. In their case there was no approaching sound to give them away.

But back to those first war years. When I was around fifteen, I was cycling home from work, trying to get home before a storm hit the area, and in desperation, sought shelter under a rather large oak tree. After a few moments, a man came along on his bike, stopped close by and warned me that it was well known for large trees to be struck by lightning which made them dangerous places to seek shelter. Taking his advice, I cycled off in the heavy rain to the first house which fortunately wasn't too far away. A few days later, I learnt that the same tree had been struck by lightning and a man sheltering under it had been killed. I knew it was the same tree because I later saw that the trunk bore the marks of a lightning strike, but I don't know if it was the same man who gave me the warning.

CHAPTER THREE

BEING CALLED UP

Life on the troop ship to South Africa and Naval traditions.

You were called up when you were eighteen and a quarter, which according to my calculations, must have been in the autumn of 1942. Do you remember that day?

Very much so. However, I went to the recruitment office in Catford six months prior to my call-up in order to volunteer as a wireless operator. Cyril came with me to do the same thing. We did this because if we didn't, then when our call-up dates arrived, we could in theory have been called up to the Army or Navy, and we wanted to ensure that we went into the RAF. But when we told the chap in the recruitment office of our desire to become Wireless operators, his reply was 'We have enough of those already, I will put you both down as pilots'.

Anyway, my call-up papers arrived around the 5th of October, and I discovered that I had been called up when I arrived home one day and my foster mother said 'Your call-up papers have arrived'. She had already opened the letter and gone through it. The letter itself detailed where I had to go, what I had to take and by what time I had to be there. I turned eighteen on Sunday the 11th July 1942, but my call-up was delayed by one day until the Monday as one was never called up on a Sunday. I had to go to Lords Cricket ground and report to entrance gate 'E' at 08:00 hours. The gate one went to was decided by their surname. So, a chap whose last name was 'Brown' would report to entrance gate 'B' and so on.

Once there, we were all assembled into a large room where we were kitted out with uniforms and RAF clothing, including footwear. When it was my turn, I was asked 'what size' for various clothing, I told him and he went to the table behind him and grabbed the relevant piece.

We then went into a big hall for refreshments, which in my case was tea. People were spitting out the tea saying how disgusting it was. I later found out that this was because they put Bromide (a chemical) in it to kill our sexual desires. Crazy isn't it. From there, we were shown our quarters for the first few nights which were dormitory-like. Many of us to a room.

My rank upon joining up was 'Aircraftsman 2nd class the lowest rank in the RAF.

On the second day we had to parade at 8am and from there we were marched to a place named Seymour Hall which we entered through the rear via a fire escape. Once inside, we had to prepare for inoculations. Most people had three inoculations though I only needed two. After that, we were all given permission to go to Regents Park and relax, though most of us were sick. In my mind, that had to be down to the inoculations. In my case, on getting back to the billets, I went straight to bed and spent most of the night still feeling sick, crying with pain. In fact, one of the older people who was in his mid-twenties, took care of me for the whole night.

On the third day, following breakfast, we had to go to another large hall and completely undress. In the hall were several tables used by doctors to carry out medical examinations. I was passing all requirements until the doctor in charge of the other doctors took me to one side. He told me that he had almost decided to fail me on the hearing side because he noticed that I had suffered two punctured eardrums. He then said that he had decided to let me proceed on the principle that the changing pressures that I would be exposed to once I started flying would heal my eardrums. His theory was correct in that at the end of the first year, when I underwent another medical, my eardrums had fully healed. My eardrums had initially been injured by our family doctor when I underwent a medical for the ATC. He had cleared both ears of wax but had been rather rough in doing it which had caused both eardrums to perforate.

As an eighteen year old, was there a big sense of impending adventure in those first few days?

Not at first. As I have said, those first few days were taken up with medical examinations and being supplied with clothing, things like that. But when I arrived home on that first weekend, I really looked forward to reporting back. There was such a sense of anticipation for what was to come. I felt as though I was on the cusp of a big adventure, but my first adventure was somewhat of an anti-climax.

On arrival back after the first weekend, we were formed into one big group, probably around two hundred, and put on a corridor less train. It meant that these carriages lacked facilities, including toilets. A few of the chaps on the train actually urinated themselves on the five-hour train journey. Our destination was a village named Ludlow, not far from the Welsh border.

Our three weeks in Ludlow consisted of manual labour, digging trenches and filling them up again, building walls and then knocking them down, things like that. We slept in bell tents, eight to a tent and discovered that the best way to keep warm was sleeping side to side, body to body. Remember, it was approaching Winter, so it was very cold and damp. We had one tap for about fifty of us and the best wash we could have was by going into a nearby river.

After about three weeks, we got the message that we were to be up at five in the morning the following day in order to catch a seven o'clock train back to London. Thankfully, that train had corridors and toilet facilities. But as we approached the outskirts of London, we became enveloped in thick pea soup fog. The train had to stop short of our destination, somewhere on the outskirts of London, as all the signals were shut down to red due to the fog. When we got off the train, we were divided into small parties of ten. The leader of each party had to navigate their party back to our residences in 'crocodile fashion', where you hung on to the person in front of you, like a chain. The group I was in got the underground into London, we didn't return to our billets until the early hours.

Nothing of any importance happened over the next few days. We were given marching sessions to learn the various disciplines in marching. It reached the stage that the sergeant in charge decided to call us on parade and then shouted out the order 'atten'. Everyone thought he was going to shout 'Attention!' but he actually said 'A ten-shilling note had been found'. Then he shouted 'about', which we thought was going to be 'About Turn!'. This is when you turn 180 degrees - there is an art to it - you swing around on your heels. Anyway, he shouted 'At about ten this morning'. The point of all this was to wait until the entire order had been given.

I had the opportunity to return home again too. Upon leaving, I told my foster parents 'I am not sure when I'll next see you again'. My foster father replied in such a casual manner, 'I'm sure you'll be back next weekend'. When in actual fact, I never saw him again as he died in 1943, on the 16th December, the same day as I got my wings. His passing really upset me; he had been like a real father to me.

We took another train, this time to Blackpool. Upon arrival, we were divided into small units. In my case, it was a total of three, billeted in a rather large house with a middle-aged married couple who owned the house. They had a daughter of nineteen. The three of us were in a rather large bedroom with a shared bathroom. Our meals were excellent. We had to parade at eight in the morning, every day. After a few days of this procedure, the sergeant called out a list of names who had to step aside of the main group and wait. It turned out the group who had been called aside, of which I was one, were destined for overseas. We were told not to reveal this fact to anyone, including our parents. It was to be kept secret. I don't know what happened to the other group.

During all of this, Ludlow, Blackpool, digging trenches and everything, what was the atmosphere like, was it a feeling of camaraderie and friendship?
Yes, we established friendships and there was a feeling that we were all in it together. During this time, we all began to learn the

differences between civilian life and forces life. Once, one of the guys misheard an order and said something like 'I thought you said…', and the sergeant replied, 'In the RAF, you don't think, we think for you'. Those of us who were in the group going overseas were looking forward to it, at least I was.

Unfortunately, when we next returned to London, which would be our last time, no one was allowed to go home. I think it was in case we spoke to someone about the fact that we were going overseas. Anyway, a few of us from the group spent many hours in the cinema whilst we were there.

Eventually, you were all sent by train to Liverpool.
Yes, eventually the day came when we, the group who were going overseas, were all put on a train and sent off to Liverpool. Once there, we joined up with other units, including those from the Army. I estimate that there were about two hundred air force and a thousand army personnel.

We were transported to the docks and told to make our way to the deck of our vessel. We were then taken below, and began getting acquainted to where we would be spending the next five weeks. We began to learn about things like hoisting hammocks, which caused much amusement when it came to things like getting into them. Bodies were falling over the place but luckily, I got used to mine fairly quickly.

We set sail on December 16th 1942 only nine weeks after I had been called up. I remember going up to the open deck as we pulled away from the docks and witnessing crowds of people waving us off. Once clear of the docks, I went below again and met a lad called Mervin. He was a year older than me and had made friends with a chap named Laurie, who was in the Army and coincidently, his neighbour. So, we became a little unit of three, two Air Force and one Army, for the remainder of the journey.

For someone who had grown up in the countryside and had little experience of the sea, experiencing the open ocean for the first time must have been quite an experience.
The freshness of the open sea, I found it to be very exhilarating, I could see the other ships in the convoy all around and I didn't suffer from sea sickness. So I took to the sea immediately, to the extent that the word 'love' came into it. I loved the fresh sea air and the sounds of the waves. There is a certain magic about the sea. I loved and still love everything about it, even if the weather is rough. I remember that once clear, out into the open sea, we were soon in rough weather, and I took great delight in hanging onto the rails at the bow of the ship, watching and smelling the sea. It was like being on a giant sea saw. But one of the crew noticed me and ordered me below saying that if I fell overboard, nobody was going to stop and rescue me.

In the following days, we had to get used to eating off long, narrow tables that would seat eighteen at a time and in the first fortnight, I ate quite well because half of my table friends were sea sick whereas I was never affected. This meant I ate their food as well. But after about ten days, they had gotten over their sea sickness and were eating normally again so I had to go back to eating just my own meals.

What was day-to-day life like on board? The threat of German U-boats must have been there.
On finer days, we as a group used to be on the open deck and given exercises to perform, similar to what one would do back in a school gymnasium. We also had lectures on various subjects from selected personnel of the crew, all of which helped to pass the time away on each day.

Our ship was named 'The S.S Rangitiki' and it was one of three troop-carrying ships in the same convoy that we were in, the main one of which was named 'The SS Britannia', which was also the lead ship of the convoy. Our convoy totalled about fifteen ships including escorts, which were naval frigates. Our ship was the slowest of the lot and could apparently only manage fourteen and a half knots at maximum speed, whereas the Britannia had a much faster maximum speed. From the day of formation, the whole convoy had to do slow zig zags from port to starboard as a defence against German U-boats. We were told by one of the crew that on two occasions, we had been attacked by U-boats and in return the U-boats had been attacked by our frigates and it was claimed that at least one U-boat had been sunk by depth charges.

Another danger that the escorts had to be aware of was high-flying reconnaissance German Condor aircraft which shadowed the various convoys travelling to and from the UK and reported their positions to the waiting U-boats. The defence against the Condors was that one of the ships in a convoy could carry a Hurricane fighter on board that would somehow be launched into the air to shoot down the Condor. After shooting it down, the pilot would fly close to his own ship, then ditch his plane and be picked up.

After a week or two, spent for the most part crossing the Bay of Biscay in very rough sea conditions, we asked one of the crew roughly where we were, and the answer he gave was, 'Approximately one thousand miles due west of the French coast'. In other words, in the Atlantic.

Judging by the time frame you have given, you spent the Christmas of 1942 at sea. How was it celebrated?
Luckily, the dinner was marvellous. Roast turkey, vegetables and potatoes, followed my mince pies and Christmas pudding. This was in stark contrast to back home where everyone had to get by on rations. It was quite a Christmas to remember and I can still picture it now, in full detail.

As we continued, the seas gradually got quieter and soon afterwards, the convoy stopped at a West African port, I believe Freetown in Sierra Leone. It being hot and humid, quite a few of us slept on the top deck which caused me to hear mosquitos buzzing around for the first time. It could have been on that occasion that I was bitten by one. It was definitely during this time as not long after reaching Rhodesia, I was taken ill with malaria, which is consistent with the period of incubation.

Anyway, once we were refuelled; we carried on, travelling to and around the Cape of Good Hope, eventually arriving in Durban. All of us airforce personnel then disembarked, but we weren't allowed to look around the city. We were split into separate groups of four. Mervin and I were in the same squad but Laurie had to stay on board, as the convoy was carrying on up the East African coast to North Eastern Africa. I believe that the troops on board were to join the Eighth Army. Laurie eventually became a tank commander. In total, we were on board for just over five weeks.

It's well known that life at sea involves various traditions and initiations. Did you or any of the other passengers have to experience anything like that?
The one which really stands out is when we crossed the equator. A couple dozen of us had gathered, not knowing why, but just on the presumption that we were going to do some exercises. That is what we had been told to dress for. But on this occasion it was the ulterior motive of the 'Crossing The Line Ceremony'. A sailor with a sort of gown on, representing King Neptune was placed on a platform with a silly sort of crown of his head, probably made out of cardboard or something. What I remember is that I was grabbed by two sailors and smeared in some sort of muck. I have no idea what it was. Everyone else thought it was hilarious until they were ordered into the well deck and were drenched with sea hoses. These were powerful hoses which would knock you over. I was up with Neptune and was sprayed down myself. An Officer soon appeared and stated that the Captain had ordered all this to be stopped as there were ladies on board, WRENS as far as I know. At the end of it all I was given a certificate by King Neptune saying that I had officially 'crossed the line'. The others down below didn't receive a certificate as they 'crossed the line' without permission.

Despite these amusing events, the risk of coming under attack must have been there. You have already mentioned being informed that two U-boats had attacked your convoy and the defences that you had in place. All of this must have been an ever- present thought in the back of your mind.
Oh yes it was, and remember that this was in late 1942 early 1943. By then the German U-boats had been operating in wolfpacks for quite a while. One time that really brought it to the forefront was when we were all ordered below deck. Questions were asked and it soon transpired that the convoy which was around three days ahead of us had been attacked resulting in ships going down. I don't know how many. The reason that we were ordered below was that bodies had been seen floating in the sea and the Captain didn't want us to see them as it might have lowered morale.

All of this happened in the South Atlantic too, far from home, closer to South Africa than to Britain.

Stepping off the ship, into a new country on the other side of the world, what was going through your mind? Your first time out of Britain, stepping onto a new continent, it must have been quite an experience.
It was indeed, I was looking forward to looking around Durban. Before the war, it was such a well-known city in Britain. It was a famous city that we even learnt about at school, though that feeling quickly turned to one of disappointment. We had heard so much about Durban and it was incredibly disappointing when we were told that we were not allowed to explore the city.

After disembarking, we were soon put on the Blue Train. Each compartment could take four people and had its own wash facilities, bunk beds and arm chairs to use. The train carried all two hundred of us. The views from the train as it climbed the mountains were magnificent. Eventually we stopped at the city of Johannesburg. The whole platform was lined with tables, stocked with chocolate, magazines and newspapers. We got plenty of phone numbers from women, but Senior Officers told us that they would be quite useless as once we reached Southern Rhodesia, we would not be allowed back into South Africa. After Johannesburg, we stopped once more in South Africa, in Mafeking. Once again, the tables were lined with things to buy.

We carried on northwards for a total of two days and two nights until we reached the Southern Rhodesian city of Bulawayo which was reputed to have the longest railway platform in the Southern Hemisphere, and it was indeed over a mile long.

When we reached Bulawayo, we were marched to an area called Hillside, which was a complete Air Force camp. To our surprise, our beds were located in small pens which had once housed pigs. We learned that Hillside had in previous times been the site for cattle markets. Each pen now housed a single iron bed and hooks from which to hang clothes.

Fortunately, things were soon to change. The cadets on Course 26 completed their course and were posted to various flying schools. This allowed the cadets on Course 27 to take over the better huts that the previous cadets had occupied. This meant that the cadets on Course 28 moved into the huts vacated by the cadets on Course 27, which were better than the ones they were in. But most importantly of all, the cadets on my course (29) could vacate those horrible pig pens. I was meant to be on course 28 but malaria put a stop to that.

CHAPTER FOUR
SOUTHERN RHODESIA

Malaria, the pilot's course, Victoria Falls.
A dice with death and two grisly murders.

Rhodesia was where you undertook the pilots' course. Did the course begin straight away?
Nearly, in that within about ten days we learnt that the actual course would start on the following Monday and that we would be on Course 28. But on the Friday before, whilst being put through army-type drills on the parade ground, I heard the Flight sergeant in charge of us call out 'Catch that man!' That man happened to be me as I had fainted, dropped my rifle and within seconds was lying on the ground beside it. I was carried to my bed and after the Medical Officer visited, I was quickly sent to hospital. What I had was the onset of malaria and the beginning of a two-and-a-half week road to recovery.

The care in hospital was great, especially in the first two weeks where a team of nurses worked on getting my dangerously high temperature back down to normal. My main memories of my stay there are of me moaning in pain and pleading to go home. Eventually the profuse sweating eased as did the pain. But by this stage, my feeling of home sickness had increased which lead me to write the following poem:

IF ONLY

If only I could tread the green of England's fields again,
and gaze upon her countless streams, her woods and rolling hills
and plains
and lay on new mown hay.

If only I could smell those flowers which I have known from birth
and walk with ease and comfort, on soft, enchanted earth,
and listen to those singing birds be near or far away,

and gaze with awe and wonder, at plumage bright and gay.

If only I could see her skies of ever changing mood,
and watch the raindrops falling, as darkened clouds do brood,
and see the lightning flashing, and hear the thunder roar,
while howling winds grow angry, and shake against my door.

If only I could welcome Spring with all its colours rare,
and when hot Summer bids adieu gaze on those trees, so bare,
and when the snow begins to fall, feel Winter's icy hand,
if only now that I could be in that romantic land.

It is a beautiful poem, so much depth and emotion flow from its words. But though you felt homesick, you were in the Armed Forces, so you couldn't just leave and go home. What did you do?
Fortunately it was a feeling that didn't last long. Once my appetite returned and I was back to full health, I was allowed to return to my unit and my homesickness disappeared. But when I was released from hospital, I had missed the beginning of Course 28 and it was only a week or so before Course 29 began so I was put on that course. On each course, there were about two hundred. My friend Mervin was still at Hillside, studying for exams. Instructors would use the results of these exams to decide on which cadet to send to which flying school, assuming they passed.

But my poem got some of the other cadets suggesting that I should have it published. But course work was taking up too much time so eventually it got tucked into an exercise book to disappear for many years. To this day, I am still surprised that I wrote that poem as when I was growing up, I never read or wrote poetry.

At the end of each course, which lasted about four months, exams covering a wide variety of aeronautical subjects were undertaken. At the end of the exams for Course 29, those of us who passed were posted to our first flying school, which involved Tiger Moth aircraft.

Going back a bit, you once told me that you almost didn't even start the pilots' course. That just before Course 29 began, you decided that you wanted to be a Wireless operator.
Well I learnt from other cadets that most of us taking part would end up with a personal interview, either by an assistant from the school staff or from the Squadron leader in overall charge and that if one was interviewed by the Squadron leader then they were a 'special case'.

I was interviewed by the Squadron leader but due to a lack of confidence in my abilities, I told him that I wanted to be a Wireless operator rather than a pilot. He became very angry and almost shouting, told me that if I studied hard then I would do well and become a pilot and to forget about becoming a Wireless operator as the RAF already had an abundance of them. So, I decided to go on the pilots' course, though he had not really given me much choice.

How was the course structured? I imagine that there must be have been a lot of theory to cover before you got behind the controls of any sort of aircraft?
Yes, there wasn't even a single aircraft at Hillside. Our time there was four months of parade drills, map reading exercises of up to about fifteen miles, some of which were purely classroom based, but on others, we were dropped off with a map and a compass, in a group of six with a leader in charge and told to report to a certain point.

There were tests on our English and Maths skills but because I had passed the ATC Proficiency Exam, I didn't have to do those tests. We also had to learn how to disassemble, reassemble and fire a Vickers Machine Gun. On top of this, we had lecture after lecture on ten subjects without even seeing an aircraft. At the end of the four months were exams on the ten subjects. They were: Airmanship, Navigation, Meteorology, Aero Engines, Flight Instruments, Signals (which included The Morse Code), Bombing theory, Gunnery theory, Pyrotechnics and Aircraft recognition. The results of the exams would decide which flying school one went to. One had to get at least fifty five percent per subject and an average of sixty percent overall to pass. I only managed fifty eight percent on my worst subject which was Aero Engines but I finished with an average of eighty-one-and-half percent overall which put me eleventh from top of the course.

Cadets who passed could select their choice of flying school, though it wasn't guaranteed that they would go there. I had heard that a school named 'Induna' was reputed to have the best instructors so that's where I chose to go. There were two other Tiger Moth schools, one was called 'Gwelo' and the other was named 'Thornside' near Salisbury, which was then the capital of Southern Rhodesia. A good friend on Course 29, Ron was rather overconfident and was sure that he would score highly on his exams and be posted to Induna. On the day that the exam results were published, we both went to a big board which had everyone's results on it to see how we had scored. He started at the top and I at the bottom, working our way down and up respectively, we found each others' names, I finished eleventh as I have already mentioned, which meant I was able to go to Induna, but Ron finished much lower, he had just about passed and was posted to Gwelo. Those exams took three days to complete.

During this four-month period of intense study, what was day-to-day life like?
Unsurprisingly, they were mostly filled with lectures. They would begin at around nine in the morning, then there would be a break for lunch and then we would carry on until about four in the afternoon or so.

It must have been quite stressful studying for all of these exams. When the time became available, how did you all relax and take your mind off it all?
In the case of Ron and I, we would often go to the gym in our spare time. Once, we came back and were making a racket, a group of older cadets studying for their exams told us to shut up or else. One of us, I can't remember who, replied something like 'Or what?!' They quickly grabbed me and pulled down my shorts, and got a

tin of 'blackie', which was black shoe polish. I had the sense to yell out that if they did anything to me, I would stop teaching them The Morse Code. They let me go and grabbed Ron and blackened the cheeks of his bottom. He ran outside once they let him go and when I caught up with him, he asked me to help him wash it off. Unlike him, I saw the funny side to it all. Another thing was to go into Bulawayo to use the swimming baths. Another was to visit the NAAFI which stood for Navy Army and Air Force Institute which was basically a glorified canteen. There was a piano there and occasionally one of the cadets would play classical music on it. He was an excellent pianist.

On one occasion I was stuffed into a laundry bag which was tied up. I had said something cheeky. Luckily I had quite sharp nails and managed to split the bag open and get out. I went and replaced the bag with one from another billet.

I remember you telling me that those who passed the exams had a five-day period in which they could go and travel anywhere within the country. Where did you spend your five days?
A group of eight of us had a joint interest in going to see the famous Victoria Falls. As this was taken as a geographical exercise, we were allowed a travel warrant to cover rail expenses. As it was a distance of nearly three hundred miles, it was a welcome help. We had to allow a full day to reach the Falls and another one for getting back, so that gave us three clear days at the Falls. The train was ordinary, nothing special about it and I was sure that the engine was log fired but I later learnt that it was coal fired. Though a day spent on the train sounds like a long time, the varied landscapes we saw made the time go by quite quickly. Rhodesia sits at quite a high altitude, exceeding four thousand feet in places. I remember passing quite a few hills. There were also a couple of towns we travelled through on the way, one of which caused us great amusement as it was named 'Wankie', well known for its coal.

When we reached Victoria Falls station, which was close enough to hear the roar of the waterfall, a Dutch man approached us and told us that if we were looking for accommodation, then he could help and when he said that it would be of no cost, it made us all wonder what the catch was, but fortunately, there wasn't one. It turned out that he had been doing this for years in return for allied forces defending his country. This Dutch man lived in a house on his own with two large spare bedrooms each having four single beds and out back, the place had its own swimming pool. It had been hewn out of solid rock, speckled with flakes of gold. One of our group even took a nail file to it but was told by the Dutch man not to bother as it wasn't worth anything. The water was changed once a week via a pump set up, so the condition of the water was good. The Dutch man told us that we were free to use it at any time but without swimming costumes to allow for the water being static. This raised a few eyebrows in our party and one commented to the rest that perhaps he preferred to see naked young men.

The Dutch man also owned a small open back van which he said we could use. But only one of us could drive so he offered lessons to the rest of us. When it came to my turn, I found it was great fun to zigzag between bushes along the riverbank but that short piece of land that we were driving on ended at a flimsy fence that if one went through it, they would end up in the river. As we approached this fence, my friend told me to press on the brake peddle but I pressed the wrong one. I pressed the accelerator which caused us to shoot forward. He managed to kick my foot off the pedal and grabbed the steering wheel, causing us to go into a sharp swerve that resulted in us stopping about three feet short of the fence. I lost interest in driving after that.

What were Victoria Falls themselves like?

It was a stunning sight, the sound was deafening and the spray went high into the sky. There were small offshoots too, before the actual waterfall. But the Falls themselves carried a large novelty value. None of us had ever seen anything like it before.

I remember you telling me that during your time in Rhodesia, you spent a good amount of time in Bulawayo, a place that you

have already mentioned. What was the city itself like? Obviously things were very different there than they are now in Zimbabwe, as the country is now known.
The place was quite lively. It had a good range of shops, cafes and a lovely swimming pool in which I taught myself to swim. There was a nice church named St Johns, which I believe is now a cathedral. There were also two cinemas. To me, it came across as perfectly safe and peaceful. You could go there on your own and be fine, though we were advised to stay out of the south side of the city, not for safety reasons but just because apparently, there wasn't anything there of any interest. From what I understood, the white population mainly stuck to the north and the black population stayed mainly in the south. However, if a white person was walking along the footpath and a black person was coming the other way, then the black person would have to get off the footpath. I never experienced this myself, but that is what I was told. But to me, it was a lovely place. I went swimming there practically every weekend.

So, having passed your exams with flying colours and having been on an interesting five- day break, what was there left to do at Hillside before your move to Induna?
The weekend after we got back to Hillside was spent packing our gear and loading it on to coaches taking us to our various flying schools. When those of us who were posted to Induna arrived, we were billeted into huts divided into rooms, with two cadets per room. A separate hut contained baths, showers and toilets. I was at Induna for just over two months. Having passed my exams and having been posted to a Tiger Moth school, I was promoted by one rank to 'Leading Aircraftsman', which also meant an increase in pay.

Induna was about fifteen miles from Bulawayo with quite a good bus service. Flying was from a rather large grass field which was kept in good condition. There were no actual runways.

My roommate was named Wally. He was a pleasant chap, one year older than me, the same height as me and medium build. He was from Brighton and surprised me by telling me that he could not swim.

On our first day, we met our instructors. My instructor was named Flying Officer Cond, a very calm man, I would say in his early thirties, who described every part of the Tiger Moth and its purpose. Then he climbed into the front 'cockpit' and the descriptions continued, including details about the instruments. Then he went through the start-up procedure but we didn't start up on the first day. FO/C tried to make everything about a plane, including the flying, very easy. The Tiger Moths used for training cadets had two sets of controls joined together. One set in the front, the other in the back, so if the cadet moved his joystick, then the instructor's joystick would move in the same way. This was so that when the cadet was flying, the instructor could take over if anything went wrong.

The next day, I was shown how to start up the engine which was done by swinging hard on the propeller. Next came a taxying demonstration before I had a go at it myself which was interesting as a Tiger Moth has no brakes or rear wheel. Instead of a rear wheel, it had a 'skid' which dug into the ground and acted as a brake. The next step was to learn the way to operate the main controls via a single 'joystick' as it was called. All of this happened over the course of a few days and each of these exercises had their own number which was useful for logbook entries. After taxiing came take-offs and landings with the instructor doing the landings. When taxiing to the take-off point, he told me that we had to turn thirty degrees to port and then swing back the other way so we could see ahead, as the engine blocked our view, and in this case, the instructor also blocked my view. This swinging motion continued until the take-off point was reached.

Anyway, my own first landing attempt was a bit bumpy but all the exercises were practised day after day until we could do them all. On the tenth day, after take-off, my instructor told me to head for 'satellite number one' which was a small airfield used for first solos. Another instructor and his cadet were already there. My instructor was going to test his cadet and that cadet's instructor was going to test me. What I didn't know was that FO/C had placed a bet with the other instructor that he would get me off solo within ten hours;

the course average was thirteen and a half. During my test, the other instructor kept asking me how many hours I had done, until we reached ten. We communicated through the Gosport, which is a rubber tube that allows you to speak to each other. He asked me to do one more circuit and to land, which I did. I was then joined by FO/C who jokingly told me that I had lost him a pound. Both of us cadets had passed our tests. As the other cadet had arrived first, he was allowed to attempt to go solo first. I watched him take off and then started my own run. I became airborne and was horrified to see that the other cadet was slightly veering to the right, which meant that when he turned left to keep on circuit at eight hundred feet, he would turn into me, so I held my climb at six hundred feet. Sure enough, he eventually turned and flew right over me. He later admitted that he had not even seen me. I continued to eight hundred feet and completed the circuit. I could see his landing approach so was astonished when he lifted away to have another go. This left the way clear for me and I did a nice landing.

It must have been quite an experience to go solo for the first time, quite exhilarating to be up in the air, the sense of achievement.
Oh definitely, no doubt about it, I remember singing to myself as loud as I could. I did a few more hours with FO/C but then, to my horror, he went on leave. I then had a much older instructor, who I will call Flying Officer T. He had been a pilot during the Battle of Britain. Each instructor had two cadets but FO/T already had two, and I believe having to take me on as a third really annoyed him. On our first introduction, we both got into a Tiger Moth, he told me to taxi down to the take-off point, in the way I had been instructed. I had hardly started taxiing when FO/T called out very sharply 'Stop! Asking me what I thought I was doing, he told me that if I had been taught to angle thirty degrees to see ahead, it was now going to be sixty degrees with him, which lengthened the time to get to the take-off point. He then told me to take off, which I did. He started telling me how it was worst take-off he had ever seen. He was in the front and we spoke via the Gosport. I carried on the circuit and soon we had landed.

When we rolled to a stop, he said that 'Your landing was the worst I have ever known'. Though in my mind, I had done quite well. He yelled at me to take off again, so I did, and on the downwind leg, he gave me an instruction, which I didn't quite understand. So instead of answering, I kept quiet. But he quickly asked me if I could hear him. Bearing in mind that I was still only eighteen, and feeling the typical anger of a teenager, I replied 'Yes I bloody well heard you!' He then did the most remarkable manoeuvre that I had seen up to that point, and haven't seen since. Somehow, he dipped the plane down, swerved steeply to the left, pulled the joystick back sharply into my body and bang, we were on the ground. I have never known a landing like it, it was truly brilliant.

He then told me to get out, which I did. He stopped the engine and got out himself, and then began the lecture. First, he asked me what I had said to him when I replied to his last question. I told him that I had responded with, 'Yes, I can hear you, Sir'. His response was, 'No, it wasn't. Try again. Do you realise that you swore at me, an officer of the Royal Air Force?' I thought he was going to scrub me, to take me off the course. He glared at me and said, 'One day, you might win the VC, or the DFC, or the AFC, and it will be all thanks to me'. He then said 'now get back in the aircraft, take off and go and kill yourself'. Those were his exact words. The awful thing was that I nearly did. On my first landing attempt, I bumped too hard on the ground and did what is known as the 'kangaroo hop'. In the nick of time I saw that I was heading towards the windsock, which is like an empty pillowcase attached to a pole. The windsock blows in the wind, thus giving the direction of the wind. Anyway, I put the throttle on full power, increased my height and just cleared it. On the second attempt I came in too high and plumped on the ground and just cleared the hedges at the end of the landing strip. On the third attempt, I said to myself, 'Please God, don't let it hurt'; those were my exact words. I turned onto the final approach; put the aircraft onto what I thought was a good landing height, and crouched into the cockpit with my arms covering my head, waiting for the crash. Instead, it was just a thump, then another. I felt the tail hit the ground, sat up quickly and saw that the plane had landed itself. I taxied back to dispersal, hoping that I had given the impression that I had done the landing myself, forgetting that the instructors on duty would have seen everything.

The red light showed on the control tower, indicating that I had to report to the Chief Flying Instructor. I did so and was informed by the Adjutant that he was at a meeting and to come back at two o'clock. I decided to go to the mess and have lunch. There I met up with Wally, who was usually a very happy chap but now seemed to be rather glum. He should have gone solo by this stage but was nervous about doing so and had decided that he was not meant to be a pilot, so his instructor had taken him off the course. Other cadets were similarly affected and were choosing to be Navigators or Flight Engineers. They were posted back to Hillside and eventually the UK.

After lunch, I went to lie down for a while and then back to the Adjutant at two o clock sharp. Yet again, the CFI wasn't there. I was told by the Adjutant that there had been a major crash that he was attending to and to come back at four.

When I returned again at four, I entered his office fully expecting to be scrubbed from the course then and there. Instead, he pointed to a single chair and told me to sit down. Then, the questions started as he told me to recount all of my experiences with FO/T. In the process, I decided to be honest about my swearing at an officer which had cause FO/T to lose his temper and send me off to fly, unprepared for his style of landing. The CFI was quiet in thought for a while and then said 'Elliott, you are not yet nineteen, so from tomorrow I'm going to place you with Flying Officer Wright. He is our most experienced instructor, so if he can't get you flying again then nobody can'. Then he added, 'Off you go and no more swearing at officers!' So I wasn't scrubbed at all.

I imagine that your new instructor was better than FO/T.
He was much better; he was a very easy man to get on with. When I first met FO/W, the first question he asked was, 'How old are you?' I replied, 'Nineteen next week sir' He then told me that he had two

grown-up sons both in their twenties. I think he was trying to imply that he was old enough to be my father.

On our first trip, he taught me several things but no landings. The next day ended up with him telling me to do the landing but I was hopeless at it. The day after, I tried again but still no good. So we got to Friday and he told me that it would be my last chance as the CFI had told him that if there was still no success that day, he would take me off the course.

After take-off, FO/W told me to head for satellite two, another small reserve airfield. He told me that it was only a long narrow strip on which planes could land from either direction. He kept stressing to look ahead in case of other planes. I did and made a perfect landing. He jumped up in excitement saying that he knew that I could do it and why had I been holding back on him.

He told me to take off again and give him, 'Another landing just like the last one'. I did it! Then he climbed out saying, 'It's all yours, give me two landings, then it's back to base where you can land there too' I did so and they were both good, so I had finally solved the problem.

What changed with your landings that allowed them to go from horrendous to successful?
The difference was that FO/T had told me to look down when I was landing; to judge my height by the shadow of the wheels approaching the ground. But my first instructor and F/OW told me look straight ahead and judge distance that way. That was the big difference which changed everything with my landings.

Did you have to study for and pass anymore exams?
While we had ten exams on the subjects at Hillside, we only had to take seven exams on seven subjects at Induna; the lectures were more light hearted too. I think that a big factor in it was that from Induna onwards, if you failed the exams, then you had another chance to take them. Gunnery Theory, Bombing Theory and Air

Craft Recognition were the three that we didn't have to study for. The other seven subjects were the same subjects as before, just at a higher level.

Was the Tiger Moth a nice, enjoyable plane to fly?

Yes, it was an easy plane to fly. It was such a simple layout with two fixed wheels, tail skidder, rudder pedals and a joystick. However, not everyone enjoyed it. We had a chap transfer from the Middle East. He originally worked as an engine fitter but somehow ended up on the pilots' course. After a while, he became sick of flying Tiger Moths or 'toys' as he called them. So, one day, as a form of protest, he came into land in the part of the airfield where the Tiger Moths were parked, in two rows facing each other wing tip to wing tip. He hit the ground just before the first one and carried on going. He wrote off seven in total including his own. He survived and wasn't even injured. Everyone thought that he would face severe repercussions and be kicked off the course. But astonishingly, he was just given a stern talking to and was back on flying the next week. It was unbelievable, utterly unbelievable.

You would have bet everything on him being kicked off the course.

Yes absolutely, seven Tiger Moths written off in such a way. I wish I had seen it really.

Having passed the ground course and completed your Tiger Moth training, what came next?

Cadets who successfully completed the Elementary Flying Training School then had to choose to go onto either the fighter or bomber stream for further training. Fighter schools were equipped with American Harvards and the bomber schools were equipped with twin engine Oxfords. Those schools had the title of 'Senior Flying Training School.

I told FO/W that I wanted to join the fighter stream, but he vetoed that and instead entered my name onto the bomber stream. When I asked him why he had done this he said it was because I was too gentle on the controls and added, 'If caught in a dog fight, by the time you had nursed your plane into a gentle turn, you could have been shot down several times.' So the next stage for me was bomber training. The school I was posted to was named 'Kumalo' and was on the outskirts of Bulawayo. So that was handy, plus I had a room to myself which was also nice. I was at Kumalo for just over four months.

Did you ever find out what had caused the crash that the CFI had to attend?
Yes, I visited the cadets involved at the hospital. I was told that FO/T was in a Tiger Moth with one of them and was warned by him that his other cadet was in the air and was coming into land and that they would collide. He was told by FO/T not to worry; that the cadet in the air had overshot the airstrip several times and would do the same again. Unfortunately, he didn't. As a result, he landed on top of the Tiger Moth on the ground. FO/T was sitting in the front and came out of it with only minor scratches, but both students suffered appalling injuries. Both had broken backs and other breakages. They were still in hospital when I eventually left Rhodesia.

Did FO/T face any punishment for what had happened?
I don't know. What I do know is that he was taken off instructing and posted back to Britain. But I don't know what happened after that.

So it was decided. You were put onto the bomber stream and posted to Kumalo. Was there much difference between Kumalo and Induna?
Very much so. Kumalo was completely different. While Induna was quite a small set-up without a proper runway, Kumalo had a main runway and a field that could be used due to Rhodesia's lack of rain. There were two hangars on the southern end and as I have said, here, we had our own room with a bed, writing desk and chair. It was a set-up I preferred.

On the 17th August I met my first Oxford instructor and was

surprised as he was only twenty-one years old. He went through the usual aircraft introductions which of course were quite different to the Tiger Moth. The Oxford was a much larger plane, able to carry six passengers in addition to the crew. So instead of a tail strut it had a conventional tail wheel. It had flaps and hydraulic brakes and two engines whereas the Tiger Moth only had one. Things like this even made taxiing different. Quite a lot of the early instructions concerned those different additions. The next stage I watched carefully as he took off, circled and then landed. He then backtracked to the take-off point and off we went again. I expected him to hand over the controls so I could have a go, but instead, he repeated everything as before including the landing. Both of those circuits were done in the morning.

By the 19th August I had been on several flights with my instructor but still had yet to take off and land on my own. This really bothered me and conjured up fears that I was on the path to repeat what had happened with the Tiger Moths; mainly the problems I went through with the landing part. I went to see the CFI and explained my issues. He told me to come with him and we went quickly to a hangar where an Oxford was stationed. He told me to get in and to taxi to the take-off point, to take off, do a circuit and then to land it. And that's what I did.

At Induna, a lot of time was taken up on lectures and the theoretical aspects of flying, which kept you on the ground. Was it the same at Kumalo or was more emphasis put on flying?

At Induna, the flying against lecture ratio was pretty much even, but at Kumalo it was definitely more on the flying side. What made it much more difficult is that we had to do the same syllabus as those before us had completed, but in our case, in much less time as the powers that be were desperate for aircrew due to the high casualty rate. While the course originally had to be completed in twenty weeks, for us, it had to be done in twelve. To put this into context, on the 27th November 1943, I flew four times. Each time I went up, I and another cadet named Jack would swap who was piloting the aircraft and who was navigator. On another occasion, after a

Saturday morning flight, I returned to my room and fell fast asleep, without even bothering to take my flying clothing off. I eventually woke up, thinking it was seven in the evening, and that I would need to get a move on to avoid missing the evening meal. I quickly changed and made a dash for the mess but soon discovered that the sun was in the wrong part of the sky and that it was actually Sunday morning. I had slept for sixteen hours! So, I made my way back and slept for another two.

If that story is anything to go by, it sounds like the course itself was very demanding.
It was, especially as we had fewer weeks to complete everything. Cadets never used to fly on weekends, but there we were, flying on Saturdays, trying to make up the hours. However, as we had already passed the various exams, the lectures we had were a lot more informal, if you will. They were more on the lines of tips and advice on the various aircraft and what was to come.

Despite having our own rooms, the last two weeks of the course were spent under canvas. The point of this was to get us used to the fact that most of us would have to experience conditions like it on our travels and postings. I remember that the rain tipped down on the second week which was unusual for Southern Rhodesia. It was so heavy that we all took the opportunity to shower in it. Unknown, to us, the camp photographer, as a joke, had photographed us doing this and to our horror, it was an elderly lady who was to have them developed.

What sort of exercises did you have to do with the Oxford? With the Tiger Moth it seemed like it was more about setting a foundation with basic flying, getting used to being in the air, while I imagine that Oxford exercises were designed to resemble the actual operations that you would soon be undertaking.
Yes, it resembled operational flying to such an extent that we would sometimes be ordered to pretend that we were on operations. We would take off, navigate to the site, drop our 'bombs', navigate back, and land. Before we took off for these 'operations', we would

all assemble and have people tell us the various facts and figures of the 'operation'. This included where we were going, what targets we were going to strike, what the weather would be like on the way there and back. The intelligence people would have their say on the known state of any defences. It was a mock version of the briefings we would have before undertaking real operations. When we returned from our imitation operations, we would even have a mock debriefing. All of these mock operations happened twice, with Jack and I swapping the roles of pilot and navigator.

There was one pretend operation where Jack was flying. We had to fly low, pretending that the enemy had radar. The ravine we were over had little offshoots and we worked out that if we took the third ravine, it would take us close to the bombing area where we would have to climb, drop the bombs and return home. Unfortunately we picked the wrong ravine and as soon as we turned, we had cliffs in front of us due to this ravine being much shorter in length. Jack had to put on full power and steeply climb over them. I was in the nose of the plane at the time acting as navigator and was absolutely mesmerised by the sight of the cliffs coming ever closer. When we got back to base we told our instructor about this experience and he told us that we were lucky on several accounts: one it was a brand new plane, two it gave us maximum power as it was new, and three, we were probably caught in an updraught which helped us to climb.

On another occasion, I was flying into the sun; in other words, the sun was ahead of me, which effects one's vision. Coming from the opposite direction was another Oxford at the same height as myself. Fortunately, it was being flown by an instructor. When we saw each other, I pulled back hard on the controls to increase height and he dived down. It was one of those things that was over in seconds. It wasn't spoken about once I was back on the ground and I never heard any more of it. Thinking about it, I must have been slightly higher than he was for myself to go up and he to go down.

During these navigation exercises, there seemed to be a risk that if you made a mistake and became lost, you could run out of

fuel, not knowing how to make it back or face a similar potential tragedy. Was that ever a concern?
Yes, it was always in the back of your mind. Two cadets force landed as they were running out of fuel while on a navigation exercise and were murdered when they wandered into a village while trying to find their way back.

That's tragic. What happened with the two cadets?
Well, during the start of the Oxford course, say a couple of weeks after it began, it became known that an Oxford had gone missing that had been in the hands of two cadets who had been on a cross country exercise. A big search party was assembled and all training flying ceased while the search was on, but after three to four days, flying continued and the search was called off as it was believed that no one could last in the wilderness of Rhodesia for that long. Eventually, around six weeks after they had gone missing, they were found after a native of Bechuanaland land had walked into the police station and had reported that he had seen a big yellow bird on the ground - Oxford training planes were painted yellow.

The authorities of Southern Rhodesia got permission from the Bechuanaland authorities to search the site. They found the abandoned Oxford, with the chocks in place and with the engine and cockpit covers on. But the two things that were missing were the navigator's maps and the compass. They had left a note which stated the direction they were going to take from the aircraft to a river that they had seen from the air. But when our people followed this track that they had marked out, they didn't find anything at all.

But then the chief navigator of the unit had a brain wave regarding all of our compasses - big magnetic ones with the needle floating in alcohol. He remembered that every fifteen degrees, the compass had to be compared with another compass at least fifty yards away to account for the magnetic pull of the aircraft. They discovered that the course that the airmen had taken was without taking into account either the magnetic pull of the aircraft or the variation between magnetic north and true north, or possibly both. As a result they ended up in a native village. It transpired that they had both been murdered and their remains stuffed into termite mounds. When the authorities arrived in the village, the chief of the village and the witchdoctor were both found to be wearing RAF clothing. The two of them were taken to trial, confessed to the killings and were then hanged in Bulawayo jail. The village was then destroyed; burnt to the ground I believe.

What a horrific story.
It must have been a horrible ending for the lads. What I don't understand is that we were all instructed to stay with the aircraft if an event like that happened. But I guess that if you crash in the middle of nowhere without any communications and you are running out of supplies, many would try and find their way back.

Before passing out of Kumalo, you had to complete the famous Wings Exams.
Yes, they were on the same seven subjects but at a more advanced level. The same rules applied as at Induna. If you failed any of the exams, you were allowed a second go. I passed first time but seven cadets failed on the first attempt. I believe that they all passed on the second attempt.

By the way, having received my wings, I was promoted to 'sergeant' which once again meant an increase in pay, as every increase in rank did.

What do you remember about receiving your wings?
It was rather a quiet affair. We all lined up next to each other and the Air Vice Marshall in charge of the RAF in the whole of Southern Rhodesia then pinned them on to our chests. We sewed them on later, and later still, replaced them with metal ones. Once given them, we were told that unless we did something really dire, they could never be taken away.

The Air Vice Marshall then gave a speech where he said that we were now pilots in His Majesty's Royal Air Force and that we think we know it all and are now are all going to show off. He told us to go ahead and do it, to go to our girlfriends or parents' house and show off. But to only do it once, as to do it a second time would be dangerous, and to do it a third time would lead to us killing ourselves. It was RAF superstition, like in the First World War where the men in the trenches were told not to light a cigarette lighter three times or the sniper would get you. Ironically, and quite tragically, immediately after this ceremony, The Air Vice Marshall got into his personal Harvard and flew back to Salisbury and due to fog, ended up crashing into hills, resulting in his death. This was never officially announced. It just was something that we learned over the grapevine, so I have no idea how true it is.

Speaking of Harvards, my friend Cyril from the ATC was a few months younger than me, so he followed me out to Rhodesia on a later course. By the time he arrived at Hillside, I was at Induna so we were unable to meet, except once in Bulawayo. He in turn went to the Tiger Moth school named Thornside, so again, we were unable to meet. I went onto the bomber stream and he went on to the fighter stream and on to Harvards. Unfortunately, he suffered a bad accident which put him off flying. Like others in a similar situation, he was posted back to Britain and received compulsory orders to join what were known as 'Bevin Boys', who were men sent to work in the coal mines. By the time I arrived back from overseas, he was out of the mines and I think he was working for a bank but unfortunately he had moved to Shropshire and as a result, I never saw him again.

While we are on the topic of friends, I forgot to mention that while I was in Southern Rhodesia, I used to meet up with Mervin from the troopship, quite regularly on Sundays as we went to church together. He was on the course ahead of me due to me being struck down with malaria. He used to give me helpful advice and tips on what was to come.

What did you think of the Oxford at the time and how do you look back on it?

It was quite an easy plane to fly, actually. It had a particularity, at least in my opinion in the sense that when you landed it, it would bounce forward resulting in the weight going onto the nose and the propellers going into the ground which generally resulted in engines catching fire. I had been flying with an instructor and was told to do an exercise or something which involved taking off. As I waited at the take-off point, an Oxford was coming into land, did the landing, bounced and tipped onto its nose, the props hit the runway and the port engine caught fire. Then a second Oxford came in and the same thing happened except with the starboard engine. The fire engine that was putting out the fire on the first Oxford had its work cut out as it quickly had double the work. It was quite common though. Our course leader wrote off three Oxfords, two during the day and one at night. On the night flight, he overshot the airfield and went between two trees causing the wings to be ripped off. The plane ended up sliding along on its fuselage.

I'm just glad that you managed to land them without any engines catching fire or ending up on your fuselage, that you never had any incidents with them.

Well I did have an incident. It's something I must confess to after seventy five years. I was on a night exercise with the object of landing at Kumalo, but as I was coming back, I spotted the lights of the Hillside area. The two areas were not too far from each other. Being young, I couldn't avoid the temptation of going into a shallow dive and roaring over them, breaking one of the basic rules of the air, not doing 'beat-ups'. I knew that I would have been seen and tracked; that any plane would be tracked - what direction it approached from and everything. So, after my dive, I climbed back up to circuit height and returned to Kumalo from a different direction to make it look as though I had returned from the exercise at that direction. Over the next few days there was a big investigation in both Oxford camps, Kumalo and Heany. Everyone was questioned and when my turn came, I made up a story about how on my return, I had seen a plane flying low down in that area. The Kumalo investigators thought that nobody who had studied at Hillside would 'beat up' his own pals. In the end, the belief was that it must have been someone from Heany, so they were all banned from leaving the camp for a while.

Another incident that comes to mind is when I landed at Kumalo on a very windy day. I had just landed and was rolling to a stop. There were two hangars at Kumalo that were quite close to each other. As a result, if the wind was strong and in the right direction, it would almost be sucked through the gap between the two and cross the runway, as it was on this occasion. When I came to this section of runway, the wind caught the tail fin and started to cause my Oxford to spin. I put on opposite rudder and increased the power of the starboard engine. I was soon out of the wind stream which stabilised my Oxford. But the air traffic controller noted it down as a bad landing and notified the CFI. Later that day, I was called to see him and I explained what had happened. He asked me if I had learnt anything from the incident and my reply was that I had, that I had learnt to take into account the dangers posed by crosswinds when I landed. His reply was that it can happen to any pilot regardless of experience and that the same thing had happened to him that morning.

CHAPTER FIVE

FROM SOUTHERN RHODESIA TO JERUSALEM

Travelling through Africa to Cairo and memories of Egypt.

What happened after you received your wings? I assume that you were posted to a new flying school that involved new aircraft. For a group of fifteen of us, three of whom were older chaps, the next stage involved a lot of travelling. We were posted from Kumalo to Jerusalem, which is obviously on another continent. We travelled by three methods: train, open back truck and flying boat. We left Southern Rhodesia on the 30th December 1943 and arrived in Cairo on the 15th January 1944 and were there until the 1st February.

We were first put on a train to Victoria Falls, the same line as before, but this time we only stayed there for a few hours. We then departed from Victoria Falls, carrying on with our train journey, but there was an incident when our train came to a loop. It would normally have gone into the loop to let the train coming in the other direction go through. But when the train crew tried this, they found out that the last two cars which were restaurant cars, blocked the line. When the other train tried it, the same thing happened, the line was blocked. Us RAF lads set to, to solve the problem. We went to the crew to tell them our plan, but we were told to mind our business. Their solution in the end was by going into the loop as far as it could go, leaving the two restaurant cars on the track. The south bound train then went through, connected to the two restaurant cars and pushed them all the way back to Victoria Falls. All of this took around three hours and for the rest of the journey we had nothing to eat or drink.

From there, we crossed over into Northern Rhodesia, now known as Zambia, into a town named Livingstone. We spent one night there and what surprised us was how cheap everything was.

The next day, we were put onto three trucks. During the journey, we were caught in the slipstream of dust being kicked back from the truck in front so we were caked in dust. On top of that, the seats were rock solid and as you can imagine all of this led to an uncomfortable journey. The journey was roughly three hundred miles and ended at an army camp where we stayed the night. Once we arrived there, a load of us stripped down and made our way to the lake, to go swimming; to wash all the muck off. Just as we were about to enter the lake, an army captain came rushing over shouting at us not to go anywhere near the water. He shouted, 'Haven't you heard of Bilharzia!' We replied, 'He isn't with us.' He then told us that it is a water borne parasite, a worm that burrows into your skin and gets into your blood stream. There were a group of natives swimming in the lake without a care in world, but still, that put an end to our desires to swim.

The captain proceeded to tell us that as we were in an army camp, we fell under army orders.

We were billeted in two wooden huts, which could house twelve people each. The three older chaps decided that they would like to stick together in one hut, and the remaining twelve of us decided to remain in the other one. Apparently, the natives who worked in the camp were known to come in and steal things, so the army soldiers told us to look after our stuff, which we did. One man stood by the door keeping a lookout and he would be swapped every hour. The three older ones in the other hut didn't do the same as us and as a result, they lost everything; literally everything. The rest of us had to give them what we could from our supplies otherwise they would have been completely naked. We were only there for one night.

The next day, we were all put onto a train and eventually found ourselves in a second army camp. The following day was another train journey to Lake Tanganyika. After crossing that lake, it took us two days to reach Lake Victoria which I remember as we had to sleep on the train. We had a chap in charge of our party, whose job it was to make sure we reached Cairo. He came up to me and asked if I wouldn't mind sleeping on the floor as they were one bed short, I agreed. So, in the carriage I was in, the chap in charge was on the top bunk, an army chap on the bottom bunk and myself on the floor. In the early hours, I awoke to this army chap trying to interfere with me. But before he had any success, I was awake and swearing and shouting at him which woke up the chap in charge. He turned on the light and proceeded to call him a bunch of explicit names and that was the end of it.

From there, we crossed Lake Victoria by boat, which took twelve hours. This boat had cabins which had two individual beds inside. Most of them were full and if you didn't have one, you had to sleep on the deck. I was relieved to find a spare bed until I saw that the kitbag that was already there belonged to the army chap from the train. I could tell by the name and handwriting on his kitbag that it was the same army chap so I chose to sleep on the deck.

We disembarked in Kasumo, but we were only there for a few hours, maybe not even that. We were told by a man that our billets were at the top of a hill, which we proceeded to climb. Within minutes of reaching these billets, we were told that there had been a mistake and that we actually had to go back down and board a flying boat named 'The Caledonian'.

The first stop was a place named Juba, on the White Nile. We spent one night there. The next day was spent mainly flying, our destination being Khartoum. We were only there for one night and had to leave at five the following morning. We didn't get to see or do anything. When we left, there was a full moon in the sky. It wasn't light yet. This caused me to recall an army song that we all knew. The part which came to mind was, 'We are leaving Khartoum by the light of the moon. We are sailing by night and by day!' So, we made our way to Cairo. On our way there, as we flew over the desert, the plane suffered horrific turbulence which the pilot counteracted by climbing.

I forgot to mention that I had developed a cold sometime during this journey that was giving me grief, especially in my ears. It had eased once the pilot had ascended but once he descended and landed, the pain came back. But luckily, I misjudged a step when I disembarked. The jolt from hitting the ground after misjudging the step somehow caused the pressure to be released from my ears which left me in a much better state. By the way, none of these flying boats were RAF aircraft; they all belonged to 'Imperial Airways'. We did ask the crew how much they were paid and they told us that they received one farthing an air mile. As a result they were refuelling and then continuing on to their next destination, as more time in the air meant more money for them.

Post-Southern Rhodesia, you didn't spend a lot of time in the African countries and cities you passed through. Despite this, were you able to form any comparisons and opinions about them? After all, it's a giant and diverse continent.
Not really. After all, we were just passing through and didn't really have the time to speak to people and explore. It was a journey of highlights and was rather boring at times. At no time did I ever feel any antagonism or disdain during this journey. But again, interactions and time to explore was very limited.

You were in Cairo for two weeks before being posted to Palestine. What did you do while you were there?
In Cairo, we stayed in quite a nice hotel named 'The Heliopolis'; five to a room. We didn't have duties during our two weeks there. It was staffed by Italian prisoners of war and they struck me as being quite depressed. There was a sad demeanour about them which was understandable.

As we had so much free time, we decided to do a lot of sightseeing. One of the first places we went to was the 'Museum of Hygiene' and it was awful. They had detailed wax exhibitions of what all these awful diseases could do to the human body, but in quite graphic detail. Once we had finished downstairs, the museum curator asked us if we wanted to see what was upstairs. One of our party asked if it was as bad as what we had just seen. We were told that it was worse which prompted us to decline his offer and leave.

We also visited the Pyramids. There were two ways of getting there back then, either by horse or by camel. My four chums had ridden horses in the past but I had not. By the time I managed to mount my horse, the other four were already way ahead which caused my horse to take off quite quickly after them. I was terrified which is ironic considering that I had no fear of going up thousands of feet in a plane by myself. Once we got there, we discovered that we were able to go inside. As you can imagine, it was completely dark. The guides profited by selling strips of magnesium which could be set alight and used as a candle, though they only lasted a few minutes, so one would then buy a new strip and so on.

What was it like to be standing in front of and then going inside one of the most significant and famous manmade structures in history?
What struck me about them was the size of them, they were huge. The tunnels were narrow but you could keep upright. We came to the edge of a chamber and had a look but didn't go inside. But just by being inside the pyramid, you felt as though you were part of history but at the same time there was certain uneasiness about it where I just wanted to get out.

The two cities that you spent the most time in on the African continent were Bulawayo and Cairo. How did Cairo compare to Bulawayo?
The people in Bulawayo were very friendly and the city was very clean and well laid out in regards to roads and avenues, while Cairo by contrast was anything but. Also, I don't recall coming across the entertainment facilities that Bulawayo had, like swimming baths and cinemas, though I'm sure they were there. Though we had free time we still had to report to a RAF office every day and to be updated on the latest situation regarding any future activity. There was also quite a big army presence in Cairo too. Unsurprising considering that the North African campaign had only been won around eight months earlier.

With all the British troops there at the time, and the history of Britain and Egypt, what was the general attitude towards the British from the Egyptian people?
To me, there was quite a strong anti-British sentiment. We were told to never get into a confrontation with an Egyptian because it would never be a fair argument or fight. It would quite quickly become you versus a group of them, a fight that could never be won. The army were always in large groups and the British and Egyptians always seemed to stick to their own.

Did you see any other part of Egypt while you were there?
Yes, we took a bus to Alexandria. Out of curiosity, one of my friends took his shoes and socks off and went for a paddle in the Mediterranean but soon came rushing out saying that it was bloody freezing. There was a feeling of age about the place, as though you were many centuries in the past, it was nice. It was a very interesting place. I remember that we found a small café and managed to find tea there. It doesn't sound like anything special but this was the tea drunk in Britain which stuck out to me. In my opinion, Alexandria differed from Cairo in that I found the place quite friendly, there wasn't the antagonism there that there was in Cairo.

Travelling from Cairo to Jerusalem was done by train I assume.
Yes, it was a rather slow journey from what I remember. We didn't stop there, but we passed through a huge army camp, there were acres upon acres of tents. One story which sticks out in my mind is that children used to run alongside the train selling peanuts in paper cones. A chap, not in our group, wanted to buy a cone and lent out the window with a banknote in his hand. The child took the banknote and made a run for it with no intention of handing over the peanuts. This man grabbed the child by his shirt but ripped a huge section of it off. The child scampered away with both the peanuts and the banknote leaving the man shouting explicit words. He then threw the ripped part of the shirt away. Amazingly, the child ran back, picked up the missing piece of his shirt and ran off again.

What was also interesting is that the landscape kept on changing; you never got tired looking out the window. While there were areas that resembled a desert, especially in the beginning of our journey, as we continued on, we would start to see small fields filled with orange trees and date palms, particularly near the coast. Small lakes were also noted.

We really looked forward to arriving in Jerusalem, it was a place that we had heard so much about.

CHAPTER SIX

PALESTINE

Exploring Jerusalem, a tragic passing and forming a crew. Converting on to and taking a Wellington bomber to breaking point. Travelling to India.

Jerusalem is a city steeped in history, a significant city for so many people around the world. It has been occupied and fought over by so many armies and empires throughout history. Even now, the atmosphere one experiences there is hard to describe. What feelings and impressions did you get from being there?
Exactly that, the sense of being a part of history. An immediate reminder of the things I had read about in the bible was observing that many of the Jews of Jerusalem wore their hair in ringlets and were touching the Western Wall. We were told that the reason their hair was worn in such ringlets was so when they died, they could be pulled up to heaven. The Western Wall, even then, had such a high turnover of people coming and going.

How long were you in Jerusalem? Was it a similar situation to Cairo where you had few duties and plenty of time to explore?
Yes, we were in Jerusalem for four weeks, staying in what can only be described as an assigned building. We didn't have any duties during this time, we just had to report to the military officials. The rest of time was spent sight-seeing and looking around. It was quite similar to our time spent in Cairo in that sense. One thing that we did everyday was to go swimming at the Young Man's Christian Association, also known as the YMCA. There was also a library there, on the top floor.

I remember exploring the old town and looking around the whole market. I remember that you could buy these delicious Jaffa oranges that they would cut open and squeeze into a glass for you to drink. They have a very strong taste to them but I must say that dates were my favourite. The market itself was constantly busy and full of life, it was great, you could quite easily spend all day there. Clothing stalls were also there and I took the opportunity to stock up on underwear as the ones the RAF supplied were quite poor.

We also took a one-day bus trip to Bethlehem, which was quite an experience. The atmosphere in the town was quite normal until you went inside the building where Christ was said to be born. Then it went dead quiet, the silence fitted you like a coat in some ways. Even my friend, who was never short of things to say, was completely silent while we were inside. There was quite a deep feeling of holiness when I was in there, a feeling of being blessed. It was a lovely feeling. I can't speak for anyone else but that's how it felt for me. But the town itself, it was quite small, there was a steady amount of people but there weren't masses of them or anything like that.

We also took a one-day trip to Tel-Aviv, I seem to remember that it was an RAF vehicle that took us there which of course introduced a time limit which wasn't the case when we went to Bethlehem. Either way, we spent most of the day on the beach.

It was during these first weeks that I received a batch of post that had finally caught up with me; around nine envelopes in total. In that batch was a letter from Bert, my foster parents' own son. In the letter, he informed me that my foster father had died on the 16th December 1943, the same day as I received my wings. It was horrible, I was crushed, I really liked him. In the same batch was a letter from Mervin's mother telling me that he had been killed. He never completed the pilots' course because he couldn't do two manoeuvres at the same time. So, he became a navigator and when returning from his first operation, over Europe, the aircraft he was in crashed into a church steeple in heavy fog conditions.

It must have been horrible to receive two letters like that.
Yes, and the five of us were just about to go out when our mail arrived. We decided to open our mail before going out and the reason I opened Bert's letter is because I recognised his handwriting. As I

said, I was crushed and just started crying. The others went out and I just stayed in with my thoughts.

The 1930s and 1940s saw an escalation in violence in Jerusalem for many reasons, the unpopularity of the British being one of them. To what extent did this situation impact you?
Well my little group always stuck together during that period, not because of any threat, but because there was an atmosphere of tension, and various groups like the Stern Gang were getting a lot of publicity. We were on alert but fortunately, nothing happened to us. One could still go around sight-seeing and visiting the market without any issue.

Eventually you were posted to Aquir.
Though fifteen of us arrived in Jerusalem, I was the last one left out of the group. How this came about is that the officials sorted everyone by age and the older ones were posted first and it worked its way down like that. Of course, new names were added which eventually left me as top of that group. As far as I can remember, in Palestine, there were three fighter conversion units, two Spitfire and one Hurricane or maybe the other way around and two bomber conversion units. These units were called 'operational conversion units'.

We were all put on a coach, about thirty of us and posted to RAF Aqir, in order to convert on to Wellingtons. After we got off, we were taken to a big hangar where many other personnel were. An officer told us to mingle and form crews. Basically how it worked is that one man would walk up to a pilot and say something like, 'Have you got a wireless operator' or whatever trade he held, and if the pilot didn't have a wireless operator and they all got on, then he became the wireless operator of that crew. I was in No. 76 Operational Training Unit.

What happened once your crew was assembled?
We were only in Aqir for a little over two months, in which time I only did around eighty-two hours of flying which is nothing really,

especially when you consider the fact that I totalled one hundred and fifty seven hours in the Oxford. Anyway, once the various crews were assembled, we started flying as a crew and started to work out how to work as a team.

At Aqir, it was tradition to have a drink when you formed your crew. This event was the first time in my life that I had drunk alcohol. At two in the morning I felt that I was going to be sick but the nearest latrine was around one hundred yards away. I made a quick dash under the full moonlight to the latrines, made it there and was sick everywhere. It was then that I realised that I was completely naked. Unfortunately, on the following night, a navigator who shared the same hut as myself disappeared. One of the others who was in our hut said that the chap who disappeared had gone to use the latrine. What we all believed happened is that he had been kidnapped by the Arabs. We never found out for sure though as no witnesses came forward and no body was found. There were no guards at this camp so it would have been quite easy for anyone to come in. Thing is, that could easily have been me the night before.

During this time, I met an Australian pilot named Carl Fristrom, who preferred to be called 'Frizzy'. He would go on to become my best friend during the coming years.

How long did it take for your crew to gel, was there instant rapport?

We all got on well quickly and this transferred into flying, where we began to work as a well-oiled machine. Though I was the youngest at nineteen, we were all within a few years of each other, except for my rear gunner who was eleven years older than me.

There was one character though, my first navigator. He was quite a maverick and was a hard drinker. He was always making us laugh and pulling practical jokes. For example, we were once in the mess and he got on the phone to the Commanding Officer and asked 'are you the C/O?' Then once the reply came, he asked, 'Do you know who I am?' Then, once the reply came he slammed the phone down and walked off saying, 'Guess he's not in' while shrugging his shoulders.

Another time, we were coming back from a night exercise when some lights appeared off the coast, quite a cluster of them, obviously boats of some sort. My navigator saw this, leant over and said, 'See those lights down there, they're Japanese trawlers, we should go after them!'

I was only with him for a few weeks before he was posted back to Britain, which I'm sure was due to his reputation and actions, which often involved drunken brawls. Even before I arrived, he had a reputation for being a maverick and had been overseas for over four years whereas a tour was set at two and a half years.

I didn't get on with my next navigator at first, which is ironic as we became good friends later. Our friendship developed quite quickly though as we discovered that we worked for the same company before being called up, just in different counties; him in Essex and myself in Kent. He was an excellent navigator; he could navigate you through the eye of a needle in the darkest of conditions. His name was Len.

Seeing as you now had your wings and were a qualified pilot, did the procedure of learning to fly the Wellington differ from when you learnt to fly the Oxford?

Well this time we didn't have any lectures or anything like that as we were now qualified pilots, but flying didn't start straight away as we had to do a brief classroom period of learning all the systems of the Wellington. It was described how to handle and fly them, how the plane worked and what to do in emergencies, alongside the electronics, the hydraulics and pneumatics. We would start by going over it in the classroom and would then go to see it in person. This stage was purely to prepare us for operations. There was a system in the Wellington of transferring fuel from a tank on one side to the other, so if one tank was running out of fuel you could transfer its contents to another one.

Another exercise was learning the emergency procedure for bailing out and we learnt this on a non-flying Wellington in the hangar. Several matrasses were put in front of the hatch, we then had to put on our parachutes and pretend that we were bailing out. In my case, there happened to be a loose screw on the side of the hatch which caught my uniform and almost ripped it off. I went back to try it a second time knowing I had to master it and the same thing happened. The third time it tore my trousers. Frizzy thought it was hilarious.

An important exercise was how high we could fly without oxygen. How they measured this was that we were sat crew by crew and had a doctor by the side of us. We were in a decompression chamber and they gradually lowered the amount of oxygen in the chamber and used that to record how high we could fly without passing out. For what it's worth, in the chamber, I reached the equivalent of twenty-three thousand feet and the rest of my crew were similar. I think the rear gunner reached twenty-five thousand feet. It was an important exercise for me as otherwise, I wouldn't have considered the possibility of passing out.

I did nearly pass out a few nights later while on a night exercise when my oxygen supply became disconnected. I started to believe that the plane was doing strange things like flying upside down as the stars appeared beneath me, but this was a false picture as I was hallucinating. I told my Flight Engineer to check my oxygen and he managed to fix it.

Learning to fly a Wellington was the same as an Oxford in the sense that the pilot went up with an instructor who showed him everything to do with taking off, flying and landing in really precise detail; alongside when to lower the undercarriage, when to operate the flaps and so on. My instructor was Flight sergeant P and I didn't like him. He used to try and make flying as difficult as possible, like turning off one engine and making you fly purely on the other one. On another occasion, we were coming back over the Eastern Mediterranean when FS/P noticed searchlights glaring in the sky, probably to do with an exercise for another unit. He proceeded to fly into them, then handed me the controls and told me to get us out of them which I did by going into a sharp dive, then putting on hard left rudder to put us back on course. My crew wasn't with me during these exercises.

I didn't see much of the crew for the first two weeks as I first had to complete the things that I have just mentioned, the exercises with FS/P and everything. Then I had to be passed to fly a Wellington solo without an instructor present. I had to go to a different airfield to practise take-offs and landings. This happened for three days beginning on April 9th 1944. Once I passed, we started a programme of regular exercises, day and night with my crew.

Going into the searchlights sounds like quite a baptism of fire as far as exercises go. Were they all so intense?
The exercises we had to do were mainly cross country in which the navigator came into his own. A lot of these exercises took place over the eastern side of the Mediterranean. Having said that, my first night exercise involved an emergency as a red warning light came on. Knowing the system, I knew it had to something to do with the electronics. I radioed base and asked them what to do. They told me that it was probably an electrical fault but to divert to Haifa, an airfield that I had never been to before. The fault turned out to be an instrument failure.

Of course all these exercises were designed to resemble actual operational flying. We had actual bombs to drop at this point, not for every exercise though; just for 'bombing exercises', though these bombs were only eleven pounders, whereas the bombs I dropped on operations were as heavy as three thousand pounds, which had to be dropped from a minimum height of three thousand feet to allow for the updraught.

Seeing as you and Frizzy were both pilots and such good friends, did you ever compete with each other on these exercises?
Well it wasn't planned as such, but if we were put on the same

exercise, we would compare results, it was a very friendly rivalry. But I do remember once, he boasted to me that he had done what I could never do, which was to go past the red line on the instrument panel, which was marked at around two hundred and seventy miles per hour which was the maximum speed you could take a Wellington before it risked falling apart in the air. So, soon after, we were on a daylight exercise at the height of around ten thousand feet when my maverick navigator started to goad me into trying to beat it. So I took it into a dive but completely underestimated the force of the slipstream and soon found myself unable to pull out as I couldn't match the force I was experiencing. As we kept diving, I luckily remembered the elevator trim tab just as we had crossed three hundred miles per hour. My wireless operator became quite scared and started frantically telling me to 'pull out of it!' By the time I operated the elevator trim tab, the speed had reached three hundred and five miles per hour and we couldn't have been much more than three to five hundred feet from the ground. All this took place just as I flew over the airfield. One of the engineers on the ground later told me that it was like 'a bat out of hell'.

That's crazy, though I guess that being nineteen, your concept of danger still wasn't fully developed.
Anything but. It was all exciting at the time. But I didn't intend to cross the three hundred mark or to come anywhere close to it, I just wanted to go one mile an hour faster than Frizzy had. But still, once I landed, the red light came on from the control tower and I had to go and see the Chief Flying Instructor who was not happy. He really gave me a talking to but I think it helped that I looked so young.

I remember on one exercise we had to do night photography. We had to fly over the target and drop the flash so the camera would work. I remember getting back and Frizzy started shouting at me, 'Bloody hell Denis you could have killed me, your flash went off right in front of my cockpit'. He then started laughing. It was that sort of competition and that sort of humour.

I imagine that the day-to-day atmosphere was quite lively, that there was a sense of impending adventure as once all of you had finished with the Wellington Conversion unit, you would be posted to another corner of the globe and find yourself on the cusp of operational flying.

Yes, that's exactly right. Frizzy and I already knew that our next step was to be posted to a Heavy Conversion unit, which we knew was for Liberators. We also knew that we would be posted to India all being well, which led to a lot of excitement and anticipation. Growing up, I had heard a lot of stories about India as it was known as 'the pearl of the empire' and was a place etched in British history.

How did the Wellington compare to the Oxford? Was it a plane you liked?

I liked the Wellington. It was such a powerful machine though not as powerful as a Lancaster. It was also a reasonably easy plane to fly. It was one of the planes that you could land smoothly with relative ease, even from the higher starting point of the cockpit. Ironically, the passenger version of it, the Warwick, was different and was not a plane I liked. It wasn't as sleek; it was a harder plane to land as its elevation wasn't good.

After you had passed out of the Wellington conversion unit, you were posted to India. Jerusalem to India is quite a distance. How long did it take to reach India?

All together, it must have taken about a week to get there. The first leg of our journey was to take the train back to Cairo, through the various fields of fruit and the desert. We were only in Cairo for a day, but while I was there, I made a visit to the dentist as my fillings were coming to the end of their lives. I was at the dentist for just under an hour where they got to work taking out the old fillings, there were about four teeth involved. Two in the front, which I remember the RAF were particular about for image reasons. The other two were molars. We were part way through the procedure when my front gunner barged in and said that the flying boat was leaving in half an hour. In that time I had to pack my kit and everything. We were like blue arse flies. The dentist wrote a note explaining what he had done and told me to find a dentist in India to complete the treatment.

Once we were packed up, we were all put on open back lorries and taken to the awaiting flying boat. Ironically, there was a small wait to receive permission to go aboard. By the way, this flying boat was an RAF Sunderland. It didn't belong to Imperial Airways. Once we took off, we were in the air for about two and half hours. We flew to Bahrain for what was meant to be a simple refuelling stop, but we actually ended up spending three days there. How this came about is that there was an important wedding there that went on for the entire three days. The noise coming from the wedding was quite something. The music and sounds of people partying went on day and night and as a result, we got very little sleep. The engineers who would have been involved in refuelling the plane were guests at the wedding and there was no one else to refuel our plane, so we were grounded. The accommodation that the fifteen of us were given, was a Nissen hut type building.

How did you spend the three days?

Well at this destination, we actually had a chance to go and explore. Even back then, the waters around Bahrain were quite busy with oil tanker type ships. Bahrain itself wasn't built up like it is now with its huge modern cities; in fact, it was all quite undeveloped back then, at least compared to now. I remember hearing the call for prayer bellow out at various times. Another thing that stands out in my mind is the night sky. Due to the lack of light pollution, the night sky was so bright and vivid, it was amazing. Night skies like that are a navigator's best friend.

CHAPTER SEVEN

ARRIVING IN INDIA

The jungle preservation course, pulling a gun on a friend's crew and converting on to Liberators. Meeting the commanding officer of 159 squadron.

Once the wedding was over, did you quickly depart for India?
Yes, one morning, three days after we landed, we were put onto the same Sunderland flying boat in the early hours and began our flight to Karachi. Despite the flight taking most of the day, the nice thing about it was that we were all given a meal on board. That was the highlight of the flight and by the late afternoon, we had landed in Karachi. The fifteen of us were put onto an open back lorry and taken to an army camp fifteen miles outside of Karachi.

Once we were in the camp, we had to queue up for blankets and the most extraordinary thing happened. In the queue next to me was a chap who I was with in the Air Training Corps back in Britain. He was two years older than me so was called up when I was sixteen. He recognised me first and it was quite a sight once we realised who the other was. We only had a few minutes to talk before having to go our separate ways but it was an amazing occurrence.

Within a few days, we realised that we were going to be there for some time with nothing to do, so a few of us had the idea to go into Karachi and rent some bicycles. This included Frizzy and his crew who had been on the same flying boat as us. Close to the huts that we were billeted in was a flat patch of land about the size of a football pitch. We crushed up a tin can and devised a game of polo using the bicycles. By the time we were finished with them, the bikes were absolutely wrecked and the chap who had rented them to us was furious. He demanded money to cover the costs of replacing them and we agreed.

We were there for a total of fifteen days before boarding another lorry that took us to Karachi train station. Our destination was Bombay but we had to go via Lahore. On the way to Lahore, I saw the most unbelievable sight. I saw a cow with five legs, the fifth leg was hanging from its chest, a few inches above the ground, it wasn't supporting the cow or anything like that. It was one of those things that caused me to do a double take as I just couldn't believe what I had seen. I spoke to a crew member of the train about this and he told me that it wasn't as unusual as I thought, that he had seen and heard of them before and that it wouldn't be killed due to the beliefs held by the Hindu population. Remember that before the migration crisis caused by the split of India in 1947, there was quite a large Hindu population in what is now Pakistan.

By the time we reached Lahore it was dark. We took the opportunity to shower, but the heat and especially the humidity were so strong that even though we took the option to shower, we found ourselves unable to dry. We dried ourselves the best we could and got back on the train. From there we travelled to Bombay, which took two days. On that leg of the journey, I noticed that I had developed a sore on my left leg that I knew required medical attention. In our medical packs, we carried needles, threads, little bandages, iodine and the like. So, I proceeded to disinfect a needle with iodine, pricked the sore, dabbed it with iodine and repeated this for the duration of the journey. Once I arrived in Bombay, I went to see a Medical Officer. I told him exactly what I have told you and he told me that I had cured it myself and didn't need any further treatment. I also took the opportunity to find a dentist where I then had the outstanding work on my fillings completed.

From what I remember you telling me, you were in Bombay for an extended period of time, did you get a chance to look around? To many, Indian cities generally come across as quite chaotic.
Yes, but it was organised chaos. We found an air-conditioned cinema which surprised us. Even back then, the traffic was very heavy, it was a very bustling city and there was always the feeling that there was so much to do. For example, it had quite a big lively market.

We were there for two or three days. It wouldn't be my last time in Bombay. It was a city I really liked.

But having said all this, there was a really poor area of Bombay which we visited out of curiosity. In this area, people lived in huts made out of basic materials with roofs mainly constructed of corrugated iron. Due to the lack of sewage facilities, there was an unsavoury smell in the air at all times. But having said all that, I never felt unsafe there.

Afterwards you had to undergo a course known as 'Jungle Preservation'

Yes, we were put in trucks and taken to 'The School of Jungle Preservation', where we spent exactly two weeks under canvas in a jungle-like environment dealing with incredibly wet conditions and doing exercises under the command of retired army officers. The area that the jungle was in was named Mahabaleshwar and in the fourteen days that we were there, we learnt how to recognise poisonous plants, which plants and shoots were edible and how to make cooking pots out of bamboo. With maps of the area and compasses, we had to do daily exercises of following trails that the instructors lay. These would include wading through rivers and streams.

In some parts, the jungle was very dense and required the use of machetes to hack our way through. The instructors would attach certain objects to certain trees so we knew that we were on the right course. Though our boots were meant to be leech proof, they were anything but. We concluded that they would get in through the lace holes - amazing really. They would also get in under your clothes. Unfortunately we were told that our boots were not snake proof, but that if we ever came across a snake, we had to kill it.

Once back at camp, we had to completely undress, dry ourselves off and put on clean clothing. Two charcoal fires provided the heat in which to dry our wet clothing. The fire also helped as we all found ourselves with leeches attached by the end of the day. Luckily, one of our party smoked so we were able to use his cigarettes and matches to burn them off. You can't pull them out otherwise the head will stay attached. How many leeches you had on you was pure luck of the draw. Sometimes you would have one or two on you and other times you would find yourself covered in them.

Though the leeches were bad, one really terrifying event did occur. We had reached a point in the trail that we were on. To our right was a rather deep ravine, at the bottom of which lay a fast-flowing river. To get to this river, one had to go down a small trail which was rather muddy and slippery. From there, one could begin to descend down to the ravine. As Captain of the crew, I went down first. I reached the bottom, but the person coming behind me was Lance, my co-pilot. Now, I was around nine stone and he was around fifteen or sixteen stone. He slipped over and let out a yelp, I turned around to see him sliding down the trail trying to grab on to anything. There was no where I could go, so I grabbed on to a small tree and braced myself. He grabbed on to me and fortunately, the tree didn't break. If it had, I hate to think what would have happened. Luckily that was the only dangerous incident that we experienced on the jungle course.

By the way, the jungle we were in was rated as 'third-rate' jungle. I would hate to find out what first- and second-rate jungle look like.

Another incident I do remember from the jungle was when I pulled my revolver on Frizzy's crew. Frizzy wasn't present as he was in Australia on leave. What happened was that we were on a map-reading exercise through the jungle. My crew was separate from Frizzy's crew. Eventually I heard gun firing in the distance. When my crew and I arrived, we discovered that Frizzy's crew were standing around a pond and shooting at the frogs that were in it. When I saw this, I immediately lost my temper at these innocent animals being shot. I shouted at them that they had better stop or I would do the same to them. One of his crew proceeded to shoot another frog so I pulled out my revolver and shot at the ground next to him, causing him to jump. He told me that it was all a bit of fun to which I yelled that the frogs wouldn't see it that way.

Did any repercussions result from that incident?
No, no officers were present when it happened, and no one reported it. It was soon forgotten.

After you completed your jungle preservation training, did you go straight onto learning to fly Liberators?
No, we were put into trucks and transported back to our quarters in Bombay. From there we went to No.3 Refresher Flying Unit in Poona, where we were for just under two weeks. While we were there, we were given lectures which were refreshers on what we had already done. There was also a lecture on Bombay itself. We were also there to receive new clothing and to deal with any outstanding medical issues.

The next stage was to be by rail which I am fairly sure was the day after we returned. The train took us to Bangalore. We were picked up and taken to the 'Heavy Conversion Operational Unit' which was named 'RAF Kolar'. It was unusual for the RAF to have such an airfield as there was a huge hill of around two thousand feet on the circuit. I can visualise it now, at the end of the runway and to the left of it. The result of all this is that it interrupted the circuit, so when one took off, one had to climb to two thousand feet to clear the hill, then descend back down to one thousand feet when clear of the hill; then complete the circuit.

As we drove in through the perimeter, we walked alongside the hangar and as we entered it, I saw a Liberator in front of me. It was such a big, majestic plane, so much bigger than any other plane I had flown. Upon seeing it, I said to myself, 'Bloody hell, I'll never be able to fly that!' Frizzy on the other hand, seemed excited, as though he couldn't wait to fly it. His attitude seemed to rub off on me as over the next few hours and days I became more excited at the prospect of flying it myself.

As a Liberator was an American plane, were the cockpit and controls any different from its British counterparts, and if so, did you have to go back into the classroom and take lectures to

learn how everything worked before being allowed to operate the controls in the cockpit?
Yes. The day after our arrival, we were taken to a Liberator in dispersal and a slow procession of us circled the plane while the instructor pointed out the various bits and pieces, what they did, how they were positioned and things like that. This is all part of what every pilot knows as an 'outside check'. One had to check the rudders and elevators, parts like that to make sure that they were all moving correctly, to make sure that there was no elevator lock in place or anything like that. If you failed to do these things, there could be serious consequences. For example, if the elevators are locked in place, you won't be able to control the rate of elevation.

If the aircraft was about to immediately fly, a shield covering the 'Pitot Head' was removed. A 'Pitot Head' is a device on the wing that measures the static air versus the speed of the slipstream air and the results are shown on an instrument on the panel inside the cockpit which tells one the speed that the aircraft is traveling. We would also have to check the tyres before any take off, to see if there were any defaults. On the inside of the tyres is a square of yellow paint. On the outside would be a matching yellow square and then on the centre rim, another one. They had to match up within reason to make it safe for flying. If they didn't match up, then it was obvious that the pressure on the tyres was unequally distributed.

There were other things too, things like the engine covers and the cockpit cover had to be removed. Apart from the pilot, it was also the duty of the engineer and the navigator to go with you.

That completed your outside inspection. Then one had to do the inside inspection. Once inside a Liberator, the rear turret is to the left. Before getting to the main part of the fuselage were the side guns. From there one could make their way through the bomb bay area. If the plane was loaded, the bombs would be either side. As one carried on, one would arrive at the wireless and radar operators' positions on the port side, and then the navigators table, also on the port side. And finally the engineers position on the starboard side.

Then there was a seat where a third pilot or second navigator could sit and then you would finally reach the cockpit. Once one was in the cockpit the instructor showed that person what each instrument and dial represented. Further instruction was transferred to the classroom.

Were there many lectures?

There were around eight to ten lectures, about an hour apiece, but it was nothing compared to the lectures in Southern Rhodesia. These were much more relaxed. There weren't interviews as such, but we did have discussions with the instructors about various instruments.

One thing I did that no one else did was I took it upon myself to go visit the airfield every day to see in person what the instructors were talking about. Walking there and back was a four-mile round trip. The first time I went to the airfield, the first plane I found unlocked was unsuitable for my needs because I found that I couldn't' reach the rudder pedals. It was probably on the third visit that a voice asked me what I wanted. It was the flight sergeant in charge and when I told him what I wanted, he told me to come with him. He said the aircraft I was looking at was useless because it was only used to provide spare parts. He told me that he would unlock one of the others, which he did. The controls on the one he opened were perfect. We struck up a friendship and when he asked me how I was getting back. I told him that I was walking back which resulted in him giving me a lift on his bicycle. I sat on the handle bars. I met up with him the next day and quickly realised that he knew as much about a Liberator as a pilot. He suggested that I sat in the pilot's seat and operate the controls so I could see what they did. The Liberator being stationary obviously. Though once he did let me taxi it, though there was no danger as he was sitting next to me the entire time.

My visits there went on for several days and each time I got back to where the lectures were, I met up with everyone else. Most of the others chose to spend their free hours in the recreation ground but by the end, Frizzy had caught on to what I was doing and accompanied me. Once, Frizzy asked me why I chose to make this four-mile trip every day and I told him that I wanted to know how the Liberator operated.

What came next?
After we had finished with all the lectures and knew how to fly a Liberator theoretically, we then went on to practical flying. Initially, we went up with an instructor who showed us everything, how to navigate the hill and complete a circuit. After he was satisfied, it was my turn. I completed my circuit but my co-pilot was told that he would never be able to fly a Liberator after he swerved off the runway twice.

After we had finished all of this, we found ourselves at the noticeboard, looking to see where we had been posted to. Frizzy and myself were posted to an airfield named 'Digri', to 159 squadron. Once we arrived there, we had to see the C/O. Frizzy went in first. After he was done, I knocked on the door and went in. The C/O looked up and said to me, 'Good lord, I didn't know they were sending school boys'. He saw that I had gone bright red with anger and followed it up with, 'All I care about is that you can do the job'.

Both Frizzy and I were told that we would have to go with an experienced captain for the first few operations before being allowed to captain aircrafts ourselves. In total, I went up with an experienced pilot five times but the last one doesn't really count as we had to turn back due to an American miscalculation. They thought that they had seen a group of Japanese naval and supply ships heading north but what had happened was that they had actually seen a very small group of islands which were being hit by northerly winds which was creating what appeared to be a wake. They were observing this from over twenty thousand feet so I can see how the mistake occurred. Still, we had to turn back.

Before we get on to your operational flying, I would like to talk about your first commanding officer on 159 squadron. As we both know, he was no ordinary C/O. He was none other than James Blackburn, a Royal Air Force officer who had been sunk

on the Laconia and held in Morocco as a prisoner of war having survived the sinking. He escaped with two others and made it to the American lines. He was also awarded the Distinguished Flying Cross and the Bar to it. On top of this he was also awarded the Distinguished Service Order and was awarded the Bar to that too. He seems like an exceptional man. What was he like in person?
Firstly, a 'bar' is awarded if the recipient has already been awarded the medal in question and is awarded it again. Anyway, as a person, you sensed that he had that air of authority about him, that sternness. He didn't take kindly to fools, here's an example. On one raid, later on, I was hit with one single bullet that had hit the nose but it didn't affect the plane or hurt anyone. We didn't even know about it until the ground crew informed us following their inspection. This was told to Blackburn in the de-briefing and a chap who was a squadron leader Flight Commander, came out with something like, 'One bullet, is that it'. He made fun of it. Blackburn turned to him and in front of all of us, intelligence people included, said, 'That proves that Denis got much closer to the enemy than you ever did'. The look on the face of this Sqn.Ldr was quite something.

As you will find out later, that was quite a prophetic statement. But at the same time, Blackburn was quite friendly too, alongside this air of authority. He had earned it though; this was his fifth tour of operations!

He seemed like the type of man to inspire complete faith and trust in himself, a true leader.
Yes, he was the type of man to inspire complete trust and confidence. If he was taking part in an operation, one felt safe, that if nothing happens to him, then nothing will happen to me. He was a rare type of chap. He was only interested in operational flying as there was a sense of danger. Regular flying did not interest him at all, he found it boring. He really led from the front.

I remember on Christmas Eve 1944, Frizzy and I grabbed all the chairs and tables from the non-commissioned officers' mess and set up a celebration with bottles of drink and everything. Blackburn walked in, took a look around and said, 'This is where I belong'. He stayed and celebrated with us, not with the other commissioned officers. Imagine it, there's a table with fifteen or sixteen of us, talking about flying, life at home and what have you. Then Blackburn asked us all what we were going to do once the war finished. One or two had ideas, I had no idea. He told us that before the war, he enjoyed sailing, I think it was with his father, and that on one occasion they were 'pooped', which is when a wave goes over and swamps the entire vessel. He then went on to say that once the war was finished, he was going to buy a yacht and sail it around the world and asked if any of us would join him. Everyone remained silent except myself. My hand shot up in the air and I said that I would. He said that he would write to me with instructions once the war was finished and I was out of the RAF.

Finally, before we get on to operational flying, what was the main role of the RAF in India and what was the main role for 159 squadron?

The main role for the Liberator squadrons on the east coast of India was to attack enemy targets then held by Japanese forces in Burma and Siam (Thailand). Our role was to attack the main imports of supplies that the Japanese wanted for their armies in Burma, so that included bombing ships, bombing ports and laying mines, though it wasn't just limited to those types of targets. We bombed railways, bridges, storage depots and targets like that too. 159 squadron was split into three flights, 'A flight 'and 'B flight' with eight Liberators each, which were operational flights. There was also 'C flight' which had four Liberators and carried out what was known as 'special duty flights' which were things like: reconnaissance, getting weather reports, and follow up photography of the results of the bombing by A and B flights. Sometimes, during night operations, C flight would go slightly ahead of us and drop flares to illuminate the area, though it depended on the target. It usually happened with bridges. The crews of the Liberators on C flight were usually made up of men who had completed a tour of operations. All three flights used Liberator aircraft.

CHAPTER EIGHT
OPERATIONAL FLYING

Bombing and mining raids, losing a friend and nineteen-hour flights. The brilliance of 159's commanding officer, dropping napalm, escaping death and the cowardice of a high-ranking officer.

You have already touched upon the fact that you had to act as co-pilot for an experienced pilot for your first five operational flights. What do you remember about your first operational flight?
It took place on the 20th of October 1944. The pilot I was with taught me a lot, he emphasised how these types of operations were supposed to be done in theory to maximise the chances of success. For example, he explained that when laying mines in a river, which we were doing, that it was important to keep the aircraft as close to the centre line of the river as possible. This was done to keep maximum distance from any gun batteries placed on either side of the river. He also taught me how to 'porpoise', which is a gentle moving of the controls forwards and backwards which causes the plane to move up and down. This was to put the gunners on either side of the river off focus.

What I remember is that we were laying mines at a section of the Kraburi River beyond Victoria Point. Before we all got into our aircrafts, I saw my good friend Johnny, who was a navigator, get into his aircraft. I waved at him and said, 'Have a good trip Johnny'. He waved back.

Victoria Point is a small town at the mouth of the Kraburi River which is at the southernmost point of Burma on the border with Malaya, which is now part of the Federation of Malaysia. We were warned by intelligence that there were gun emplacements on the banks of the river. It was a pretty straightforward operation. We arrived at the mouth of the river and flew up it. Fortunately, the anti-aircraft fire we came under wasn't too heavy, though the real concern for us is that we were in the range of Japanese Zero fighter planes so the crew had to be on a constant lookout for those. Anyway, we had eight mines to drop in a pre-determined location. Once the mines were dropped, we were to carry on going for a short distance, then turn, head back to sea and to base.

But one terrible thing happened that I must mention. I told you how I waved to Johnny and wished him a good trip. Well, as we began to climb and bank away, I saw the Liberator that Johnny was in begin to descend in order to lay its mines when it suddenly exploded. It had obviously suffered a direct hit, most likely in the bomb bay. The only reason I saw it is because I happened to be on right side of the aircraft and had seen it in the distance. However, at the time, I didn't know Johnny was in that Liberator.

How do you deal with something like that, losing a close friend in your first operation and actually witnessing it?
My crew and I went to the mess for an after flight meal where we found out about the missing plane and who was on it. After the meal, Frizzy's crew and mine went back to our billets; we were all in the same hut. All I can really say is that I kept my feelings to myself. After a while, you harden yourself to it.

Does it affect personal relationships with comrades and the friendships you make?
It does, but it's such a depth of feeling that it's hard to describe. One way that losing Johnny affected me is that to this day, I have never said to anyone taking any journey, 'Have a good trip', whether it is a plane or a car.

Were these little superstitions common in the RAF?
Yes, I think a lot of it went back to the First World War. Even then there were superstitions about things, like not lighting a cigarette three times or a sniper would notice and get you on the third light. Though I believe that they were quite common, they were not something that was advertised and really spoken about. After all, they are quite personal.

Was your second operation as eventful as your first?
The second operation took place on October 23rd. It involved bombing a town named Taungup. In this town were Japanese supply depots which contained weapons, ammunition, food supplies and the like. Our objective was to bomb these depots. Unlike the first operation which was fourteen and a half hours in total, this one was only seven and a half hours and not a single shot was fired. We flew there, dropped our bombs and came back with no opposition. On the way back I said something to myself like, 'Boy this is a piece of cake, I hope they are all like this'. That was another thing you shouldn't really say.

Your third operation was a very important one. This operation was mining Penang Harbour. Would you mind talking about everything that went into it and explain why it was such an important operation?
It took place on October 26th and it wasn't the harbour itself but the approaches to the harbour that we had to mine. There were two approaches, from the north and south. We were mine laying in the northern approach; other aircraft were mining the southern. Due to the distance we had to travel, a three-thousand-mile round trip which took nineteen hours of non-stop flying, each aircraft was only able to carry four mines as opposed to the usual eight. What made Penang Harbour so important is that it was a vital place for Japanese warships to come and be repaired, re-fuelled and re-supplied. It was our objective to deny the Japanese this essential repair depot.

It was a very complicated operation to carry out because our own runway was too short to try and take off from. This was because of the extra weight involved in carrying overload fuel tanks; which were extra fuel tanks fitted to the aircraft. As a result, we had to take off from an American airfield that had a longer runway. The day before taking off for the raid, our planes were loaded with the four mines and the overload. Fuel tanks were filled, with the main tanks only being partially filled. We then took the planes to this neighbouring American airfield which was about forty miles away and was named Kharagpur. It had a runway of two thousand, and five hundred yards which was six hundred yards longer than ours. The planes were lined up wingtip to wingtip along the perimeter track. The Americans were trying to get in every drop of fuel they could and by the time they were done, a few were resting on their tailskid, front wheel in the air, though once an engine was started, the slipstream from it was enough for the Liberator to tip back on to its front wheels. Each plane, including the extra fuel tanks carried three thousand gallons of fuel. The fuel from the extra tanks were used first and once all the fuel had been used, the flight engineer ditched the extra tanks in order to lighten the load on the aircraft and to achieve maximum efficiency with the remaining fuel in the regular fuel tanks. This was all worked out by Blackburn.

What happened next is that we had to be returned to base by Dakota aircraft to spend the night in our own quarters. The next day the same Dakotas took us back. Each aircrew was lined up next to their plane. The American air men went around offering us sweets and snacks. Also, the Americans didn't believe that it could be done; they didn't believe that the Liberator had the range, even with the extra fuel tanks and were expecting a minimum of a fifty percent casualty rate.

Penang was a three-thousand-mile round trip. The range of a Liberator without extra fuel was two-thousand-four hundred, so their view was understandable. Not only did we have extra fuel, but Blackburn ordered that each Liberator was to have all its guns and turrets removed, except for the front and rear guns. He also ordered that the armour plating behind the captain's (pilot) seat was to be removed because of its weight. However, the crew stayed at seven. They were: captain, co-pilot, navigator, flight engineer, wireless operator and front and rear gunners. An American Liberator crew usually numbered eleven. Even with all of that, no one knew for sure if we would actually be able to even take off.

Blackburn had all the captains around him for a final discussion. What he was waiting for was the arrival of a Liberator that had already been to Penang to get the latest weather forecast. It returned and informed him that the weather report was good. He told us the situation, and informed us that he was going to take off first and that if he didn't make it, it was up to the captains of each aircraft if they wanted to attempt the take-off. That's the sort of man he was, leading by example. Also, before I forget, it was Blackburn who planned the entire Penang operation, by himself, without the support of the Americans or the higher echelons of the RAF.

So Blackburn taxied to the runway and did what is known as a precautionary take-off. That is, when one has both feet on the brakes as hard as one can and opens up the throttle to maximum power, including the turbo boosters. Then when the plane begins to creep forward, one releases the brakes and the plane shoots forward. It enables one to reach take-off speed quicker, using less of the runway. We noticed that his take-off took about two thousand two hundred yards and his climb was painfully laboured. After that, each of us took our turn to take off. In the case of my aircraft, we took the same amount of runway to take off as Blackburn did. With all of us, it was a painfully laboured climb. We had been told in the briefing that the Royal Navy were also taking part in that submarines were positioned; the first one a third of the way to Penang and the second two thirds. Our Navigators were given the coordinates of these submarines with the idea that if anything went wrong and we had to ditch, to do so as close to those coordinates as possible. It takes a mind like Blackburn's to think of something like that, of having help available if anything goes wrong.

It was a nineteen-hour round trip. What was the atmosphere like among the crew on the way there? Did the scale of what you were attempting to undertake reflect the atmosphere inside your Liberator?

Very much so. With such long hours sitting there doing nothing, the realisation of what we were doing really hit us and the tension rose further and further as we got closer. The last half hour or so was very tense; everyone was on edge. We had no idea what defences Penang had; we had no idea if they had any fighters on standby, if they had any gun emplacements. I can almost feel it now. The navigator in the last few minutes had to be sure that we were over the exact point and when the mines were finally dropped, you could feel the tension just disappear, like someone sticking a pin into a balloon.

When you reached Penang harbour, did you have specific sites to target within the harbour complex?
There were two deep water channels feeding Penang harbour. A and B flights were each assigned one of the channels to drop their mines. Each Liberator was carrying four magnetic mines which meant thirty-two mines were dropped in each channel; sixty-four mines dropped in total. We approached at probably no more than two hundred feet in case they had radar. Even so, we had to climb as the ideal height to drop these mines was four hundred feet.

There was huge tension as the navigator counted as each mine was dropped. Once the last one was dropped, there was a huge sigh of relief, we turned sharply to port and began another nine-and-a-half-hour journey back to base. Because we took off at ten thirty in the morning, we arrived just as the sun was setting and arrived back at base just as the sun was beginning to rise the next morning. The timing of it all was planned so we would arrive just as the Japanese were winding down for the day; when they would least expect an attack to happen.

I imagine that the atmosphere inside the aircraft on the way back was a lot more joyful than on the way there.
We were totally relaxed. Though I was only co-pilot on the first Penang trip, I'm sure I flew the Liberator on the way back as the captain had a nap, up until we reached base. It was always tradition for the captain of the aircraft to land. By the way, we didn't land at Kharagpur, we landed back at our own airfield. One thing I should mention is that as I was acting as co-pilot to the captain, we were with his crew, not mine.

Out of interest, how did Kharagpur, the American airfield and its standard compare to Digri, the RAF airfield you were stationed at?

Apart from its size, I got the impression that the atmosphere was a lot more relaxed. Take Digri - if you met another airman, depending on their rank, one would salute the other. There was that formality in place, while with the Americans, they didn't seem to care about that at all, they were really laid back. Also, they seemed to enjoy a higher standard of living than us, they had more money, more consumer products and a lot more imported for them. There also seemed to be more activity, more men and hustle and bustle on Kharagpur compared to Digri.

The RAF seemed to only have the bare minimum amount of men on its airfields while the Americans seemed to have a surplus. The UK had to be careful with what it imported, even the estimated fuel consumption of our Liberators was calculated for every trip, which decided how much fuel each Liberator would receive. The Americans didn't seem to face those restrictions. They were very kind though, offering us sweets and the like, nice chaps.

What was the aftermath of the first Penang operation?

The next day, American B-29 aircraft bombed the trapped Japanese ships from high altitude and reported that several were sunk or badly damaged from the bombing and that others had suffered damage or had sunk after hitting mines when they tried to escape from the harbour.

One thing I find amazing about it is that we were so overloaded with weight, yet not one of the Liberators suffered from an engine failure or anything like that.

Your fourth operation, a bombing raid on Bangkok was quite eventful wasn't it.

Yes, it was on the 2nd of November and it was a night time raid. I couldn't tell you how many Liberators were involved but I can tell you that we were bombing a bridge in Bangkok. All was going well, we attacked the bridge from the north with the idea that after our one run, the sergeant who was captaining the aircraft would fly out to the Gulf of Thailand, turn West, and climb to ten thousand feet and cross Thailand and Southern Burma. From there we would continue on our way home.

But what actually happened is that the sky over Bangkok was clear and there was a full moon which silhouetted us and as we had just finished dropping our bombs, we were still quite low when we reached the Gulf of Thailand. We were met with a horrific sight: four Japanese naval ships that were anchored next to each other. All hell broke loose as they proceeded to open fire on us. There were shells exploding all around, it was like being in the middle of a firework display. The sergeant's reaction was to take violent evasive action which resulted in the plane being thrown around. Honestly, it really scared me. That was the only occasion that I was so scared. I was quite nervous on other occasions but that was the only time that I was truly scared. After all, even at twenty, I appreciated the fact that it only took one shell to bring us down.

Did the plane suffer any damage?
The aircraft sustained very minor damage as luckily we weren't hit directly. The only damage suffered was when a shell fragment struck a blade of the propeller on number two engine. It gave us some vibrating trouble on the way home but didn't impede us or anything like that.

What a frightening experience it must have been.
Yes. Though it only lasted for about three minutes, it was a frightening experience, especially at my age. I was scared stiff.

You didn't complete your fifth and sixth operational flights. What happened?
Yeah, but before the fifth operation, Frizzy and I became captains in our own right as we had finished being screened. As a result, we were promoted to the rank of 'warrant officer' by Blackburn, skipping the rank of 'flight sergeant' completely. I was grateful for the promotion but the reason he did it was because he wanted all of his captains to be commissioned officers, or at minimum, to hold the rank of warrant officer, which is the highest non-commissioned rank that one can hold in the RAF. Prior to that, while we had been

screened, we were 'acting warrant officers'.

Anyway, the fifth operation, on the 4th of November which was also my first operational flight captaining an aircraft resulted in the flight engineer reporting that we had a fuel leak. We were at five thousand feet and over Burma, on the way to Bangkok which was our target. The flight engineer backed up his claim by the fact that there was a smell of fuel in the plane. But what had happened is that the navigator had kicked over a small tank holding fuel for the Auxiliary Power Unit, which gives a boost to the electrical supply when it comes to landing. All of this coincided with the flight engineer telling me about this apparent fuel leak.

What did you decide to do?
Can you imagine the situation, five thousand feet above the Burmese jungle. Do we carry on to the target believing that we could run out of fuel and crash or do we turn around, jettison the bombs and return to base? I asked the flight engineer to use the Aldis lamp to light up the outside of the aircraft to see if we could find the source of the leak. No leak was found but the instruments showed that there was a drop in the fuel supply which pointed to a leak. Combined with the smell of fuel, it led me to decide to turn around, jettison the bombs and return to base. Ironically, as we approached base, the instruments showed that everything was normal and not long after landing, we were told that it must have been an airlock in the pipe connecting the fuel tank to the engines.

I am sure that you had to explain yourself to the senior figures. What was their reaction to it all?
Well, my report had to be given to the flight commander, who was the squadron leader that I have already mentioned. His reaction was one of fury. He told me that I was a disgrace to the Royal Air Force and accused me of cowardice in the face of the enemy; that I could face a court martial. Remember that I was only twenty, going through all these new experiences, so all of this had quite an effect. Anyway, this infuriated me so I went straight to Blackburn and explained what had happened. He assured me that given the circumstances, he

would have done exactly the same as I did. He told me that he would much rather have a full crew and plane back than having a target hit and losing the crew and aircraft. He also told me not to worry about the Flight Commander and that there would be things I would discover about him in time.

Did that claim ever come to fruition?
Yes, I said earlier that Blackburn's statement after the bullet in the nose incident, which happened weeks after this fuel leak incident was prophetic, I'll explain how it was. There were rumours going around that the Flight Commander would jettison his bombs just before reaching the target. This came about because he was always the first one back whenever he flew operational flights. He claimed that this was because he had a faster plane than anyone else, which is utter nonsense. For it to go on for as long as it did, his crew must have been in on it too. I guess the fact that they wouldn't face a fraction of the risk that everyone else would was too much to pass. Not long after the Flight Commander mocked me for being hit with the single bullet in the nose of the plane, Blackburn replaced two of the Flight Commander's crew with two men from his own crew, men he trusted. Once again, the Flight Commander came back early. It was confirmed that he was jettisoning his bombs and after that, he completely disappeared from the squadron.

A year or so later I ran into him at an airfield called Bagarchi, outside of air traffic control. He was in a white uniform. He had become a private pilot for a high-ranking air official. I was quite deliberately trying to draw eye contact but he wouldn't look me in the eye and quickly scurried off somewhere. He must have had contacts in high places. What he did was a Court Martial offence, cowardice in the face of the enemy, yet he became a personal pilot.

But to have the gall to speak to you in such a manner when he was acting in the way he was is unbelievable.
Quite agree. During the war there was a process of automatic promotion. I'm sure that's how he got to the rank of squadron leader. I can't imagine him passing any of the exams that one had to take in

order to be promoted in peace time.

Do you think he was projecting himself in such a way in order to make one think that he would never be capable of such an act himself?
Yes, I think he was trying to place himself in a higher place than he really was and create an image of how brave he was. His crew were slowly drawn into his web.

Did his crew ever face any sort of punishment?
No, I don't remember them facing any sort of punishment. Blackburn put it all on the Flight Commander's head. He was a true coward. I would have loved to have been there when Blackburn was dismissing him. Blackburn was a nice man but if you got his rag up, he was a force to be reckoned with. As an example, a sergeant on the squadron was once a Warrant Officer but due to a drunken brawl he was in one night, was stripped of rank by Blackburn. To put it into context, when I first joined the Squadron, I was a sergeant.

We have just covered why your fifth operation had to be abandoned but why did your sixth operation have to be abandoned? From what you have already mentioned, a group of islands were mistaken for a group of Japanese ships.
As I mentioned earlier, the Americans were conducting reconnaissance from high altitude when they thought that they had seen a group of Japanese naval and supply ships heading north but what had happened was that they had actually seen a very small group of small islands which were being hit by strong northerly winds which was creating what appeared to be a wake. The result was that on the 7th of November, all sixteen of our Liberators were sent to attack this convoy and when we reached the target, discovered that they were in fact islands. We had to jettison our bombs as it was too dangerous to land with bombs on board, turn around and return to base. The Americans had observed these islands from over twenty thousand feet so I can see how the mistake occurred. We took it in quite good humour and were quite relieved. Imagine having to attack a convoy of ships, including heavily armed naval ships with

bomber aircraft in the middle of the sea. It's one thing with nimble fighter aircraft, but imagine doing it with lumbering bombers.

If memory serves me correctly we had a party that night to celebrate the fact that they were islands and not ships.

I assume that your seventh operation was a success and that the target actually existed.
Yes, it took place on the 11th of November and was a pretty ordinary flight. It was mine laying at a small port named Moulmein in Burma, south east of Rangoon. The following two operations were very similar. For the eighth operation, which took place on the 15th of November, a few of us bombed a port named Mergui which was also on the Burmese coast. For our ninth operation, on November 18th, a few of us returned to Moulmein but this time with bombs. The reason I say 'a few of us', is because with these types of raids, the squadron wouldn't all concentrate on one target as was the case with Penang. What would normally happen is that out of the sixteen operational aircraft in 159 squadron, three or four planes would go to one target, three or four to another and so on. The Japanese tended to use large numbers of small ports as opposed to concentrating their incoming supplies to Rangoon or to another big port. The idea was that supplying their forces via scattered smaller ports and not concentrating incoming supplies into one area would make it more difficult for us to target, thus giving them a greater chance of resupplying.

The three operations I have just mentioned were fairly simple. Nothing went wrong with the aircraft and we never came under enemy fire. The atmosphere on board was calm and cool. Though it wasn't really talked about for superstitious reasons, these types of raids were known as 'pieces of cake' operations. This is because these types of targets were generally very lightly defended. When Frizzy and I would compare the targets we had been to, some of them were quite different.

Your tenth operation was to mine an area of the main river that flows through Bangkok.
Yes, it took place on the 23rd of November, and fortunately, the journey to the target went without incident. But as we were preparing to drop the mines, that is when a big incident occurred. As I dropped down to four hundred feet, I prepared to turn to port in order to reach the starting point for dropping the mines, when we were suddenly caught in search lights.

Considering that being caught in search lights spelt the end for many aircraft, did it scare you being caught in them?
Honestly no, I was so focused on the operation at hand that I didn't really focus on it as much as one would think. There was a degree of apprehension though, being so close to the enemy under those circumstances.

I immediately told Blondie, my front gunner to take out those lights. He didn't need asking twice, he immediately started firing at them and the lights went out. I then lined up for the mining run and Len, my navigator, duly dropped the mines. Once done, we turned west and climbed to ten thousand feet and began our journey back to base. In the debriefing, the intelligence people told us that the men manning the lights probably fled for cover. I'm not surprised really, .5 bullets being fired from such a low height hitting the ground around you can't be a nice experience.

But one thing happened on the journey back. The rear gunner told me through the intercom that he could see an aircraft on the starboard quarter. I then turned to look in that direction and sure enough there was an aircraft there. It looked like a Japanese fighter to me. As I saw it, it banked towards us so I immediately went into clouds and when I came out of them a few minutes later, it was gone.

Your eleventh operation was a return to Penang, but this time it didn't go so well.
What an understatement that is. It was the first time I was involved in a really vicious storm. This combined with my inexperience led

to what happened.

The reason we had to return to Penang was to repeat what we had done the first time. It was assumed that it would take a month for the Japanese to sweep the mines and repair the damage we had caused the first time. So, exactly a month later, on the 26th of November, we took off from the same American airfield, with the same type of mines and again, extra fuel tanks. The only difference is that I was captaining the aircraft this time instead of acting as co-pilot. The same applied to Frizzy. Both of us had our own crews. The other aircraft involved had different personnel on board as in the last month various men had finished their tours and other new crews were starting theirs.

The main difference target-wise is that we had to negotiate stormy conditions. The aircraft that had returned with the weather report had reported that a big storm had been over Penang and was drifting away but in reality it was still there.

Taking off and travelling to Penang went without incident but in the final few miles, everything changed. As we approached Penang, it was still dark so I was relying heavily on instruments. Once I noticed the storm, I quickly had to decide what to do. I decided to try and penetrate it and so reach the target. Once into the storm, we were tossed around quite violently, to the point where I didn't have the strength to hold the control column level. I told my co-pilot to help me keep it steady, but he made the potentially fatal error of trying to bank to the left, which could have ended in disaster as this would have resulted in the wings not being level and would have put us at risk of being rolled over if caught in an updraft. So I shouted at him to stop and to keep it level. Alongside this there was lightning flashing and thunder booming all around us, illuminating the cockpit for seconds at a time as heavy rain battered the fuselage. From there we were caught in an updraught at one thousand feet and the storm threw us out at three thousand feet. Once we were out of the storm, I decided to jettison the mines as I felt it was too risky to get to the target. It was still dark, I was completely flying on instruments and to reach the target, Len would have needed to work out where we were and set a new course which meant flying back into the storm as it was still over Penang.

We began the flight home but we had to reach deep, open water before we could jettison the mines. Before they were jettisoned, the parachutes were removed from the mines which were always dropped via parachute. Later on we went into Digri and had the parachutes, which were made out of silk, made into shirts.

What was going through your mind on the flight back to base?
Not a lot as I was down on the rest bed having a nap. But I was quite nervous that everyone else reached the target successfully and that I would be the only one to have jettisoned and would be ridiculed as a result.

What happened to everyone else?
After landing at Digri, I went to the debriefing meeting with everyone else as we had all landed at around the same time. Blackburn made an appearance just as I was explaining what had happened with the storm to the authorities. I was a bit nervous because I thought that there was a good chance that no one would believe that we were caught in an updraft, thrown off course and had jettisoned as a result. I told everyone that I had been thrown out at three thousand feet, Blackburn looked at me and said, 'I beat you Denis, I came out at five thousand feet'. At that point, a big sigh of relief came over me as I knew that the account that Blackburn gave would squash any doubt that may have existed about mine. By the way, it transpired that every other aircraft had jettisoned their mines too.

Looking back on it, the fact that Blackburn and I were the only two to enter the storm and attempt to get through it leads me to believe that we were the only two who tried to reach the target and that the others looked, saw the storm, and decided that they didn't want any part of that game of marbles. You can't blame them though, I only attempted it out of ignorance and because at that point, I didn't have a fully developed appreciation of danger. Blackburn was different;

it was just pure bravery on his part.

For a while, there was a lingering sense of disappointment around the aircrews that took part due to the fact that we had not been able to successfully complete our objective.

Now, many people don't know that the RAF did drop Napalm during the war, one such occasion being on the 2nd of December 1944 during your twelfth operational flight where you and your squadron dropped Napalm on a target in Bangkok.
Yes, and the reason we did was because the target was so compact that conventional bombing from regular height could cause blast damage to the surrounding buildings. The target housed a tremendous arsenal of weaponry and supplies in support of the Japanese forces in Burma and the rest of the region, so its removal would put a severe strain on those forces, thus giving the Allies an instant boost.

However, before an attack could be launched, pilots of the Liberators taking part would need to be trained for the unconventional approach to the target area: dive bombing! But not in the famous nose down vertical dive like the German JU87 Stuka would perform.

Photos taken of the target showed a road bridge bordering the west side beyond which were many huts and buildings of all sorts, mostly constructed from wood; all housing weaponry and supplies waiting to be forwarded on to the Japanese army units spread across Burma and the region. That bridge became the focal point of the entire raid as it marked the boundary between the target area and non-target areas but also because it marked the point where we would release our bombs. The bridge itself was heavily defended by a nest of machine guns.

As a pilot taking part in the raid, I can describe in detail how we trained for it. A line of empty oil drums were spread across our airfield. They represented the bridge. We then practised a shallow dive towards it from eight hundred feet. It was like making an approach to land except that we maintained a speed of one hundred and twenty miles per hour. Our Liberators had been modified in that the pilot had the button on the control column to release the bombs. The 'dive' continued until the nose of the plane reached the bridge (or the oil drums on the practice runs). At the exact moment where the nose reached the bridge, the pilot pulled back the control column and at the same time pressed the button to release the bombs. The result was to 'throw' the bombs beyond the bridge and into the target area. The bombs used by each plane in the actual raid were incendiaries, conventional high explosives and one napalm.

During training, an observer on the ground told each pilot via radio whether he was short of the 'bridge', beyond it or just right. We trained like that for several days with eleven-pound practice dummy bombs until Blackburn was satisfied.

Did Blackburn organise this raid like he had done Penang?
Yes he organised it himself and I think he had more cooperation from the higher ups than he had received when trying to organise the first Penang raid. The target area was so small that a high accuracy rate was required to ensure that none of the surrounding buildings were damaged, which ruled out high altitude bombing so I imagine that they were more open to other ideas.

Was the raid a success?
The raid was a complete success with the whole target area being virtually wiped out. To avoid any danger of collisions, each plane was given a time to attack. Even so, the gunners on the bridge plus others elsewhere opened up on us. A few of our Liberators fired back and for once, Blackburn had to break radio silence to shout, 'Stop firing or you'll shoot yourselves down!' After everyone had dropped their bombs, we all then climbed to ten thousand feet to begin the journey back to base. But the amazing thing is that we could still see the firestorm the raid had started fifty miles away. A few of the planes were hit, but all of us taking part returned safely to base.

What was going through your mind during it all? What you were expected to do required such precision.

We had been practising it for so long that I felt quite confident about it. Intelligence had told us of the machine gun nest on the bridge and the suspected ones in the surrounding buildings. So of course there was tension on the way to the target due to the potential of coming under heavy enemy fire and all the consequences that can result from that. But once we arrived at the target itself, all the tension disappeared and everyone just completely focused on the job at hand. However, unlike on our return journey from Penang, the tension didn't exactly dissipate on the way back from this raid. The reason for this is because we had to be on the lookout for Japanese fighters. Luckily none appeared.

Talk me through your next operations.
Number thirteen took place on the 5th of December, we returned to Mergui to lay mines. This was a night time raid that took thirteen and a half hours. It was a straightforward raid. We didn't meet any enemy opposition.

Number fourteen, on the 8th of December was a return to Victoria Point to lay mines. I estimate that there can't have been more than half the squadron - eight planes - attacking it. The mine laying was straightforward but it was once the mines had been laid that things became interesting. In the briefing before we set off, we were told about an island close to our route back that had Japanese sea planes stationed there, attached to little wooden jetties. A few of the planes on this operation were detailed to attack the seaplanes on the return leg. We were making our way back following a successful dropping of our mines when I remembered the islands and decided that I couldn't miss out on the opportunity to attack them. It shows the type of person I was back then, it was all good fun to me, one big adventure. So, once we reached the island, I noticed that two out of the three planes were already on fire, from a Liberator that arrived before ours no doubt. I descended to no more than twenty feet and told Blondie to let rip. Blondie began firing and hit the one remaining seaplane, setting it on fire. What we didn't notice was that there was a machine gun nest that began firing on us, but it was quickly put out of action. Despite hitting the seaplane, Blondie also hit the jetty, causing pieces of wood to be thrown into the air. As all of this happened, I turned to Lance, my co-pilot, and said something like, 'We are going to be the first plane shot down by pieces of wood'. He found it funny and we had a good laugh about it. All of this took place while travelling at one hundred and fifty miles an hour or so.

The island was quite bare and narrow so we quickly approached the other side. I came around for a second run and noticed a supply boat, which I told Blondie to open fire on. He did and the two or three men on board began diving into the water. But one man had a rifle and let off a shot, which ended up imbedded in our nose. It was this bullet in our nose which I mentioned earlier, that the Squadron leader mocked me for. Anyway, after that I came back for a third time. There was a parade ground in the middle of the island with a Japanese flag blowing in the wind so we flew back across the island at the same height. This time I told Blondie to hit the parade ground and the few huts surrounding it which he did. After that we left and returned to base leaving most of the huts and all of the seaplanes on fire. Interestingly enough, during all of this, my rear gunner, Sammy, didn't fire a single shot, claiming that his gun had jammed.

Was the fifteenth raid as exciting and exhilarating?

The outstanding memory of that raid on the 17th of December was that the entire squadron took part. Our target was one island in a group that made up the Cocos Islands, off the coast of Malaya. The reason we targeted this specific island is because the Japanese were building a radar station there which could have given them advance warning of any incoming allied air attacks or movement of allied naval ships.

It was a straightforward case of arriving at the islands without a specific target other than the island itself. Due to the impact that these bombs would have we were ordered not to drop them from less than three thousand feet.

The entire raid was a success; the entire trip only took ten hours and twenty minutes. We took off, flew to the islands, dropped our bombs and then came home, without any incident.

There can't have been much of the island left.
Yes, absolutely. The island was absolutely pulverised, every building was destroyed and we didn't face any opposition. On top of this, every Liberator made it back safely.

Was your sixteenth as straight forward and without incident?
Yes, it was to the Martaban dockland area on the 21st December. Martaban was a small port to the south east of Rangoon. The squadron was to take off at ten in the morning with a load of ten one-thousand-pound bombs on each aircraft with orders to drop them in two clusters of five; one to the southern area of the port, the other to the northern area. But those instructions were soon to change quite simply because one of my engines would not start up. It had to be completely replaced.

Blackburn had already taken off, but by radio I was notified that his response was a complete change of orders. All ten bombs already loaded were to be removed and replaced with three bombs, each weighing three thousand pounds, and photography equipment. But Blackburn stated that if I had not taken off by one in the afternoon then I was to remain at base. I really wanted to go so I kept on pestering the ground staff and eventually, at twenty past one, after a complete engine refit, I took off.

My new orders were to first make two photographic runs over the port. The first in a west to east direction and the second on a north to south. Both Len and myself were then to agree where to drop our bombs, from a minimum height of three thousand feet. This was because of the powerful up blast created by bombs of that size.

During the photographic run, Len and I noted two fires, probably set off by our previous bombers. Those fires were probably two small ships which were about three to four hundred yards apart. After we had finished the photographic run, we decided that we would make a run over the port flying from south to north. Len released the first bomb to land near the first fire and the second bomb near the second fire. I then turned around and on the reverse course. He then set our third bomb to land between both fires.

Regarding opposition, there was none during our photo runs, but from the first bomb onwards we were subjected to considerable anti-aircraft fire. However, once the third bomb had dropped, I went into a starboard dive so we were soon out of range and heading for home.

When I met Blackburn in Malta after the war, when I was with 38th squadron, he told me that the Martaban operation I have just told you about, was the only time he was worried about me, simply because had things gone wrong, he would have been asked to explain why he had sent a twenty year old to carry out such a dangerous mission.

However, the next operation, number seventeen, mining the Irrawaddy river near Rangoon, the capital of Burma - that was quite an experience.

What happened?

It took place on the 29th December 1944, and it was a disastrous night for 159 squadron. Blackburn devised a plan to mine a specific section of the Irrawaddy river between the mouth of the river, known as 'Elephant Point', and the city of Rangoon itself. At the time, Rangoon was the most important port for the Japanese to supply their army in Burma. If we could cut this vital supply line, it would put the Japanese army in Burma into a lot of difficulty.

Five aircraft would be required, each with its own length of river in which to lay its eight mines. Five of the most experienced pilots of the squadron were chosen to fly the five Liberators that would lay the mines. Laying mines is an art in itself as you have to be completely steady and dead on the course that your navigator has laid out for you. On top of this, timing the release of each mine is essential. All of this is in order to ensure that each mine lands where it is supposed to. I was well into my tour, and having laid mines on several occasions already, I became one of the five.

The plan that Blackburn had devised involved fooling Japanese radar in the Rangoon area. The idea was for the whole squadron of sixteen aircraft to deliberately fly in loose formation on a course from west to east. Once we arrived south of Rangoon, the five Liberators with mines would rapidly drop height out of the formation, one after the other, all the way down to four hundred feet. The hope was that the Japanese radar operators would only see the main 'blip' of the formation still heading eastwards and not be aware of the mine laying aircraft.

But it did not work, as I saw from my number five position. Once we reached Elephant Point and had descended to four hundred feet, the first two Liberators came under intense anti-aircraft fire and were damaged, though they still managed to lay their mines. The third Liberator however, was shot down. Before my eyes, I watched that Liberator suddenly explode into a ball of fire and crash into the river. What had probably happened is that a shell had gone through the bomb doors and hit a mine. That's the only explanation I can think of that explains how it suddenly exploded like that.

Having seen all of this, I was struck with a brain wave. I knew that with mines aboard, I was a sitting target as I couldn't take evasive action for risk of a mine detaching and exploding. So I took my Liberator off course and out of range and asked Len to rework the calculations so I could come around from the opposite direction. We could then release the mines in reverse order. The mines would still be in the same place but mine number one would become mine number eight and so on. In doing so, by the time the last mine had been dropped, the bomb bay would be empty and I would be able to take evasive action and manoeuvre my Liberator out of the range of the anti-aircraft fire. They were in fixed positions, facing out towards the mouth of the river, in the direction of which I was supposed to come in from.

Once Len had worked out the calculations, I came around into range and dropped the mines successfully. However, we came very close to being hit. As the mines were being laid, I saw the flashes of the guns. I said to Lance my co-pilot, 'Those bods couldn't hit a barn door from ten feet', and in that instant we heard from our left, a low hum turn rapidly into a loud roar before fading to our right. A shell had only just missed us. I reached the end of my section, went into a dive to the right, down to one hundred feet then levelled out and began the journey back to base. From then on, I gave more respect to the accuracy of the Japanese gunners.

To say something like that under those circumstances, it's unbelievable.
The thing is, nothing up until that point in this operation had really frightened me, not even seeing the third Liberator shot down. By that point, I was nearing the end of my operational flying, and I guess you could say that I was becoming a bit blasé about the whole thing.

What was the aftermath of it all?
Our intelligence people rated it as a successful raid because the idea was to fester the Irrawaddy with mines, which we did. We got all the mines down with the exception of the Liberator that was shot down. We put that section of the Irrawaddy out of action for quite a while. To top it all off, during debriefing, when we were giving our accounts, I explained to everyone my brainwave and how it was successfully implemented, then Blackburn congratulated me and told me that he would never have thought of it.

By the way, I met up with the pilot of Liberator number four and he told me that he had also been hit by antiaircraft fire but had managed to lay his mines and make it back. Number one and two had made it back too, despite also being hit.

Your eighteenth operation was absolutely incredible but for other reasons. It's quite a story.
Blimey, yes. It took place on the 1st January 1945 and we must have had a guardian angel overlooking us that night. Our operational orders were simple enough. Bomb the Nakhon Pathom bridge which

crossed the River Kwai, North East of Bangkok. Like the other Liberators involved, we had an exact time to make our bombing run. Overhead and to the north of us, a couple of planes kept the area lit up with flares for the duration of the raid.

The journey there was fine; the approach to the target was fine. It was once we reached the bridge that everything started to unravel. As we were approaching it, Len said, 'Bomb doors open', in preparation to drop our bombs. At that moment I glanced up to see another Liberator almost sitting on us, also with its bomb doors open. This time I was scared, I had no choice but to slide away using only the port rudderpedal, so as to keep the wings flat. We were that close that if I had tried to use the control column to steer, it would have caused the right wing to raise and hit the other Liberator. We were on time; it was the other Liberator that was either too early or too late.

Still, this caused us a lot of problems. The reason was that in the initial briefing, we had been told that should any Liberator miss its attack time, it was to circle until all the others had cleared the area, like being told to go to the back of the queue. So, after this incident, we had to wait and eventually the way was clear for us to make our run. We successfully dropped our bombs on the bridge and began to make our way home. We were ordered to return via the Preparis Island which we did; it wasn't our first time using it as a reference point. Whenever our target was situated in southern Burma or Thailand, the Preparis Island was used as a navigation point. However, on this occasion, going in that direction lead us into a huge storm chain. I tried to get through at different heights which were no good. So I warned the crew that we faced a bumpy ride and ploughed into the storm. Hailstones battered us and lightning bolts hit the sea but fortunately, not us. Eventually, we made it to clear skies but we were one hundred miles off track. It meant that we no longer had enough fuel to reach base. I decided to head for Cox's Bazaar, an airfield on the north east coast of the Bay of Bengal. But when we were about thirty miles away, we came into range of a British fleet that were on their way to retake the port of Akyab.

They mistook us for a Japanese aircraft and began to open fire on us. Anti-aircraft shells began to explode around us which caused me to immediately start flashing the navigation lights to tell them that we were a friendly aircraft. The firing stopped.

When we finally made it to Cox's Bazaar, it was still dark and I realised that we had enough fuel to make it to Chittagong. The journey there was short and without incident until we approached Chittagong. Suddenly a huge shape seemed to glide past our port side, then one on our starboard, then another on our port side, then then another on the starboard and so on. We had flown straight through a balloon barrage in foggy conditions which was hoisted to protect the ships moored in the harbour below us.

Once we were around three miles away, I realised that the airfield was covered in fog, though I could just make out the runway lights. By the time I had descended into the fog, in order to begin my final circuit, I could no longer see the runway lights. In basic training in Southern Rhodesia, we had learnt how to get down in fog by means of timed runs on a stop watch. How this works is the navigator has a stop watch, then the pilot flies the length of the runway from the beginning until the end. The navigator times this and once at the end of the runway, the pilot goes into a rate one turn which is also timed and brings him to the opposite direction, still level with the runway. The navigator times it again, from the end of the rate one turn to the beginning of the runway. At the end of the time from the first count, the pilot once again goes into a rate one turn that is a copy of the first one, just from the other direction. This brings the plane to the beginning of the runway, so it can make a safe landing.

Once this manoeuvre was implemented, you must have been relieved beyond belief once the plane touched the tarmac.
Not entirely, intelligence had told us that if we had to land at another airfield, we should turn on our landing lights in order to identify to the people there that we were a friendly aircraft. So, once we had lined up with the runway and were descending, I turned on the landing lights and to my horror, there was a steamroller sitting at the

beginning of the runway. I pulled back hard on the control column which guided the plane over the steamroller. The problem I faced is that I had lost about two hundred yards of runway in which to come to a stop in. Once the wheels touched the runway, I had to slam on the brake pedals as hard as I could, which caused the brake shoes to start catching fire. This meant I had to release them, but only for a few seconds so the flames went out. Then it was back to engaging them as hard as they would go, but not for as long as before because we had slowed down by quite a speed at that stage. We only had two or three yards of runway left, so I swerved on to the perimeter track and finally, we came to a stop. From there, we followed the airport jeep to the control tower.

To summarise, during that operation, you had a Liberator with its bomb doors open sitting on top of you, you had to navigate a storm chain, came under friendly fire, made it through a balloon barrage, landed in fog and barely managed to avoid a steamroller sitting on the runway. You must have been in quite a state once you were out of your Liberator.
I breathed a huge sigh of relief to say the least. We had landed at four in the morning, and by the time we taxied to the control tower, it was just beginning to get light. In the distance, we could make out the balloon barrage that we had flown through and boy did they look clustered. Lance commented that he wouldn't like to fly a Tiger Moth through there let alone a Liberator and he was not wrong.

We later discovered that we had twenty gallons of fuel left in the tanks, which is nothing for a Liberator. Some people would say that once I saw the steamroller, I should have aborted that landing, done another circuit taking the steamroller into account, and landed that way. But with only twenty gallons of fuel left, it's doubtful that another circuit and landing would have been possible. Besides, in a situation like that, you don't have time to think.

What I forgot to mention, is that during all of this, we were hit by a low calibre shell in the bomb bay which damaged the structures that held the bombs and mines in place. They were damaged to such an extent that my Liberator was downgraded to a training plane and I received a new one. It was named 'Britannia V'.

The good news in all of this, is that not long after the raid, we were told that we had successfully wiped out our section of the bridge, which was the northern part. How this came to be is because for that raid, we had cameras fitted onto the aircraft which, we were told, confirmed it.

Did you ever discover why there was a steamroller sitting on the runway? Was it there due to negligence or was it purposefully placed there?
Yes, I was talking to an officer there and he told me that it was put there to stop Japanese aircraft landing there, in the event that they needed to. Even at this stage of the war, Japanese aircraft were still in range of Cox's Bazaar and Chittagong. What surprised me is that I was not told about it in advance. It's the sort of thing you would expect to be told about.

I assume you were only there for a day at the most before you returned to Digri.
Yes, we went back the same day, we were only in Chittagong for a few hours. Remember, the senior staff had to wait for all of the planes to return before they could start preparing for the next operation.

Once I was back, I had to go through the regular debriefing and explain what happened.

Wasn't it around this time that Blackburn left 159 squadron?
Yes, he was promoted from wing commander to group captain, which took him to Alipore in Calcutta. On the morning of the 9th January 1945, I was asleep and he walked in with a group of officers, ripped off the covers and told me that I was taking him to Calcutta.

So, we took off, me as pilot and him sitting next to me in the co-pilot's seat. He didn't interfere or anything but when we landed, he told me that he wanted to taxi to air traffic control and blimey did he taxi at some speed. I must tell you, before we even took off, Blackburn told me to bring my entire crew.

Once we arrived in Calcutta he invited us all to lunch at the Firpos hotel. It was a high class, luxury hotel. During the meal, he noticed that I was eating the bread rolls dry, and he told me to put butter on the rolls. He was surprised when I told him that I didn't like butter, therefore never ate it. I still don't like butter, all these years later. After we had finished, he told us to go and do our shopping and to meet him at the Firpos once we had finished. We met him there again, and from there we all went to Christies for tea. Christies was another luxury, upper tier hotel. He paid for it all, the lunch and the tea. Afterwards, he phoned up airfield transport and organised us a taxi to take us back to the airfield.

Once we had returned to the airfield, we went to the mess to eat and drink before returning to the aircraft and flying back to Digri, except we didn't, because number one engine wouldn't start, so we had a whole extra day to spend in Calcutta. We didn't return to Digri until the 11th. Ironically, Blackburn later told me that he had phoned Alipore on the 11th to make sure that we had returned safely, only to discover that we were still there. This annoyed him as he told me that he would not have let us sleep in the Nissen hut that we all did. He would have put us all up in a hotel if he had known that we were going to be stranded there for a few days.

How much of Calcutta did you get to see?
Quite a lot, with almost two days and nothing to do, there wasn't much else to do but explore. It was a large, sprawling city, but quite an interesting one. It really was a city of hustle and bustle, very noisy and very busy. To give an example, the buses were always heavily crowded, even the double decker buses had people sitting on the roof.

We spent most of the day looking around the shops and there were plenty of places where one could find a cup of tea. There was one main street that was particularly packed with people though I always found it to be a safe city and the people to be quite friendly. It's hard to believe that two years later, India would erupt into violence. One interesting fact though, we were not allowed to drink milk on its own anywhere in India, as the milk was not pasteurised. If the RAF police caught you drinking milk you would face punishment for it. It was a city I liked and one I would return to more than once in the following year.

When you returned to Digri on the 11th, you had a new Commanding Officer in charge of 159 squadron, what was he like?
I didn't see much of him actually, but he was nice enough, but didn't have the charismatic force of personality like Blackburn. He was Canadian and we soon had a few Canadians join the squadron which changed the makeup of it. There was somewhat of a divide between us and them, though it went unspoken. They came across as more arrogant; they were loud and seemed to look down on us. I screened two of them myself and I got the impression that their training was not as rigorous as it was in the RAF. One chap I screened had poor instrument flying ability which I discovered when we were flying in cloudy conditions. This can potentially be very detrimental because if the pilot is even a little bit off course, it impedes the navigator.

Did this divide affect morale in any way?
It did in the sense that to many of us, the Canadians wanted to be in charge, to be the top dogs, not to work with us as equals. But then again, I was only there for a few more weeks as by this stage, my tour was coming to an end, so I don't know how their arrival impacted on the squadron long term.

Your crew didn't change in the last few weeks though?
No, I had the same crew right to the end. But I was on course to reach the required number of operational flying hours before they did. To complete a tour, one had to do three hundred hours of operational flying. Though we had become a crew in Palestine, I had more hours than them because of the first few operational flights I did as co-pilot

when I was being screened. I didn't do those flights with my crew; I did it with the crew of whoever was captaining the aircraft.

So you flew an extra operation so you could all finish together.
Yes, I completed one extra one. It was once again returning to the site of my very first operation, Victoria Point, to lay mines.

After leaving 159 squadron, I completed a one-off operational flight a few months later when I was based in Cox's Bazaar. I will enlarge on this later on.

But before we talk about your final operation with 159 squadron, you had another five to complete.
My nineteenth operational flight, and the first operation I undertook after returning from Chittagong was to bomb the Rajburi bridge in Burma which also crossed the River Kwai. This took place on the 14th of January. The operation itself was fairly straightforward. It was also the first time I screened someone. Basically, I was supervising and advising a new pilot who was acting as co-pilot, like I was when I first joined the squadron. We carried out our run dead on time, we hit the target and from there, we turned around and headed for base. The photos that were developed from the cameras that were timed with the dropping of the bombs informed us that we had scored a direct hit on the support structure of the northern end of the bridge, which was our designated target.

Were cameras a common fixture on your operations?
No I don't believe so, the only reason I knew about the cameras on this occasion is because intelligence told us about the direct hit. For all I know, there could have been cameras fitted for the operations that took place before and after the Rajburi bridge one. I know that the Americans used cameras a lot. For example the Americans would attach cameras to their P-51 Mustangs and would show the films in their camp cinemas.

Operation number twenty was bombing the Martaban railway sidings.

It took place on the 18th of January and the operation itself went well. We came in, dropped our bombs and came home. But what really stands out is that after completing the raid, we climbed to five thousand feet for the return trip. When I levelled out, I saw another Liberator on my starboard side, about a mile away. A few seconds later, it just exploded into pieces. It must have come under anti-aircraft fire, but luckily, we did not. I didn't know anyone on board.

On January the 20th, for your twenty-first operation, you returned to the site of your first and fourteenth operations, Victoria Point.

Yes, everything was going well until we reached the intended starting point where Len was going to drop the first mine. The problem was that the starting point was close to an island which was situated in the middle of the Kraburi River. We had received wrong information somewhere along the line. We were told that the maximum height of the island was around three hundred feet but in reality, it was closer to four hundred. The problem this caused meant that we had to alter our flight path as we were supposed to descend to four hundred feet, fly over the island and then drop the mines into a specific area of deep water before the water breaks on the island. If we had stuck to our original flight path, we would have crashed into the island. So what I had to do was circle around the area until Len had recalibrated the course to drop the mines. We had eight mines in total, it was a timed run, so Len would time it and each mine would be dropped at the same interval.

During this operation at Victoria Point, I was screening a Canadian pilot. I told him exactly what I was told when I was screened and what I did whenever I was mining a river. That was to stay in the centre of the river so the aircraft would be at the furthest distance possible away from any guns stationed on the banks either side of the river. I also explained and showed him how to 'porpoise' so it would be harder for any gunner to get an aim on him. I later learnt that he had completely ignored my advice and had flown directly over the river bank on the port side, over gun emplacements and had been shot down.

You twenty second operation was the third trip to Penang.
It took place on the 24th January; I captained the aircraft and acted as a screen to the same Canadian pilot as I had on the previous Victoria Point operation. On the first occasion, they were taken by surprise so there was no anti-aircraft fire. The second time we were caught in the storm, but the third time, the squadron did face anti-aircraft fire. Luckily, the target that our aircraft was given was a target on the northern end of the northern section, so we faced very little anti-aircraft fire. It didn't interfere with us laying the mines. Two Liberators were hit but they laid their mines and made it back, as did every other aircraft involved.

Even though Group Captain Blackburn was no longer with us, we followed his routine from the first two trips. We flew to the American airfield the day before with the extra fuel tanks fitted. On the day of the operation, the fuel tanks were filled and the mines were fitted. We then took off and completed the operation. There isn't really much to say about the third Penang trip as it was an exact copy of the first one.

Now, as you have already mentioned, your last operational flight with 159 squadron was a flight that you did not actually have to do.
Right, as I have already mentioned, I did it so the rest of the crew could reach the three- hundred-hour mark which would mean that we would all finish our tours together. It was another mine laying operation at Victoria Point.

We came under fire and one thing I noticed is that the Japanese seemed to have more powerful guns as their shells seemed to reach further. But still, it was a success, the mines were laid and we made it back. This final operational flight took place on the 27th January 1945.

You and your crew must have been elated once you landed back at base and the reality that your operational flying was over fully sunk in.

Yes, we had all passed the three hundred hours required and were all very happy for it. However, we didn't party or do anything to celebrate. One thing we were all wondering is where we were going to be posted. Even though we had finished our operational flying, the war was still going on. As it would happen, Frizzy and I were posted to Bagarchi as we had finished our operational tours at the same time.

Do you know where the members of your crew were posted to?

No, but I believe that they were all posted back to Britain. I know that Len was and so was Jock, my wireless operator. I know this as I kept in touch with them both. In fact, on more than one occasion, I went to visit them at their homes, and they came to visit me at mine. While we're on this topic, another visitor was Laurie from the troop ship.

CHAPTER NINE

REFLECTIONS ON OPERATIONAL FLYING, FELLOW CREWMAN AND FRIENDS

Being robbed of receiving awards.

When you look back on your operational flying, what do you think about it all? After all, you were only twenty years old, in the Far East, captaining a Liberator against a ruthless enemy. The things you did and witnessed are quite unbelievable in many ways.

What I have probably mentioned to you many times is that I had finished a full tour of operations by the time I was twenty and a half. It's amazing to me that in such a short amount of time, I had gone from a clerk in an electrical store to having completed a full tour as captain of a large bomber aircraft. It's amazing, really. One thing you have to remember is that at that stage, the average age of a Liberator pilot on 159 squadron was twenty-four-and-a-half. I think that the fact that I was so young helped me in the sense that I didn't have a fully developed sense of danger. To me, many of the operations were exciting, like with operation number fourteen. I did not have to attack those sea planes but to me, it was all one big adventure. But trust me, I did appreciate the Japanese as an enemy, I was under no illusions there.

The rest of the flying I did in the Far East seemed so tame by comparison, as I wasn't actively facing the possibility of being shot down every time I took to the air.

Did you ever feel any guilt for what you were doing? When you were dropping bombs on places like docks and targets within urban areas like Bangkok, there was inevitably going to be civilian casualties.

I find it best not to dwell on that subject, because what's done is done and I was only doing my job. The hope was always that any loss of life would be the enemy and not civilians. I never felt guilt, but when we bombed targets in urban areas or dropped high explosive bombs, it was always in my mind that there would inevitably be civilians caught up in it all, whether it would be in the total fatalities, casualties or things like manning the hoses or fighting the fires caused by incendiary bombs. Don't forget, growing up so close and being so close to London during the Blitz, I knew what it was like to be on the other side. After all, I was blown off my bike by the blast of a bomb. Dropping napalm shocked me due to the tremendous power and effects of it, to see the target go up in flames like that. However, I looked upon it all as a job that had to be done; I had to comply with orders. Also, it has to be remembered that we were fighting a ferocious and fanatical enemy that were trying to kill us and many others.

You have mentioned that you lacked a fully developed sense of danger, but did you ever contemplate the possibility that you could be shot down and taken prisoner, or killed?
Yes, once or twice it happened at the beginning, before take-off even, wondering what we were heading for. But once we were in the air, it disappeared. One thing that would occasionally be contemplated was engine failure, which was not common, but at the same time, wasn't unheard of. Once, not long after the Flight Commander I told you about had left, another Flight Commander was appointed who told all of us pilots that a Liberator could fly just as well on three engines as four and that it was no reason not to carry out an operation.

Ironically, on the operation following that lecture, I noticed that I was catching up with the Liberator in front of me. Their number four engine had failed. I contacted them via radio and asked if I could be of any assistance. I received an abrupt reply telling me to maintain radio silence and to carry on my way. So that's what I did. They completed their objective and made it back alright. But honestly, at that age, I never comprehended those types of scenarios. I was excited more often than not. Though operation number four when I was being screened by that sergeant really did scare me.

But to put into context how high the possibility of being shot down was. Soon after arriving at 159 squadron, Frizzy and I had asked Wing Commander Blackburn how many Liberators had been lost in the past four to five months, the average length of a tour, and the answer was eight. This was half the number of operational aircraft on the squadron. Frizzy and I agreed that we had about a fifty-fifty chance of surviving, though luckily, both of us did survive. Receiving those figures didn't really have an effect on me, though I have known pilots become scared before their last operation. A superstition that they had survived all of them so far, so was this the one where they wouldn't make it back.

Amazingly, Frizzy's Liberator wasn't even hit by a single bullet or shell once, while another pilot on the squadron returned from an operation with around twenty-five bullet holes in his aircraft. In my case, I was only hit twice, in the nose and in the bomb bay, and a third time when I was being screened and we came under fire from those Japanese naval ships.

But I was injured once, though I can't remember on which operation it was. On the journey back following a night operation, I had gone to lie down for a nap, handing over the controls to my co-pilot. I landed the aircraft and we were transported to the debriefing. My crew and myself walked in and Blackburn looked at me and said, 'Bloody hell Denis, what has happened to you?' Unbeknownst to me, there was dried blood down the side of my face. While I had been sleeping, something had fallen on me, cutting me just above my left ear. I was taken to the Medical Bay to be checked over and was taken off flying for a week. Fortunately, that's the only injury I or my crew suffered.

What did you and your crew do when you weren't flying?

It's a difficult question to answer for the simple reason that there weren't many things to do because Digri was in quite an isolated location. There was a village in the immediate area but that was it really. A lot of our time was spent writing letters, playing cards, playing badminton and occasionally, myself and my wireless operator would go out on bicycle rides. I mean, we didn't even have to wash our clothes as there was a laundry team for that.

Sometimes I would have to take up a Liberator for an air test to confirm that it was able to go on operations. Whether or not any of my crew would come up with me would depend on what it was being tested for.

How important was the camaraderie between you and your crew when you were flying operations, and to what extent did it contribute to your operations being successful?

It was very important. Flying a plane like a Liberator is like a well-oiled machine working successfully. Every piece has to do its job to keep the machine working and it was like that in the Liberator. Every crew member had to do his part to keep the plane in the air. Communication between everyone is vital to ensure this and if two or more people don't get on, then that can affect the entire atmosphere inside the aircraft and can potentially have consequences like lowering morale, which can lead to a disastrous outcome.

Fortunately, my crew got on very well, and to the best of my knowledge, so did the other crews. However, I didn't really get on with Len when I first met him. As I have mentioned, I lost my first navigator as his drunken brawls and antics became too much for his superiors, so he was taken off flying and returned to the UK. On another crew however, the pilot, who was from New Zealand, became seriously ill and was returned home. So, I gained the navigator from his crew; it was Len, who was twenty-four at the time. The reason why we didn't immediately get on is that Len was full of praise for his previous pilot, who was also twenty-four and obviously thought that at age twenty, I still had a lot to learn. But a chance remark soon improved our feelings towards each other. I had asked Len about his job prior to being called up and his reply was that he was 'learning the ropes' with a firm known as 'South East Essex Electrical Supply Co'. By coincidence I was learning the ropes with a firm known as 'North West Kent Electrical Supply Co'. Both of our firms were under the umbrella of a larger firm and were only separated by the River Thames.

Talk me through your crew, what were they like as people?
They were nice chaps, we all got on very well. For example, Jock, my wireless operator was from Scotland. He was a classic example of how generous the Scots are. Len was an excellent navigator; he had outstanding accuracy and could quickly recalculate if anything went wrong, like how he recalculated dropping the mines at Victoria Point. My front gunner Blondie was a great gunner as he was very accurate and really enjoyed shooting at targets. Lance, my co-pilot was a nice chap, not fat but heavily built - the type of guy you would want by your side in a fight. But Sammy, my rear gunner… to this day I'm still not sure about him as his guns would never work when they were needed. I never once heard him fire a shot at an operational target, only when the guns had to be cleared. He was the oldest one out of us all, he was thirty-one when he joined the crew, eleven years older than myself. Also, I am still slightly suspicious of the flight engineer. I was never happy about his story that we had suffered an air lock in the fuel system, so for the rest of the tour, I would keep an eye on it myself, via the instrument in the cockpit.

I know you kept in touch with Len and Jock, but what became of those two and the rest of your crew after the war?
Well Lance was killed not long after returning to the UK when a Tiger Moth he was flying crashed. My flight engineer I never kept in touch with but with Len and Jock, I did. We met quite a few times and I became the godfather to Len's daughter. However, he got promoted within his job and moved to Wales, and I lost touch with him after that. I didn't keep in touch with Blondie or Sammy. I kept in touch with Jock up until he passed away, which I believe was only a few years ago. I visited him in Scotland and he visited me in Kent. He was from a town named Stanley, which is around ten miles outside of Perth.

Now, you have mentioned him quite a few times already. Let's talk about a man who you said was your best friend during your years in the Far East, a man named Carl Fristrom, but who went by the nickname, 'Frizzy'.
As a man he was confident, easy going and had a couldn't-care-less attitude about him. Frizzy was the type of chap who one never forgets, he was so easy to get on with, I cannot think of Cox's Bazaar without thinking of him. The only time he had any trouble, was when he had a disagreement with George Livingstone, my post operations co-pilot in the Far East, which resulted in Frizzy being put in a headlock. Frizzy's co-pilot and myself had to pull them apart. Though we had been friends since meeting in Palestine, it wasn't until after operations when we were posted to Bagachi and later Cox's Bazaar that the friendship really became strong. During operational flying, we had our own crews and had operations to complete, although we would socialise in the mess or play sports or something.

The Penang operations were great feats. A lot of it was down to the intuition of Blackburn. What are your thoughts about them now, over seventy years later?
The first was a great success, the second was a washout, and the third was basically a repeat of the first. The organisation behind it was huge. I remember Blackburn telling me years later, that he had received very little support from senior RAF officers or the Americans, who were convinced that it couldn't be done with Liberators. They were right, at least with the way that the Americans flew Liberators. They carried almost double the crew that we did and our Liberators were stripped of their armoured plating, which was only behind the pilot's seat. All the guns and turrets were removed, except for the front and rear guns. The whole plane was stripped back in order to reduce the overall weight and so allow the extra fuel tanks to be fitted. I have already mentioned this. It was quite a baptism of fire for me. The first one was only my third operation.

Honestly, I highly doubt that Penang would have happened without Blackburn. He had to do so much pre-planning and a lot of it was purely down to him. I think a lot of it was down to his sheer force of personality. He had a forward-thinking brain and seemed to think in advance of the problems we would face and come up with solutions for them, like our short runway, and the extra fuel needed, being two examples.

What sticks out in my mind now is that I can so vividly remember the last half an hour of our approach on the first trip. It was getting more tense by the second. It was a completely new target, we knew nothing of their defensive capabilities, and we didn't even know if they had radar.

The Americans were so impressed with the raid, how it was planned and executed that they gave Blackburn their Distinguished Flying Cross. In fact, they wanted to give every crew member who took part in the operation their DFC. But the RAF vetoed it, so Blackburn accepted it on behalf of the Squadron.

Why did the RAF veto it?
Quite simply, it wasn't in the nature of the RAF to hand out medals like that. They never awarded medals easily. I mean, Non-Commissioned Officers couldn't be awarded the DFC, that was only for Commissioned Officers. Non-Commissioned Officers could be awarded the Distinguished Flying Medal, the DFM. It symbolises the rules, requirements and achievements needed to be awarded a medal.

How did Blackburn commemorate the awarding of the American DFC?
He threw a party in Calcutta, but I don't know much about it as I wasn't able to go as I had been posted to Bagarchi by that point.

In the years preceding your first meeting with him, Blackburn had been through a lot. Did he ever talk to you about any of it?
On the flying side, no. When he was on the Laconia, he described how close he was to being sucked down into the sea by the drag of the sinking ship. He said that he had to swim really hard that night.

He never spoke about his time as a prisoner of war or his escape either. Years later, I was in contact with his former navigator. We exchanged letters and in one, I wrote to him about our squadron dropping napalm and he told me that he remembered it due to the fact that it was the pilots dropping it and not the navigators themselves.

While we are on the subject of medals and the DFC, you were supposed to be awarded the British DFC, but it never happened.
Frizzy was too. As far as I know, each squadron on frontline duty was allowed to award one or two pilots: the DFC for things like outstanding service, outstanding flying, and things like that. Blackburn told me after the war, when we met in Malta, that he had put our names down for the DFC before he left for Calcutta, but that the Canadian C/O who took over 159 squadron scrubbed our names and replaced them with the names of two Canadian pilots.

That's unbelievable.
Yes, and Blackburn was quite annoyed about it too. At first I was quite rankled about it as well as I had screened both of the Canadian pilots, but eventually, I realised that there wasn't anything I could do about it. Now, it doesn't bother me.

One of those Canadian pilots was a chap who I had screened and shown how to porpoise and where to position the aircraft when mining a river. Incidentally, as I have mentioned, he had taken over my Liberator and was shot down on his second operation.

Your willingness to take risks and throw caution to the wind during your operational flying has been mentioned a few times already. How do you look back on it now?
I suppose I look back on it as a manifestation of a period of excitement and novelty. One story which symbolises this was once, I was taxiing around the perimeter track at Digri when I noticed that two trees were exactly opposite each other on either side the perimeter track, which was unusual. I started to weigh up in my mind if I could fly between them and estimated that I could, just about. I asked Len if he thought a Liberator could fit through that gap. He

saw right through me and said, 'Don't you dare Denis. I have a wife back home!' Another one which springs to mind is when I was in Bagarchi. C/O Trumper called me into his office and asked if I had been low flying again, when I said that I had not, he asked me how I accounted for all the twigs and leaves around the tail wheel.

I had a ground crew member ask me if I ever felt nervous about flying an aircraft, especially taking off and landing. But I wasn't; to me it was simple and fun.

Looking back on it now though, I can't now see myself doing half the things I did back then. However, I would love to go back into the air again, I really would.

What is your standout memory from your operational flying?
The night when we bombed the Nakhon Pathom bridge, where we escaped death so many times. How we made it through a balloon barrage covered in fog is just down to pure luck. It's unbelievable really.

What are your thoughts on the Liberator?
The Liberator on first sight frightened me, it looked so big. But in actual fact, I found the controls quite easy to manipulate and I took quite a liking to it. It did handle well. But one problem I experienced was that if the autopilot was in and a fuse blew, it could completely throw the autopilot off and the aircraft could end up in any position. It happened to me three times. The first two times it happened to me, we ended up in a half roll before I managed to switch off the master switch that controlled autopilot. On the third occasion, we almost ended up on our tail before I managed to turn the master switch off and fly the plane manually.

To many people, autopilot is a very modern concept, not something that many think of being in a Second World War aircraft. How did it work?
It was all to do with the control column and the trim of the aircraft. Whatever you had set the plane at, it would lock it in that position.

So, if you were flying straight and level, then by putting the autopilot in, it would maintain that balance. So if you got it wrong and you were flying in a bank and turned on the autopilot, it would maintain that position.

What were final figures for your operational flying?

I joined 159 squadron on the 15th October 1944 and I left on the 10th of February 1945. In that time, I did a grand total of three hundred and twenty-five hours and forty minutes of flying. Three hundred and fourteen hours and ten minutes of those were operational flying. Within those operational hours, seventy-three hours and fifty minutes took place during the day and the other two hundred and forty hours and twenty minutes took place at night. The eleven hours and thirty minutes of non-operational flying was taken up by air tests and taking Blackburn to Calcutta.

CHAPTER TEN

FLYING THROUGHOUT INDIA AND THE FAR EAST

Setting up transportation links, saved by a dog and a friend's terrible accident. Passing out at the controls, hospital, meeting old friends and arriving in Singapore.

You mentioned that after finishing operational flying with 159 squadron, you were posted to Bagarchi. Though you were no longer flying on operations, the war was still going on. What was the aim of your flying during this time?
The aim was for us to eventually go on to Cox's Bazaar and set up a system of flying soldiers from places like Chittagong and Akyab to Calcutta, or to be more accurate, Alipore, for a week's leave. But the reason we were posted to Bagarchi was to learn to fly Warwicks, which were non-operational counterparts of the Wellington bomber, mainly used for things like transport and carrying military personnel.

What surprised both Frizzy and myself is that one day, a public display was put on. The highlight of this display was that Mosquitos were going to bomb an old Anson that was no longer being flown due to age. They were to shallow dive bomb the Anson but only with eleven-pound practice bombs. So when it came to the six Mosquitos, the first four released their bombs and missed the target. But the fifth aircraft came in at a steeper dive from which he failed to pull out, and flew straight into the ground, killing both men on board. The last plane being flown by their C/O went ahead with the 'attack'. The Anson exploded, so it seemed like he was successful with his bombing, either that or it was detonated from the control tower with explosives connected by wires. Who knows? Also, I have no idea why the display was put on.

What was the conversion unit like? I imagine it must have been a different experience to prior conversion units in the sense that

you were much more experienced and had completed a tour of operations.

Quite right, because we didn't have any classroom exercises at all. The first time I even saw a Warwick was with Frizzy and our instructor and we immediately began flying it. The instructor did a circuit and landing, then Frizzy did one and finally, I did one. We actually began flying on the same day as we arrived, the 11th February 1945.

How did the Warwick compare to the Wellington and Liberator?

I didn't like the Warwick. It was meant to have Bristol Centaurus engines. But because those engines weren't available, they were fitted with American Pratt & Whitney engines. The snag with that was that the Pratt & Whitney engines required longer propeller blades to absorb the power from the engines, which were more powerful than the Bristol Centaurus engines. This meant that when you were taking off, the propeller blades were only around eight inches or so from the ground. So, if you hit a bump, the blades could hit the ground and ruin the engines in some cases, and definitely bending the blades in all cases. On top of this, I didn't like how the plane handled, it's hard to describe why. To me, you either take to a plane or you don't.

So, what came next?

We were there for nine days and in that time, we just learned how to fly the Warwick, which was the whole objective of our stay there. However, on the eighth day, we transported passengers and freight.

How many other pilots were in this conversion unit?

Believe it or not, there were no other pilots there; it was just the two of us. The entire point of us being there was to set up the system that I have already spoken about.

What happened once the two of you had learnt to fly the Warwick?

We were posted to Cox's Bazaar, which was the main station of the RAF Bengal Burma Communications Squadron, with a small detachment further south at Akyab. Frizzy and I each had our own Warwick. Cox's Bazaar only had one runway, it was around two thousand yards long. It was operated by the RAF and the American Airforce. There were no hangars; all the planes were kept out in the open. The Americans had P51 Mustangs and Thunderbolts and six small single-engine aircraft named the Sentinel which could carry three people. The RAF had our two Warwicks and three of the single-engine Argus aircraft. This was slightly bigger than the Sentinel and could carry four. The six Sentinels there were flown by us as the RAF had leased them from the Americans.

Did the British and the Americans get on well?
Yes, we socialised, though I didn't know any personally. The American unit was to the north of the runway and we were on the southern end. They had a cinema there, and it was there that we would go and watch them shooting down Japanese planes on the films that their Mustangs had captured on their flights. Normal films would be shown too. They also had a store there where one could buy anything, within reason, which we could use. Things like that really contrasted the differences in the standard of living. The Americans definitely had a lot more money and a greater opportunity to spend it. Though they only had coffee, we had tea.

During this time of transporting troops and freight, did you experience any hair-raising moments like you did on operations?
Nowhere near to the same extent as on operations. But once, the Japanese sent four Mitsubishi bombers to bomb Cox's Bazaar. They were each carrying a single one-hundred- pound bomb, but their bombing was all wrong. They forgot that when a bomb is dropped, it doesn't fall straight down, it carries on moving forward as it falls. As a result of all this, only one bomb hit the runway, and that was on the northern end, the American side. The other three bombs went into the sea. The Americans sent up Mustangs which shot down all four Japanese bombers. What little damage to us was caused, was repaired within a few hours, and life carried on as normal.

On another occasion, I was preparing to land at Akyab. At the time,

Akyab was a busy RAF base, also used by the Americans as a staging post. There was a paved runway and a dirt runway, which were parallel to each other. We had to land on the dirt runway as three Mustangs had crashed on the paved runway. What had happened was that they were landing one after the other, quite close, from what I heard, when one of the wheels on the first Mustang came off. This resulted in the Mustang 'collapsing'. The second went into the first and the third went into the second. Fortunately, all three pilots were OK.

Anyway, we came into land on the dirt runway. I was on my final approach when for some reason, I could not slow the plane, at least according to the speed dial. So I went through normal procedures, but ended up landing with a big thud and at greater speed than I should have. Once I had hit the ground, I slammed on the brakes and while I knew that the aircraft was slowing down, I was still travelling at a higher speed than I should have been at this stage of the runway. At the end of the runway was a gully, and I'm sure that I had the speed to overshoot the runway and go into it. As we carried on slowing down, I noticed a Dakota pulling out of the area where the planes were parked. Once I reached this area, the space was free and I performed a manoeuvre that is the aircraft version of a handbrake turn in a car. I did this by putting full power on the port side engine while applying the brakes on to the starboard engine and somehow made it into the gap. Even completing that manoeuvre was pure luck.

Did you find out what the problem was with the speed dial?
Yes, a bird had been impaled onto the 'Pitot Tube' which resulted in a false reading on the air speed indicator. The speed on a Warwick is worked out, as it is with all aircraft, by a calibration between actual speed and static speed. Static speed is the air that you are flying in. So, there was nothing wrong with the dial itself. The impaled bird just resulted in it giving a false reading.

Oh yes, there are two I forgot to mention, which I believe took place on the 20th and 21st March 1945 when I 'beat up' Digri, which is when you fly in low across the airfield. A parcel had to be delivered to Digri, my old operational airfield, so I volunteered to do it. As I approached Digri, I came down to around three hundred feet and roared over the airfield but then my starboard engine failed which didn't cause me any problems in the air. I came around and landed without incident, but taxiing proved more difficult as I had to open up the port engine to move forward then steer against it once we began to turn; it was a zig zagging motion. The ground crew managed to fix the engine, I returned to base and fortunately, I didn't face any punishment.

But the next day, I was returning to Cox's Bazaar from Akyab with freight when for some reason, I decided it would be fun to come in on my final approach from a really low height. I approached from below tree height; I knew this as I couldn't see the runway. At the last second I hopped over the trees and it was then that I saw a crashed Thunderbolt on the runway with the ground crew trying to extract the pilot. I said some explicit words, and went in to a steep climb, up to circuit height and waited for the Thunderbolt to be cleared off the runway before landing.

You must have faced serious repercussions for that incident.
Yes, as soon as I landed, I knew I was in serious trouble. In fact, the C/O came right up to the aircraft; he was furious. When my crew and I came out of the aircraft, he immediately asked who was piloting it. I told him it was me and he proceeded to tell me how he could easily strip me of my rank and the repercussions I could face. He then told me to report to his house that evening in my 'best blue' which meant that my official uniform had to be spotless. His house, which was a bungalow, was around two miles away.

So, that evening, I went to his bungalow. It was dark, I had no torch and I was quite nervous. I arrived, knocked on the door and he told me to enter. I saluted him and it was at this point that I noticed he had a dog, an Alsatian. I gestured to it and it started to wag its tail. The dog came over and I began to pat its head. The C/O told me that the dog obviously liked me and asked me if I had one back home. This turned into a conversation about dogs which lasted quite a while. Eventually though, the incident was brought up. I told him that I had no idea that the Thunderbolt was there and that if I did, I would never have done what I did. He gave me some stern warnings and that was that. Looking back on it now, I'm sure that what worked in my favour was the dog liking me, the conversation about dogs and the fact that I looked so young. Even now I can't really get over it. I went there to be reprimanded and ended up talking about dogs.

Though the number of hair-raising situations were significantly less than on operational flying, you did actually fly one operational flight during your time at Cox's Bazaar.
Yes, it took place on March 23rd. Frizzy and I had to deliver chemicals to Imphal, in India, but he opted out of it. I was entitled to have an escort there and back because we were told that we would be flying into airspace that was still within range of Japanese fighters.

As I climbed away from Cox's Bazaar, a Hurricane joined me on my starboard side, but after about ten minutes, the pilot called me up on the radio to tell me that he was running low on fuel so was going to return to base. Also, this Warwick was fitted with turbos to both engines. This was a system where a plate closed off the exhaust pipe in order to divert the energy created. How this worked is that a dial was fitted in the cockpit which controlled plates, which when activated, would gradually close off the pipe carrying the exhaust gases, the power being diverted back to the engine. The dial went from one to ten, depending on how much extra power you wanted. The reason for turbo being fitted is that the aircraft would have to climb to ten thousand feet to cross over a range of mountains. All of our flying during this stage usually took place at around a thousand feet or so.

So, aside from this, did the set-up of transporting troops operate smoothly?
Well as I have mentioned, our instruction was to set up a system for getting front-line soldiers to India for a week's leave, then returning them to their unit. Frizzy and I would both depart from Cox's Bazaar

but we flew to different airfields. Frizzy would fly to Chittagong and I would fly to Akyab. The destination was usually Alipore. During any stopovers, Frizzy and I were free to do as we wished as long as we transported the troops on time.

The system worked quite well for a few weeks during which we got several hundred battle- weary soldiers away from the front line. But as you can imagine, the inevitable happened. Frizzy's Warwick became unserviceable through an engine failure. The replacement had to come from the UK but none were available. At the beginning of this arrangement, Frizzy and I agreed that if one of our aircraft became unserviceable, that its pilot would not harass the other pilot to fly his aircraft. So, I continued from my end while Frizzy was stuck on the ground, only able to fly the single-engine planes that were available. Eventually, Frizzy begged me to let him do a run in my Warwick. Fortunately for him, a separate run occurred where I was taking non-military passengers to Akyab but returning empty, so I suggested to Frizzy that he be my co-pilot on the way there, and then on the way back, he would fly the plane with me as his co-pilot.

The war in Burma was a hard and brutal conflict. Did you ever speak to any of the soldiers that you transported?
No. Aside from the odd chit chat as they were getting on and off the aircraft, but the topic of war was never mentioned.

What was life like for you in the few months that you were stationed at Cox's Bazaar?
I enjoyed myself. There was a really relaxed atmosphere, it lacked strict formality. Frizzy and I were the only ones who were allowed to fly the Warwick. We did around five flights a week, transporting troops and freight.

When I wasn't flying, I spent a lot of time playing cards, relaxing on the beach, which was very close by, watching films in the cinema, socialising, things like that really. One amusing event that stands out is that I was once sunbathing on the beach when a jeep load of nurses were being transported along the beach. They saw me sunbathing there and a group of them started whistling at me.

Strangely, I was the only one who I can remember that enjoyed swimming in the sea. Very few of the other chaps ever went in, and if they did, it was just for a dip.

With Frizzy's plane stuck on the ground as a result of its engine failure, what happened to this troop transportation service?
It still operated, but the service was reduced. I took up some of the slack for about three weeks before mine went unserviceable due to it having to be refabricated and sprayed with a chemical, which stopped insects from eating away at it.

So, what did the two of you do, seeing as there were no big planes to fly?
I took the Warwick to Cawnpore on May 4th to be refabricated, but there was no aircraft to take me back so I was stuck in Cawnpore for a while. A random Dakota showed up and I hitched a lift. We stopped in Calcutta, so I checked in to the Salvation Army, and there Frizzy was, but he looked ill, all shaken up, and wasn't himself. He proceeded to tell me that while I was away, a new Warwick had been sent to Cox's Bazaar to replace his. He allowed his co-pilot to do the acceptance test, but on landing, he crashed straight into stanchions, which were big iron pillars embedded in front of the control tower to protect it. The plane was a write-off and the co-pilot was seriously injured and needed several weeks of hospital treatment. Frizzy came away from it with minor injuries, but he was suffering from complete shock. He had been sent to Kathmandu, to a place where they dealt with cases involving a loss of nerves and other psychological issues. But when I met him in Calcutta, he was awaiting a plane which would take him back to Australia.

I could not believe that all of this had happened in the time I was away. At Alipore, a small plane had been sent from Cox's Bazaar to get me back there and Frizzy came with me to sort out his belongings. A few of us threw him a small going-away party. One memory that really sticks out in my mind is that George Livingstone, my co-pilot, who had got Frizzy in a headlock, poured him a drink and the two of them made up. I was really happy to see that. The next day, I took him back to Calcutta, but he was only a passenger on this occasion. In Calcutta, he was to await his flight which would be the beginning of his journey back to Australia. We both knew that we would probably never meet again, so it was quite emotional. Both of us were almost in tears.

Did you keep in contact with Frizzy?

We kept in touch for a while. He soon left the Royal Australian Air Force, got married and began working as a pilot, flying small planes that sprayed crops. We eventually lost touch. But a few years ago, around 2010, a chap in America was writing a book on notable figures from the war, and Blackburn was one of them. He put adverts in newspapers and on the internet and Frizzy saw this and wrote in with what he knew about Blackburn and mentioned me. A few years later, a chap who lived on the same street as I did saw that Frizzy had mentioned me and brought it to my attention. I managed to acquire his phone number, but when I phoned him; his wife answered the phone and told me that he had died the previous year. That really upset me.

How did you spend your time in Calcutta, it seems like you spent a good amount of time there?

I would check into Salvation Army accommodation, which back then was a Rupee a night. Back then it was fourteen point something Rupees to the Pound. By the way, in the Calcutta Salvation Army they had quite a set-up of single rooms and they served breakfast. Obviously, non-military personnel could stay there. But if the guest couldn't stump up the Rupee, they could still get a single room without the breakfast for a cheaper price. If they couldn't afford the room then they could pay a cheaper rate where many people shared the same room, many to the floor. They would get a cup of tea and a biscuit with that too. But if they couldn't afford that, then the cheapest option would be to pay for a spot on one of the support beams, which were situated on the bottom floor. There, you could drape your arms over and lean on it, to sleep that way. During the monsoon season, the place was absolutely packed, especially the bottom floor where the beams were situated.

When I wasn't there, I mainly spent my time relaxing and shopping, buying clothes and whatnot. There wasn't a big military presence in Calcutta at the time.

Soon after you had dropped Frizzy off, you had to fly all the way around the Bay of the Bengal.

Well, a signal came through to Cox's Bazaar saying that all of the six Sentinels and the three Argus aircraft had to be taken to Yelahanka in southern India. The night before, on May the 21st, I had taken a doctor to Akyab in one of the Sentinels. I didn't know anything about the signal until I returned to Cox's the next day. It was scheduled: the first leg was to Chittagong, the second leg was from Chittagong to Alipore, the airfield in Calcutta. The third leg was from Alipore to Cuttack. The fourth leg was from Cuttack to Vizagapatam, then from Vizagapatam to Gannavaram, then from there to Donakonda, then to Madras and finally from Madras to Yelahanka. This journey was scheduled to begin on May 22nd and it was a lot of flying. On the 23rd, on the leg to Vizagapatam, it was just myself flying a Sentinel.

I started getting light-headed from heatstroke and knew I had to get down quickly. I knew that the Americans had built several airfields down the East side of India, but the one I could see was covered with cattle. I remembered a salt flat that I had seen from the air, so flew there and performed a precautionary landing. I taxied close to a small bungalow that I had seen and then passed out. A while later, I awoke to noise - a load of angry men had appeared brandishing big sticks. When I saw this, I restarted the engine, and started spinning the plane full throttle with the right rudder pedal pushed as far as it could go. All of this caused the plane to spin a circle, kicking up dust and salt, keeping everyone away. At this point, an Anglo-Indian chap, an inspector type of person there, came and calmed everyone down. He told me that I should lie down and sleep and invited me to his house. When we arrived at his bungalow, he offered me a drink of whiskey or brandy, something like that and I was quickly asleep. When I woke up, I was in a lovely bed, and in pyjamas that his servants had put me in. I got dressed and went to speak with this chap. He let me phone Madras, which was where the big regional RAF offices were. I gave them the position of where I was and informed them that I needed fuel to replace what I had lost searching for a landing site.

That night, we sat down and ended up talking about the future of India. He told me that it was inevitable that the British would have to pull out of India within a few years, that the British occupation of India was unsustainable. What also became apparent is that he didn't like the British system of rule. He made intelligent arguments and what he said made a lot of sense. I liked him, he was an intelligent man, he had a way of making his point without insulting people and was capable of strong arguments regarding the British leaving India which in time, proved to be quite accurate.

Anyway, the next day, word came from Madras that a plane would be coming in with a five-gallon fuel drum. I decided to make life easier for the incoming plane, so I got around twelve turbans and laid them out in the shape of a runway. But before the plane came, the wind changed direction, so I had to move them all into the direction of the wind. When the Sentinel landed, I was surprised to see that there were two pilots. The idea was that the second pilot would take over my plane and I would be the passenger. I strongly opposed this so I carried on flying it. Once the plane was refuelled, I made a precautionary take off and headed for Vizagapatam. Over high ground, I started to feel dizzy again, but managed to reach the airfield and land. When I landed, there was not a soul there. So, I got out of the aircraft, walked into town and went to the hospital. I was there for three days. They wanted me to stay longer but I left and walked myself back to the airfield. From there, I conducted a pre-flight inspection of the plane and found that a bird's nest had begun to be built in the air intake. I cleared that, and took off for Gannavaram and then went on to Donakonda where I stopped to refuel. I carried on to St.Thomas Mount which was the airfield that serviced Madras. I was there for two days where I spent most of my time swimming. I then finally made it to Yelahanka on May 29th.

What was the objective of this flight path?
Well that puzzled all of us taking part. The point of these aircraft was to get injured people out of the jungle. Yelahanka was nowhere near the jungle. As it turned out, there was a miscommunication somewhere along the line as these aircraft were supposed to go to Rangoon, which by this stage had been liberated from the Japanese.

It was quite an adventure, flying all the way around the Bay of Bengal, then back around again, then, I was supposed to go on to Rangoon, but I didn't do the Rangoon leg. I stayed at Cox's Bazaar.

Why didn't you go all the way to Rangoon?
The reason was that another Warwick had been delivered to Cox's Bazaar with the instructions that as the only pilot available to fly it, I was to do the 'acceptance test', which the aircraft has to pass before it can be accepted into the squadron. So, while all the others were on the way to Rangoon, I did the acceptance test and asked for permission to land, which was accepted. I then put the undercarriage down and nothing happened. Three green lights were supposed to light up, showing that the undercarriage had come down and locked in place, but they didn't light up. Also, if one lowered the undercarriage lever, but the undercarriage didn't come down, a loud horn would sound, which it did. So, I aborted the landing, raised the undercarriage lever, did another circuit, and once again, went through the preparations to land, but the same thing happened again - the undercarriage wouldn't lower. So, I contacted the control tower and told them that I wanted to fly past them slowly with my undercarriage lever down, so they could see if the undercarriage was down or not. They allowed this, so I flew past them slowly and they told me that it appeared to be down but that they couldn't be sure that it was. I then asked them for permission to do a 'fast landing' in which I would come in fast, with the undercarriage supposedly down, then purposefully hit the wheels on the runway with the idea that it would dislodge anything that could be interfering with

the electrical system. Permission was given. It was a dangerous manoeuvre, especially because the tips of the propellers were so close to the ground, as I have already mentioned. But I decided to do it anyway. As I approached the runway, no green lights were showing and the horn was blowing. But once I hit the runway, the green lights lit up and the horn stopped blowing, so I did another circuit and landed, and the plane was accepted onto the squadron.

Was there anyone else on board this Warwick with you?
It wasn't just me on this Warwick. There was also an RAF corporal and a young chap who had only recently been called up. The corporal was apparently quite the boxer. When the horn was going off and it became apparent that something was going wrong, the young chap completely panicked and tried to open the door in order to jump out. The corporal ended up knocking him out.

The day after the acceptance test, on an island off the coast of Burma named Ramree Island, you had the most unbelievable encounter.
Oh yes. I had taken passengers to Ramree Island for a meeting. I was to wait at Ramree until another plane arrived, then I would take its passengers back to Cox's Bazaar. However, the monsoon weather had other ideas. We managed to land just as the monsoon broke. The runway, which was built from coconut matting and metal strips was obviously hit by a lot of rain which caused it to flood and as a result, become lumpy and uneven. It also caused the metal plates to buckle.

So, we were stuck there, and it was there that I had the most unlikely of encounters that you will ever hear about. The fact that I met this person on this tiny island is so unlikely that it's almost the stuff of fiction. One day, I heard a voice asking if he could come in and have a look around as he had never seen a Warwick before. My head shot up as I recognised his voice. It was Clive Woods, the man I had worked with in the electrical showroom back in Kent. We had not seen each other in four years, since I was sixteen. A lot had changed since then. It must have been quite a sight for him as I was just in my underwear due to the fact that it was so hot and humid.

He asked me if I was named Elliott which I confirmed. This took place in the cockpit. He proceeded to ask me if I was the Wireless operator, I said no. Then he went through training for all of the positions one can have in an aircraft before finally arriving at pilot. He didn't believe that I was a pilot, so I told him that when he got the runway fixed, I would show him who flew the plane. He was an Airfield Engineer. Originally, he was an Air Gunner, but a nasty leg injury on an operational flight put an end to that. Even now, I find it unbelievable that I met him on a small island off the coast of Burma.

How long were you there for?
We were there for four days, we arrived on the 10th of June and left on the 14th. The passengers we had arrived with were taken to accommodation and we were stuck in our Warwick for four days. Clive was kind enough to keep us supplied with food, water, books and things like that during our time stuck there. We read the books, played cards and just tried to find ways to pass the time. There wasn't much else to do as it was monsoon weather which meant heavy rain and strong winds. After four days, the rains had eased off, so the matting was replaced and we were able to take off. I never saw Clive again.

What happened with the two groups of passengers?
The ones who were coming from Rangoon were taken directly to Cox's Bazaar in a Dakota. The passengers we took to Ramree Island stayed there. I flew with an empty plane back to Cox's Bazaar to pick up passengers to take to Akyab.

While we're on the topic of chance meetings, you also met Vera Lynn.
Yes, she was part of a group that I collected at Chittagong. Honestly, not much was said between us, we only exchanged a few words as she embarked and disembarked the aircraft. She came across a nice person though.

During your time flying Warwicks, Germany surrendered. Were there any celebrations where you were?

No, the war with Japan was still going on, so everything carried on as normal for us.

After Ramree Island, your time with the Warwick was coming to an end.
I only flew the Warwick three more times after leaving Ramree Island: Cox's Bazaar to Akyab and back covered the first two on the 16th June, and the last time was a big trip going to Alipore, starting at Cox's which was on June 21st on which I was the captain. We flew from Cox's Bazaar to Chittagong, from Chittagong we flew to an American airfield named Dum Dum and from there to Alipore. Once at Alipore, I handed over the Warwick to another British pilot who was taking it to Cawnpore. From Alipore, we took a train to Bangalore, which took two days. From there, an RAF vehicle took us to Yelahanka.

From then on, I was stationed at Yelahanka. Horler, another pilot, delivered a Dakota which he was supposed to fly to Bombay with myself as Co-Pilot, but it had to be aborted due to bad weather; this was on the 7th of July. We tried again the next day, but once again, bad weather meant that it had to be aborted. We managed to complete it on the 11th. On the way, I asked the navigator what the date was and he told me that it was the 11th of July. I thought about it and eventually realised that it was my twenty first birthday. The navigator told me that I needed to celebrate and fortunately, there was a crate of beer on board in cans. Everyone got one but we forgot about the change in pressure so when we opened them, they sprayed everywhere, though we managed to drink some of it.

On the 14th we came back to base with the Air Vice Marshall, The Earl of Bandon. Rather to my surprise, Blackburn had sent me a very nice fountain pen, which was waiting for me upon my return to base. Knowing that he was still in Calcutta, I was able to write to him to express my thanks.

Our next trip was the next day, July 15th. We took the Earl of Bandon from Yelahanka to Kandy, in Sri Lanka to meet Lord Louis

Mountbatten. I didn't fly the aircraft though; Flying Officer Horler did. The Earl of Bandon was in the Co-Pilot's seat and I was in the third seat. From my position I noticed that both had forgotten to put the undercarriage down, so I leaned forward without saying a word and pulled the small lever that lowered the undercarriage; they didn't notice. If I had not done so, then we would have crash-landed. Imagine the sight: the Earl of Bandon coming in to meet Lord Mountbatten and the aircraft he is in crash-lands!

What did you do during the duration of this meeting?
We left Kandy on the same day and took passengers to Ratmalana, then returned to Kandy the next day.

On the 17th July, from Kandy, we went to a place named Madurai. From Madurai we went to Chettinad and returned to Madurai. I can only assume that these two extra stops were due to passengers and refuelling. The next day we took the Earl back to base.

The rest of July was taken up with three round trips from base to Santa Cruz. It doesn't sound too eventful but on the 19th I was scheduled to fly a Dakota for the first time because a second Dakota had been delivered to base. On the 19th, Horler was detailed to take fourteen officers to Santa Cruz, and I was to take fourteen non-commissioned officers to Santa Cruz. We had heard that there was a storm on our route, so I decided to fly out over the Indian Ocean and to approach from the sea.

Horler's Dakota had gone unserviceable so the C/O put all of his passengers on to my plane, which left me with twenty-eight passengers, instead of the fourteen that I was meant to carry. As a result of this, some of them had to sit on the floor. On every flight in a Dakota so far, I had only been the co-pilot. I had not flown, landed or taken off once in a Dakota. I went to see the C/O and told him all of this. He was so calm and laid back about it. He looked at me and said, 'Oh you'll manage'. He showed incredible faith in me. Why he didn't just order Horler to fly my Dakota I don't know.

How did the flight go?
Before I left, Horler told me not to forget to set the elevator trim to number four. That set the cross piece on the tail at the right angle for take-off. One event I recall is that when all of the passengers were on board, I walked down the length of the plane, checking off the passengers against my list when a squadron leader asked me if I was flying the plane, which I confirmed. He then asked me my age and I replied that I was twenty-one. He then asked me how many hours I had flown. I told him the number and he turned to the chap sitting next to him and said something like, 'He has already flown more hours than I have in my entire career'. Fortunately, the flight went well and was a complete success.

The rest of July just involved flying to Santa Cruz and back and was largely uneventful.

Was August as uneventful as the second half of July was?
August was a busy but uneventful month that involved crisscrossing India. There isn't much to say about that month in terms of flying.

But one thing did happen. If you remember, I told you about the time that I flew a Sentinel around the Bay of Bengal and had to perform an emergency landing on a salt flat due to an onset of heatstroke. Well, the same thing happened again on the 8th August. I was taking fourteen passengers to Santa Cruz. We were cruising along nicely when I started feeling off. George, who had fought and then made up with Frizzy, took over the controls and I went and sat next to the navigator and promptly passed out. When I awoke, I made my way back to the cockpit, sat down in the co-pilot's seat and discovered that George was preparing to land. He could fly an aircraft well but had never actually landed one. What I noticed is that he was rounding out at too high an altitude. So, I leaned over, took over the controls and landed the aircraft, and then promptly passed out again.

What happened once you had landed?
An ambulance was called and I was taken to Bombay Military Hospital where I was for the next ten days. Over that time my health

improved. I was finally eating good food and the hospital itself was very good. But what happened is that the Brigadier General came and spoke to me; he was furious. He told me that I had been doing too much flying, had not been eating enough and that he was going to contact my C/O and tell him that I was not to fly at all until I had passed a full RAF medical. He did have a point, though, I was no more than eight and a half stone and had been flying almost every day for months.

Did the medical take place at the hospital?
No, once I was discharged from the hospital, I was taken as a passenger back to Yelahanka, and was then taken into Bangalore to have the medical. Not long after, another Dakota had been delivered that had to air tested, which I wanted to do. I nagged and nagged my C/O but he said that I couldn't fly until the results of my medical came through. I told him that I had passed and that the results were in the post, when in actual fact, I had no idea if I had passed or not. He relented and told me that I had twenty minutes, but I went up for about two and a half hours. Fortunately, the letter confirming that I had passed my medical arrived while I was in the air.

Did you face any punishment for exceeding the twenty minutes' limit by two hours?
No, fortunately I didn't. My C/O during this time only really cared about the paperwork side. Flying didn't interest him. He hated it, though he knew how to fly aircraft.

Two events took place on the 6th and 9th August 1945 that changed the world forever, the dropping of two nuclear bombs, 'Little Boy' and 'Fat Man' on Hiroshima and Nagasaki respectively. Do you remember where you were when news came through of these new weapons and the effect it had on everyone?
During this time, I was here there and everywhere so I can't remember exactly where I was when the first bomb was dropped, though I was in hospital when the second bomb was dropped. Though the bombs had been dropped thousands of miles away, it affected all of us as it virtually brought the war to a close. Even before the Japanese

surrender was announced, in our minds, the end of the war was a forgone conclusion as there was no way that they could carry on after that. Prior to the bombs being dropped, the Japanese were still holding out in parts of Malaya with no end in sight and it was in the back of our minds that we could have been dragged into that with all the risks that it would have entailed. About a week after both bombs had been dropped, word came through that Japan had surrendered.

In September, purely by chance, a funny thing occurred. At Yelahanka, there was a long table in the mess where we ate our meals. At breakfast time, I said to a chap that I wanted porridge as opposed to cornflakes. Then I heard a voice a few feet away say, 'Are you sure you don't want cornflakes?' It was my friend Ron from Rhodesia days. After Rhodesia, he had gone on to a Spitfire training unit at the same time as I was on Wellingtons. Anyway, I had an air-test that day so I took him up in my Dakota. He was amazed at the speed. Later on, Ron and I were in the cinema when a message on the screen appeared telling me that I had to go to the foyer. So, I went with Ron and was met by the C/O. He told me that I had to go to the sergeants' mess and pickup four airmen to take to the airfield. I was to drive them all to the airfield in an RAF vehicle, the British equivalent to the U.S jeep. I apologised to him and told him that I couldn't do it as I had never driven a car before. He looked at me and said, 'Oh you'll manage' - the exact same phrase as with the Dakota. There were a few vehicles parked and he didn't exactly remember which one it was but he told me that the second half of the number plate began with the number '7'. So, myself and Ron went to the mess, found the car and then went and picked up the airmen, though I didn't get above first gear. Though my driving was bad, I managed to get to third gear, but one of the airmen said something like, 'Does this thing only have one bloody gear?' My reply was something like, 'Well do any of you know how to drive it?' As it transpired, none of us knew how to drive. Between us, we could fly a wide variety of aircraft, but couldn't drive a car. It's quite funny really.

How did the car hold up? The gears weren't synchronised back then.
Well, it transpired that I did damage the gear box. I know this because the next day the Station Engineer complained that someone had damaged the gears in his car. Not only that, but it wasn't even his car that I was supposed to drive.

It's quite amusing that you had completed a tour of operations and had flown a good number of aircraft, many times in quite demanding conditions, yet you didn't know how to drive a car.
Yes I know. But the flying by this stage was more of the same, crossing India with few stops in some other countries in the region. For example, we did have a few stops in a place called Morib, which is in Malaya, not long after the Japanese surrendered on the 2nd of September. But, the most exciting thing in the first part of September as far as flying was concerned, was when a tyre blew up upon landing at Mingaladon, the airfield that serviced Rangoon. We ended up swerving off the runway, no one was injured, and the aircraft was fine, but the whole wheel had to be replaced.

Anyway, the war was over at this point, the Japanese had surrendered, including in Malaya and No, there were not any celebrations of the Japanese surrender from what I saw; things carried on as normal.

Didn't you also meet your friend, Laurie, your friend from the troop ship you were on when you were transported to South Africa?
Yes, since we had parted ways, when I disembarked from the troop ship in Durban, we had kept in touch via letters. He had become a Tank Commander and fought in North Africa. By this stage, he had been posted to India, to Delhi, so we arranged to meet. At base, there was an urgent parcel that needed transporting to Delhi so I volunteered to deliver it. Dakotas also had autopilot so for the duration of the flight, I had autopilot on and my crew and I sat in the back and played cards. Every once in a while I would go into the cockpit to make sure that the slight oil leak in the starboard engine wasn't causing any problems. As long as the oil pressure remained

within limits, I could just carry on. Of course, if it had dropped, I would have had to have landed somewhere. Fortunately, it remained within limits.

I was so determined to reach Delhi while Laurie was there that I contacted the airfield we were supposed to stop at to refuel and told them that I was going to continue on to Delhi. I made it with not much fuel to spare. Once there, I found a fault so the plane would be unserviceable, which meant that we would remain there for another day. Afterwards, I went to the Army camp, which was quite large and was told where to find my friend. I went to where they were billeted and found the Nissen hut that he was in. Unfortunately, he wasn't there. Another chap told me that he had gone to the cinema. So I left a note saying that I would be in Delhi until tomorrow, and that he should come to the airfield. He read my note and we met up at the airfield the next day and went to the cinema. All of this happened between the 30th August and the 1st of September, only a day before the Japanese officially surrendered. Laurie and I met after the war. We returned to Britain at roughly the same time and we met up in Farnborough.

Not long after I met up with Laurie, I became the co-pilot of a Flight Lieutenant Stevens, who became our Flight Commander. The only reason I became his co-pilot is because he held a higher rank than me.

Before we move on from your time in India, I would like to ask you something. You left India in 1945 and in 1947, India would gain independence from Britain and during this period, would go through a period of horrific violence as Pakistan and Bangladesh became independent countries. During your time in India, did you notice anything that gave an inclination of what was to come?
Well the name Ghandi comes to mind. He and other Indian leaders had stirred up quite a lot of anti-British sentiment during the war period. There was definitely an anti-British feeling in India at the time. I got the feeling that it was worse in southern India, Bangalore,

that sort of area. Though I never felt unsafe, there was certainly a tension in the air, in the country and this lead many to stick closer to the unit than they normally would and to avoid going out.

The violence in India, once it erupted, was well known for being on religious lines, though I can't say I saw any ill feeling or violence between people of different religions.

As you have mentioned, the Japanese officially surrendered on the 2nd of September 1945. Without a war to fight, did the role of the RAF in the Far East change, and if so, how did it affect you?
Though I was only in the region for a few months after the war, the discipline, adherence to hierarchy and formality seemed to continue. But without the need to help fight a war, or to supply a war, things changed in the sense that I was involved with carrying passengers to several new locations, to places like Burma, Sumatra, Java, Malaya, and Singapore. A lot of it was to reclaim control of our colonies and reinstate our influence in the region.

For example, British troops arrived at Morib to reclaim control and to either fight or take the surrender of the Japanese troops stationed there. I do have strong memories about this. On the 11th September, we went from Rangoon to Morib. Before going there, we were issued with .8 pistols. The ground crew were all armed with rifles. When we were coming into land, we had to have our pistols ready as we had no idea what reception we were going to receive. Even though the Japanese there had already surrendered, they completely outnumbered the British personnel there, so it was always in the back of your mind that they could revolt. Fortunately, everything worked out OK.

We later learned that when British forces landed on the beach closest to Morib, the Japanese had four divisions there.

Thirteen days after the Japanese officially surrendered, you flew to Singapore for the first time.
If my memory is correct, I believe we went there to deliver mail and we spent most of the day there. We delivered mail across the region a few times.

The city wasn't bombed out or anything like that though there was damage in places. Still, despite this, it was very noticeable that Singapore was an opulent city. But one thing I noticed was that morale was very low. My only theory on why that was so is because they realised that they had an awkward few years ahead of them to rebuild. What was outstanding right from the start was the cost of living, it was very expensive. We were issued with tins of cigarettes and many of the men would sell theirs or exchange it for other goods. In a way, they were a form of currency.

The standout story of my first time in Singapore is that four of us went into the famous Raffles Hotel. We went to the bar and asked what they were serving for drinks. Just then, a young man appeared and told us that we couldn't be served. I asked why. He looked us up and down and told us that because we were wearing jungle greens, we were not suitably attired and therefore wouldn't be served. I then asked if we could get a glass of water and were told that we couldn't. What's amazing about it is that as this was going on, Japanese prisoners of war were being marched past outside.

The Flight sergeant in charge of the ground crew asked me if I liked boxing. I told him that I enjoyed watching it and he informed me that there were three fairgrounds in Singapore, one of which specialised in boxing. So, if we had time and boxing fights were scheduled, we would go and watch. There would always be a few fights of different weight classes. One fight which stands out was a heavyweight fight, two big chaps. One had the other against the ropes and threw an uppercut from the waist with a lot of power which caught the other guy perfectly and threw him out of the ring.

What was happening with the Japanese prisoners of war during you time spent in the region?
They were slowly being shipped back to Japan. They were also used as manual labour. The first time I landed at Morib, it had a dirt airstrip that had been hit by heavy rain and as a result, we sunk into the mud. It was Japanese prisoners of war that dug out our Dakota.

After being dug out, we were shown to our accommodation which was very bare, so a few of us went to look for furniture. We had come out of a hut and were walking back when we came face to face with a King Cobra that was coming from the opposite direction. Once it saw us, it reared up so we started to throw things at it which caused it to seek shelter in a shed. An Army chap then marched passed with a group of Japanese prisoners of war. One of our party asked him if we could borrow his rifle to which he obliged. The rest of us took shelter behind trees as he went in to the shed and blindly shot into the area where he heard movement and by sheer luck, he blew the snake's head off. The bullet carried on going and ended up embedded in the tree I was hiding behind.

At the beginning of this period, we had seven Dakotas in our unit. Eventually, four were leased to the Dutch, which became the nucleus of the Dutch East Indies Airline, which left us with three. Then two were taken away and converted to chemical spraying aircraft, against mosquito sites, so that left us with one.

Were there any interactions with the Japanese prisoners?
No, the only time I saw any was when they got our plane out of the mud, on the occasion with the King Cobra and when we were in the Raffles hotel. But on the occasion when we first landed at Morib, when we were dug out by the Japanese prisoners of war, a funny thing did occur. Upon surrendering, the Japanese had handed over their tools and items they had been issued with. From this collection, we could take whatever we wanted and in this collection was a counter weight scale. One of the officers in our group exclaimed, 'I have always wondered how much my testicles weighed' and then and there, he got them out and weighed them.

That's unbelievable, what a sight that must have been.
There was a ring of us standing around him watching this, we were really surprised. It was quite funny; a lot of us were in stitches. When he had finished, he asked if anyone else wanted a go, but we all declined.

For a very short time, before being stationed in Malaya, you were stationed at Kallang, in Singapore.
Yes, during this time, it was mostly transporting personnel around the region. A lot of time was spent watching the boxing matches at the fairground whenever they were on. We didn't visit all three fairgrounds that were there, just two. The one with the boxing and another one which I believe was run by Chinese, or maybe Malayans. It showed plays in their own language. There was one time when we misinterpreted something and began to applaud, which drew the attention of the crowds as he we had been applauding at the wrong time.

I just want to clarify something before we move on. You have spoken about transporting 'passengers' more than once during this period of flying. I assume that they were all Armed Forces personnel and not civilians?
Yes, they were Armed Forces personnel with the overwhelming majority being from the RAF. The rest were from the Army, and the one civilian doctor I took to Akyab.

CHAPTER ELEVEN

STATIONED IN MALAYA

Saved by the British Army and landing an overloaded Dakota on one engine.

In October 1945 you were posted to Kuala Lumpur, in Malaya. What state was the city in, so soon after the war had ended?
The atmosphere in Kuala Lumpur itself, you couldn't call it normal, but it wasn't anything abnormal. Though I can only speak for Kuala Lumpur, I can't speak for the country as a whole.

The airfield at Kuala Lumpur when we arrived was in a very bad state. It didn't have any runways; it had a very wet field which you were supposed to land on, though they very quickly did get it in order. What surprised us is that we were told to go and find our own accommodation. We ended up staying in a large house, which lacked furniture, close to the airfield. Speaking about furniture, a rat had burrowed its way into the sofa and came popping out. The cook in the house saw it and threw a knife at it, killing it outright. During our time in this house, we had to keep guard. We were taught how to use and were issued with 303 rifles for this purpose.

What was the role of your flying while based in Malaya?
The same as it had been prior to coming there, taking passengers around the region. The reason why so much of my flying was taken up with passengers is that there was so many people who were being posted home as their tour had come to an end, people being promoted, and personnel being moved around the region to reclaim control of colonies and the like. However, we weren't always moving men, once we had to collect a lawnmower.

You had to collect a lawnmower?
Yes, a Group Captain had seen a Japanese lawn mower in Kota Buri that he wanted. He wanted it transported to Kuala Lumpur, where he was stationed. So, the on the 13th November we went and

picked it up.

Are there any standout moments from your flying while in Malaya?
Well the weather was quite volatile while we were there, so on more than one occasion, we would have to abort a trip.

On November 16th we travelled to Batavia in Java to pick up wounded personnel and take them to Singapore. Java was in control of the Dutch and the atmosphere there was very volatile. During our one night stay there, we checked into a hotel close to the airfield. During the night we heard gunfire going off throughout the city. The manager of the hotel warned us not to go out due to the violence. The airfield itself was very close to a canal, in which dead bodies were floating.

The next day, we were transporting wounded men back to Singapore, I was waiting for the Dakota in front of me to take off, but as it did so, it came under machine gun fire. This resulted in several of the wounded being killed and the doctor on board was wounded.

So what did you do?
I took off and kept as low as possible, just skimming the boundary hedge, still on full power and waited until I was well clear of the airfield before climbing.

Even though the Malayan Emergency would not begin until 1948, the Malayan Communists, who had fought the Japanese during the occupation, were still well-armed. All of this was on top of the general turmoil a country goes through as it begins to recover from war and occupation. With all this in mind, what were relations like between the local populace and the British?
It seemed pretty normal actually. I suppose a good indicator was when on one occasion, my Wireless operator and myself walked into the city centre as he wanted some clothing. We did this without carrying any weapons on ourselves. It was quite a relaxed walk, without looking over our shoulders. It was on this journey into the

city that we saw a group of children kicking a ball around on a school playing field. It was little things like that made me think that things were beginning to return to normal. But of course, armed conflict would erupt once more in 1948.

Also, a lot of British personnel were coming down with venereal disease so I guess you could say that relations with the local women was good. I didn't realise how widespread venereal disease was until I walked into a bathroom and saw an army chap who was in quite a state, cutting off strips of carbolic soap and trying to force it down into his penis through the urethra. It transpired that he was a married man with a child. Not only would his wife have questions in why he wasn't expressing his interest in her, to put it in a nice way, but back then, venereal disease was quite a serious thing as antibiotics were not then available, and if one went to the Medical Officer to receive treatment, then everything was put down on to their medical record.

However, it wasn't all rosy. We had an arrangement with a garage owner that in exchange for a few tins of our cigarettes and half a bottle of whiskey or whatever, we could use his car, running costs included, for as long as we were in Malaya. We took quite a few trips in this car. Once, we were returning from a dance about ten miles outside of Kuala Lumpur. The dances practised there were the Waltz and Fox Trot. There were two of us in the car, George and I, when the axle caught fire. We pulled over and stopped and luckily, the fire went out. A short while later, as we were debating who was going to walk into Kuala Lumpur, another vehicle came past and pulled over ahead of us. Four men with bad intentions came out brandishing guns. My co-pilot and I got behind the doors of our car. Fortunately we had pistols on ourselves which we had drawn in preparation for a gun fight.

What a frightening situation that must have been.
I can't speak for George but I was scared. Fortunately, we heard another vehicle approaching, but thankfully it was a British army lorry full of soldiers. Once the other men realised this they got in their own car and sped away, pursued by the army lorry.

George got a lift into Kuala Lumpur to tell the garage owner what had happened with the car, and I was left on my own. Despite what had just happened, I wasn't scared of being left there on my own. Besides, at this stage, it was starting to get light.

George and the brother of the garage owner returned and it was then that we learnt that his brother, the garage owner, was missing. We later learnt that the garage owner had been murdered. Apparently, a group of men had asked for a test drive and the garage owner had agreed. At some point during this drive, he had been shot and left in the back seat. I know this because a search party had been organised. I wasn't taking part in the search as I had to do an air test. However, George took part, and that's how I know that the owner was found as I described, lying dead in the back seat having been shot.

Did anyone know why he had been murdered?
It was believed that he was murdered by the Communists because of his view on the British, his actions towards us, and possibly for holding anti-Communist views.

Not long after this chap was murdered, your last ever flight in the Far East took place, and it was quite eventful. What happened?
Yes, on the 21st of December, I had flown from Kuala Lumpur to Calcutta, via Rangoon. We had picked up a lot of Christmas freight, with the goal of transporting it back to Kuala Lumpur. I had landed at Dum Dum to refuel as it had an extra long runway which we needed as we were carrying seven thousand pounds, which included Christmas freight. On top of myself, the navigator, and a different co-pilot (as George was helping with the search for the garage owner), we were also carrying nine passengers, made up of Army and Airforce personnel who had gone Christmas shopping on behalf of their units and squadrons. We stayed the night there, and the next day, we took off and made it to Mingaladon airfield, Rangoon, without any incident.

Though I intended to refuel and carry on, we stayed there the night as a meteorologist had warned me that an inter tropical storm was on our flight path. The next day is where things went wrong. We took off from Mingaladon and an hour or so after take-off, we had to go through a violent chain of storms that took about half an hour to get through. Soon after we were out of them, I handed over to my co-pilot and told him that he only had to maintain the height I had set. I went back to chat to the navigator to confirm where we were and it was at that point that a cylinder exploded on the starboard engine. I noticed that the cylinder affected was still receiving fuel and still being ignited, I knew this because I could see a little flame shooting out of the engine. I realised that I wouldn't get any power from that cylinder but knew I could get some from the rest of the engine but I had to cut the revolutions down to lower the risk of fire. The co-pilot was terrified, he had only flown Spitfires prior to this, never a big aircraft. Anyway, I put the aircraft into climbing power on the port engine and kept the starboard engine going on much lower power. Then, I climbed to a height of nine hundred feet knowing that it would get me over the coastal hills. Once we had cleared the hills, I deliberately feathered the starboard engine, knowing that we wouldn't have to climb anymore. After that, I deliberately turned north to head to an old Japanese airfield near Tavoy, (present-day Dawei). I knew there was an airfield there as we had been warned of it and others when we bombed Tavoy while on war time operations. Once there, I steadily descended but came into a layer of low cloud which was really fog, originating from the sun heating the soaked ground. At four hundred feet, I saw that the airstrip was only a few hundred yards away. We were much too high so I went into a falling leaf manoeuvre, which reduces one's height much more quickly. At the boundary, I was still about fifteen feet too high, so I forced the plane down with a heavy landing so I could bring the brakes into use. At the end of the strip, I purposefully used the port engine to turn around and give us more airstrip to brake. When we finally came to a stop, I was almost in tears due to the relief. A few of the passengers actually got out and kissed the ground.

What was the aftermath of it all for everyone involved? To survive something like that must elicit strong emotions in people.
We had to spend the night at Tavoy, there was a four-man meteorology

unit station there so it wasn't an abandoned airfield. That night, everyone involved had a celebration in the mess and it was the only time in my life that people sung 'He's a jolly good fellow' to me. During this celebration, I asked my co-pilot what he would have done if I wasn't able to fly the plane when the event occurred, and he admitted that he had no idea. The incident itself was put down to metal fatigue.

The next day, six Expeditors, a twin-engine Canadian plane were sent to transport us, the passengers and the freight back to Kuala Lumpur. Three of them had to make a second trip in order to ensure that all of the freight had been recovered. Even the radio and cockpit instruments were removed from the Dakota and taken back to Kuala Lumpur to ensure that the Communists didn't get their hands on them.

An army chap told me that I had been very fortunate because at Tavoy, there were two airstrips, one running north to south, and a shorter one running east to west. I had landed on the north to south strip, but according to this army chap, the east to west strip was still mined.

Many years later, I read in an RAF magazine that I receive three times a year, an article by an RAF chap asking if anyone had any information on Tavoy airfield. I wrote in with the story I have just told you and the sergeant that was there when this took place saw my article and remembered the incident. He replied to my letter.

What you did was quite a feat. I'm surprised you didn't receive any awards for it.
Well I received a 'Green Endorsement' in my log book from the Group Captain praising me for what I managed to do, the same Group Captain who I picked up the lawnmower with. Funnily enough, when he was talking to me about it, he looked at me and said, 'Aren't you glad that I taught you how to fly a Dakota?' 'Bloody cheek' was my response, which could have put me in trouble as I had technically sworn at an officer. Luckily he saw the funny side to it.

So why was this flight your last one in the Far East?
Because it was the only Dakota we had in this unit. I have no idea why another one wasn't sent. By the time I left the Far East in March 1946 it still had not been replaced to the best of my knowledge.

Your last flight in the Far East took place in December 1945 and you left three months later. In that time you did no flying, so what did you do?
I would have been at Kuala Lumpur during that time, I was stationed with a communications squadron. Honestly, I don't remember a lot during this period so it must have been uneventful. The atmosphere was more relaxed; we had the freedom to go into Kuala Lumpur itself. The only story which really sticks out is quite random. For a joke, a chap and I were trying to whip each other with wet towels. Why that stands out so vividly I don't know.

What's your opinion on the Dakota? It's a plane that is held in high regard by many. Do you agree?
Yes, it was a lovely plane. It handled really well and was a reliable plane that could do long flights. It was also built very well and could fly in all conditions, anywhere in the world. It was a great plane, it really was, and in some places, it still is!

CHAPTER TWELVE

POSTED BACK TO BRITAIN

Adjusting to home, becoming an Adjutant and an interesting letter.
An unbelievable driving test, leaving and re-joining the RAF.

On the 27th March 1946, you boarded the SS Capetown Castle to begin your journey home. When did you find out that you were going home and were you happy to receive the news?
No, I was not happy. I was in Kuala Lumpur. I was called into the Adjutant's office. He looked up and said, 'Good news Denis, you're going home'. I looked at him and said 'home? I don't want to go home'. But it had been decided; I was going home. I was having such a good time out in the Far East, it really was an adventure, while the updates from home told me that Britain was going through a bad winter and that rationing was still going on. But a new rule had set the period for an overseas tour at two and half years and by this stage, I had been overseas for well over three years.

I went back to the billets and packed my things. I boarded a night train to Singapore and it was absolutely packed with people. The only place I found to sit was between the carriages. So that's where I slumped with all of my gear. At first, I sat on my large pack and put my smaller pack and suitcase either side of me. But when the movement of people between carriages stopped, I rearranged things so that the smaller pack acted as a pillow, which enabled me to lie down. During the night, I was partly woken up by the sounds of rattling, which I assumed was the train going over points. But when I woke up in the morning, I became aware of a draught coming into my back which turned out to be a bullet hole. I found the bullet itself on the floor and threw it away in disgust. I found out that the train had come under machine gun fire overnight, presumably by the Communists.

Once in Singapore, I left my luggage somewhere. I'm not entirely sure where but I think it was most probably on the ship itself. Once

I'd dropped off my luggage, I went shopping where I brought a tea set made of pewter for my foster mother, and for their son, a smoking set which consisted of a specially decorated cigarette tin and a small frame into which you could slide a box of matches. There was also a gap in the frame that was covered with the rough coating used to strike matches against.

What feelings did you have knowing that you would probably never see the Far East again?
I was quite sad. I felt a greater sense of freedom out in the Far East, as opposed to the stiff air of authority back home. If there had been a way that I could have avoided going home I would have done it; the longer I could have stayed out there the better. But at the same time, it wasn't that bad, because in my mind, I was not going to leave the RAF, so there was always the possibility that I would be posted back overseas, and potentially, back to the Far East.

What were conditions like on the Capetown Castle?
The conditions on board were really good. The food was excellent; it was back to typical British food. You could have cereals, porridge or things like bacon and eggs for breakfast. Stews and Roasts were the type of food that would be served for lunch and dinner, things like that. There was a library on board so there were plenty of books to read, but in all honesty I was just happy looking out to sea. The mood among the passengers was quite joyful as well. I think that many of them were looking forward to going home.

But I will tell you what made the voyage really good. On board, there were men of a wide variety of ranks, including Officers of various ranks. There were around twenty of us that were Warrant Officers, which is the highest rank one could be without being commissioned. All the Commissioned Officers had duties as did all the other ranks, but for whatever reason, us Warrant Officers did not. So, for us, it was three weeks of relaxation.

Many of us had been on Mepacrine tablets for the duration of our time in the Far East, in order to combat malaria. We chucked them overboard thinking we wouldn't need them anymore, which for me was a big mistake because once I was back home, I started getting one cold after another, which became quite bad. When I went to the family doctor, he noted my yellow skin and asked if I had been on Mepacrine and if I still had any. I told him that I didn't, which was bad as anyone who took them had to gradually come off them. He gave me some more and I gradually worked my way off them over the course of ninety days.

Anyway, on the same day that we left Singapore, a troop ship left Bombay. We caught up with it just before reaching the Suez Canal, in an area known as The Great Bitter Lake. Our captain tried to overtake the troopship but ran aground on sandbanks. Our fuel tanks had to be emptied before we could be re-floated on the next high tide. They were then re-filled by which time the troopship was well ahead.

By the way, while on the voyage home, I got to know another Warrant Officer who was in a bunk on the next row. It turned out that he had also flown Liberators, but on Coastal Command. They got their three hundred hours patrolling the Bay of Bengal and according to him, in all of his tour, his gunners never had to fire a shot in defence, and they never dropped a single bomb or depth charge. But their three hundred hours still qualified as a 'tour of operations'.

After we exited the Suez Canal, we made our way across the length of the Mediterranean, which within three years, I would be flying over while on patrols in conjunction with the Royal Navy.

Eventually, we reached the Bay of Biscay which was cloaked in dense fog, which both ships had to crawl through with fog horns blaring every few minutes.

How did it feel to be back on British soil?

I disembarked on the 16th April 1946 at Southampton and honestly, I wasn't too happy. You can imagine what it was like, all these men trying to disembark with all their kit and cases.

I arrived at London at nine at night. It was dark and foggy and there were no buses to Farnborough. I managed to persuade a taxi driver to take me the fifteen miles home, though. The charge was twenty five pounds which was a lot in those days. I arrived home at half past ten and rang the doorbell. I heard my foster mother say, 'Who can that be at this time of night?' My younger foster brother Billy answered the door and called back, 'It's Denis'. My foster mother replied, 'It can't be'. You see these images of parents being overjoyed at being reunited with their children who have been serving overseas, but there was none of that in this case. Despite being away for over three years, I didn't experience any of that. My foster mother was as stern and emotionless as ever, and of course, my foster father had passed away while I was overseas. So in all honesty, I wasn't too happy to be back. I would much preferred to have stayed overseas.

After about half an hour, Billy, who must have been around seventeen at that time, had gone to bed. I tried to get my foster mother to open up but to no avail. I looked around the walls, expecting to see Geckos like I had been so used to seeing in the Far East. I then made a comment about how small the room seemed, which it was after what I had experienced. Still, it took her by surprise. In the end, well after midnight, she told me that she would put a hot water bottle in my bed and that was that.

What was it like adjusting to life back home after so long away?
Well it was sort of halfway between civilian life and forces life in the sense that I was at home and had all this free time as I was on leave during this period. But at the same time, I was still in the RAF.

All this leave meant that I had a period of great relaxation. I spent a lot of the time with the dog but when I first arrived home, I don't think he recognised me. Then, on our first walk, he was off the lead, and I whistled to him in the same way I used to. He stopped dead in his tracks, turned around and after a second or two, bounded towards me at full sprint. He jumped up and wouldn't stop licking me.

My foster mother had also complained to me about her gas oven.

So I took her into Bromley and into a gas showroom for kitchen appliances and asked her which one she liked. She pointed out which one and I took out my cheque book and bought it for her on the spot. They came and fitted it the next day, showed her how to use it and that was that. But still, she didn't show any gratitude, no hugs or anything like that.

The standout event though, was that Laurie from the troop ship, who I had last met in Delhi, came to visit. Laurie was from East London, so the distance wasn't too far. We had lunch and then went out for a walk and caught up on events. While being stationed in the Far East, we had played chess by post, though due to the time it took for each other's letters to arrive, we only had completed about three moves each. Anyway, we set up the chess board at the same stage as it was in the last letter, and he proceeded to wipe the floor with me.

I also got back into cycling. Before passing away, my foster father had taken apart my bicycle, lubricated everything and put it in the loft. So, I got it downstairs and reassembled it. One day, when I was riding it, I came across a bicycle shop and in the window was a racing bike. So, I bought it on the spot and gave my old bike to Billy, who I spent a lot of time with until he too was called up for National Service. In his case, it was the Army.

I went out with Joan a few times, our guardians were still dead against it so we would meet in public and go to the cinema, or the swimming baths, places like that. In fact, once when I was at the swimming baths with her, I ran into my first set of foster parents. Unbeknown to me, they worked there and the look on their faces when I showed up in uniform was quite something. They had not seen me in well over a decade, since I was a child and there I was, twenty-one and in full battle dress.

What came next for you after your leave was over?
I was posted to an airfield in Norfolk named Swannington on the 14th June 1946, and worked in administration. I worked there for a little over a year because sitting in an office bored me to tears. With

every C/O, I told them that I wanted to go back onto flying. Every single one told me that they would organise it for me. But with the Armed Forces going through a period of mass demobilisation, we had a high turnover of C/Os.

However, while I was in Norfolk, I was notified that my commission had come through. I had completely forgotten about it, and it wasn't until I went to London for a final interview with senior officers that I learnt that the original application had been dated from December 1944 and signed by a 'Wing Commander Blackburn' of 159 squadron. Blackburn had encouraged me to do it, and had even filled in a large number of the forms on my behalf. Why he was so personally interested in it I don't know but one clue was that on one operational flight, I took off with bombs on board and did what is known as a 'rate four turn' which is where you turn to the greatest angle possible, where you end up practically on your side. Blackburn had not taken part in this operation but was most likely watching from the ground. The next day he called me into his office, I saluted and he asked me if I wanted a commission. I told him that I wasn't really interested and his reply was something like, 'Well if you're not up to taking the responsibilities of an officer, then we'll forget about it'. This really riled me as I knew that I was just as good as they were, so I agreed to apply for it and he told me that he would even do most of the work for me.

Anyway, it had now arrived. But in order for me to accept this commission, I had to sign on for another year. I passed the interview and the medical, but I was very clear that I would only sign on if I was put back on to flying. This was agreed and I signed on, but now, as a Commissioned Officer, with the rank of 'Flying Officer'. But still, I was not put back on to flying.

Now that you were a Commissioned Officer and an adjutant, how did things change for you?
I was given a cheque to cover the cost of the uniform change, and then it was back to Norfolk. The adjutant I was replacing was demobilised a few days after I returned and I took his place as a

flying officer adjutant. The sergeant in charge of the admin staff was a great help in those early days of 'learning the ropes', so was the C/O. So, imagine the shock when a message came from Air Ministry that the C/O was to resign his commission with immediate effect. On that same day came a message to inform us that an Anson aircraft would be bringing previously ordered equipment. The C/O jumped into his vehicle and went out to inspect the runway, which was officially out of use. He was at the far end of the runway when I received news that the delivery would be the next day. I needed to pass this message to him but there were no mobile phones or anything like that in those days. I spotted a Verey pistol and took it to the outside platform and let off a shot to get his attention. I had allowed for the wind but a gust took the shell further than I had anticipated so it only landed a few feet from the C/O who via the vehicle, was back within minutes. In a frightful temper, he roared, 'Were you trying to kill me!' I showed him the message concerning his dismissal and the one regarding the Anson, which calmed him down.

The next day, the sound of distant Anson engines filled the air. I quickly contacted the senior equipment officer who was expecting the equipment that he had ordered and he took me in a vehicle to the control tower. However, en route, our view of the bend was disrupted by big banks of earth, which were designed to protect our aircraft from enemy fighters. Our airfield was still set up as it was during the war. Just as we reached the bend, so too did the Anson. The pilot had landed it in the wrong direction, diverted on to the perimeter track and just headed for the control tower. At quite a speed, he reached the bend just as we did. Sitting in the passenger's seat, I was suddenly confronted by the Anson's port propeller heading straight for my head. Fortunately, the pilot cut off power to that engine and my driver slammed on the brakes so the two machines finished up only a couple of feet apart. Just as well, otherwise it could have been my head cut to pieces or even cut off! The pilot never did explain why he had landed downwind. The ground signal board was showing the right direction plus there was of course the windsock.

What was your role as an adjutant?
Well as an adjutant, I was, to put it in civilian terms, like a secretary for the C/O. I basically assisted him and dealt with any mail that came to him. As being an adjutant was a commissioned rank, I was also in a position to give orders. I didn't really like being in a position of authority; it was unnatural to me, not to mention that I was now moving in circles that weren't familiar to me.

Swannington at that time had around two hundred and fifty airmen. Officers consisted of the temporary C/O and his junior assistant, a senior equipment officer, also with a junior assistant, an admin officer, an accounts officer and me. Like myself, the junior officers were in their mid-twenties.

So was there really no flying at all for you during your time as adjutant?
Well there was one occasion that I flew. I don't know what the purpose of his visit was, but an officer did stay the night. He had arrived in a single engine aircraft, a Proctor. I asked him if I could go up in it and he agreed, telling me not to bend it. It was great, at that time, flying any aircraft was joyful.

However, out of us junior officers, none of us could drive but I did learn to drive during my time in Norfolk.

Tell me about it.
One of our officers at Swannington was an Argentinian who rented a local cottage. He soon got accommodation in our own officers' quarters, so he no longer needed the car to get to and from the cottage. At breakfast one morning, he asked if anyone would like to buy his car. I immediately put my hand up and said that I would. He remarked that I couldn't drive, to which I replied that he could teach me. So I became the owner of a Ford 8, a three geared car with a reverse gear too. At the traffic-free airfield, I soon got the hang of driving, but for further afield, on to main roads, I needed 'L' plates and insurance. It was already taxed in his name so that was

transferred too.

So, it was off to Norwich where Woolworths had the 'L' plates and then to Norwich Union Insurance Co. The motor section was not in one of the high-rise offices of later days but was up a narrow staircase to a single office where an individual soon dealt with my needs. So, there I was, taxed, insured and ready for the high road. We spent most of that day in Norwich. Parking was no problem back then and I soon passed my driving test. I took an instant liking to Norwich, lots of changes to modernise it were already taking place. There were numerous shops and stores staffed by helpful and friendly people and a marvellous market. I liked the city so much that in 1974, my wife and I bought a little terraced house with a nearby swimming pool, a great attraction to me as I am someone who loves swimming. We moved into the house in 1978 which was four years after that the wonderful group ABBA won the Eurovision song contest with 'Waterloo', which by coincidence was the name of our road.

I assume you passed your driving test in Norwich?
No, I took my test in South London during leave when I went home to Kent. A corporal was also on leave and wanted to get to London so I agreed to drive down with him, he driving through the towns and myself on the country roads. Our plan was going well until we reached London and parted ways at the underground station in Tottenham. He gave me directions but before long I was lost as I did not know that part of London. I soon ended up in a cul-de-sac and performed a horrible three-point turn trying to get out of it, gears crunching and everything. I then had the cheek to ask a policeman who was standing nearby if he knew the directions to Bromley, which back then was a part of Kent. He advised me to follow some tram lines which terminated at Herne Hill. Fortunately, from there, I knew the way home.

Bert was there so I went out with him a few times and he gave me some advice and tips on how to pass the driving test.

So, the day of my test came. The test centre was in Catford, I went with Bert as he was expecting to be able to come round with me on the test, but the examiner told him that that wasn't allowed. From there, it was just a case of following the examiner's instructions. I remember that we came to a crossroads where a policeman was standing on a plinth directing traffic. I didn't even see the policeman so just drove right past him. The instructor said to me, 'Do you always drive past policeman giving stop signals?' I honestly had not seen him. Later on, he told me to take the next left which I did, but too sharply, causing the wheels on the left side to bounce over the curb. Not long after that he told me to do an emergency stop which I did, so efficiently using both the brake pedal and handbrake that the instructor almost went through the windscreen. I had stopped so sharply that the braking system seized up. The examiner turned to me and said, 'I suppose that one of us will have to get out and rock the car, and I suppose it will be me'. He did it and the brakes relapsed into their normal positions. He got back in the car and once back at the test centre, referred back to his notes and commented on my RAF uniform and I'm not kidding, said these exact words, 'I see you can fly aircraft so you must be able to drive a car so we'll put it down as a pass'.

I can't believe that he actually passed you.
I know, it could never happen now. But before long, I was back at Swannington in my Adjutant position, a role I have already explained. But one thing I did not mention was that I also had to look after German prisoners of war.

German prisoners of war were held there?
Yes, there were around twenty-five there and they were very well behaved, I think that they just wanted to get home. I had to visit them twice a day, morning and afternoon. I conversed with them quite a lot though it never went beyond small talk and basic conversation. Incidentally, a lot of them could speak quite good English.

Also, it was during this time that a very interesting letter arrived.
After I had become an Adjutant following my commission, a letter

arrived for me, it was from Blackburn. I've mentioned how when we were on operations, he asked us all what we were going to do after the war had finished. He had said that he was going to buy a yacht and sail it around the world and asked if anyone of us wanted to join him, to which I said that I would. Well, this letter was regarding that. In the letter, he told me that he now had a yacht and was in Marseille with detailed instructions on how to reach him. Unfortunately, as I had already signed on again, I was unable to take him up on his offer.

Looking back on it, do you regret that circumstance meant that you were unable to go to Marseille?
Yes, very much so. The mental image of being out to sea, on a yacht, had even more appeal than flying, I really loved the sea. If I had not signed on again, I would have been off to Marseille in a flash.

Once your year was up, you actually came out of the RAF.
Yes, I came out in September 1947 because I wasn't flying. I wanted to fly, it's the entire reason I joined the Air Training Corps and went into the RAF. Once I was out, I did a number of jobs but couldn't take to any of them. I applied to be a bus driver but they had stipulations about age, height and weight of which I didn't meet any, though I was offered the job of inspector. Back then, there were strict rules and stipulations regarding bus punctuality. So I would have to go to random bus stops and see if the buses came on time. But the job never transpired as it meant having to do a period of conducting, which I had no interest in doing.

I also had an interview for a job with an engineering firm that worked on the London underground.

I also applied for a job with British South American Airways. I thought that I had done well with over a thousand hours of flying but at the interview, it transpired that they wanted all of their pilots to have at least five thousand hours of flying, which I did not have. So I was turned down on that.

Honestly, it was a period of odd jobs and once my leave was over, of trying to adjust back into civilian life. I think it's something that almost all ex-service people go through. You see it with those who return from the Middle East campaigns today, trying to adjust back into civilian life. In total, I would estimate that I was out of the RAF for just over a year.

Fortunately for you, the Berlin airlift soon started, which for you, was a potential opportunity to start flying again.
I thought so. That was my intention and why I re-applied to join the RAF. But the process of the application took so long that by the time I had passed through the flying schools, the Berlin Airlift had been over for quite a while.

My foster mother was not happy at all about me going back into the RAF and told me that I should not do it. She was quite angry about this, and told me that she was going to write to Air Ministry herself and put a stop to it. She had this inflated ego and seriously thought that her words and wishes carried such weight that she could influence things like that. Even when I went shopping with her as a child, I had to be a couple of paces behind her. Anyway, I told her that I had re-enlisted and there was nothing that she could do about it.

My application was eventually processed, I was accepted, and on the 19th April 1949 I was posted to Cardington in Bedfordshire to be kitted out. By the way, I didn't have my commission, I went back in as a non-commissioned officer, with the rank of 'Flight sergeant'. From there I was posted to Finningley in south Yorkshire on the 27th April 1949, to a refresher flying unit, flying Wellingtons and I was the happiest man alive, back on flying. I took to it like a duck to water once I got back behind the controls of a Wellington. There wasn't any dust to shake off, so to speak. This unit was made up of all sorts of men, many of which were on national service. For me at least, there were no exams to go through. For me, it started off with circuits and landings then eventually turned to cross country exercises and bombing practice, in order to test my skills with those.

From there, on the 6th of June 1949 I was posted to Kinloss in Scotland for three months on a Lancaster conversion unit. I was fortunate. I took to the Lancaster straight away without any problem.

Basically, I was taught how to fly a Lancaster from scratch, like I had done with all the other aircraft I had learnt to fly. I became familiar with the layout of the cockpit, then the effects of controls, taxiing, straight and level flying, climbing, descending, stalling, medium turns, gliding and climbing turns, taking off into wind, approaching and landing. Then I would move on to my first solo, then steep turns, then instrument flying. It became more complex the further you went, so near enough every possibility could be prepared for.

I remember, one thing I had to do with the instructor was to practise low level flying, this was over the sea. I came down to fifty feet, then twenty, then he asked me to perform a sharp turn to port, which I did, and it revealed a wake being blasted behind us, like a ship at sea, all done by the slipstream of course. Instrument flying came into it a lot too which pleased me as I liked instrument flying. It carried a lot of value as you learnt to fly in fog. I did have to take exams while I was there, on things like the inner workings of a Lancaster.

There was one scary incident while I was there, where the air traffic controller saved us from catastrophe. I was in the Lancaster with my instructor at the controls and we were coming into land in heavy fog, so heavy that you couldn't see the other end of the runway, when the air traffic controller called out, 'Aircraft just landed, turn right immediately!' The instructor did and a few seconds later, another Lancaster appeared from the fog also turning right. What had happened is that as we were landing, another Lancaster was landing from the other direction. As there was no wind, you could land from either direction. Both planes came off the runway but there were no injuries.

I passed all of the exams and was passed to fly Lancasters. I then left Kinloss on the 27th September 1949. I had around a month's leave, but once it was finished, I was posted to Malta on 4th November, where I would serve with Coastal Command 38th squadron for the next two and half years.

CHAPTER THIRTEEN

STATIONED IN MALTA

The role of the RAF, aging Lancaster bombers, removing a 5-year-old's thumb and exploring Malta. Meeting an old friend and rubbing shoulders with royalty.

So, after you had finished at Kinloss, you had a month's leave before being posted to Malta.
I was posted to 38th Squadron and knew that I was going back overseas so the first thing I did was sell my car. I sold it to my old friend from choir days, Reg Pattison. Aside from that, the month was mainly taken up with getting ready to go back overseas.

We were taken to Malta in a basic Dakota. By basic, I mean it did not have any cushioned seats or anything like that.

I made two friends on the way out there and once we arrived, we noticed that the Maltese Times printed the temperature of the sea. It didn't bother us that it was November, the apparent temperature was enough, so the three of us went to Sliema harbour and dived in, then promptly came out within a few seconds.

What was the role of the RAF in Malta at the time?
Well, I arrived in November 1949. At the time; our main role was to work with the Royal Navy. We did numerous exercises with the Navy, learning how to cooperate with them. The Cold War was in its first few years, and the powers that be seemed to believe that the Russians would flood the Mediterranean with submarines, so learning how to hunt and destroy submarines was also a big part of it.

We also had to be on standby for Air Sea Rescue. There were two squadrons stationed at Malta at the time, 37th and 38th Squadron and each were on standby for Air Sea Rescue duties on alternating weeks.

However, my first flight in Malta involved none of those things. Freshly arrived pilots had to go through 'the Flight Commander's Check', which was a formality more than anything. It was just to make sure that the pilot could handle the plane efficiently. But mine turned out to be quite eventful. I was flying the plane with the Flight Commander in the co-pilot's seat. At RAF Luqa, there were two runways, north to south and east to west. Though the east to west was the most used runway I landed from north to south, due to the wind direction. I didn't know it, but on the southern end of the runway was quite a bump. We landed, and just as I pulled back on the control column to settle with the nose up and on all three wheels, I hit the bump, which launched the aircraft about four feet or so in the air. On landing a Lancaster, the pilot sets the throttle, but for the last bit of the landing, the co-pilot controls the throttle. This is because both of the Pilots' hands are controlling the control column. Now this bump threw us around four feet into the air, and I knew that we would come back down, nose first if I didn't do anything. So I just knocked the Flight Commander's hand off the throttle and then put on maximum power so I could land it with the nose up. From then on I knew about the bump so would always allow for it whenever I landed there. By the way, the bump came from a filled in crater which was caused during the bombing raids on Malta during the war.

What examples can you give of the type of exercises that would take place with the Royal Navy?
All of these exercises took place as though we were at war. The waters around Malta were divided into boxes and given a number and letter to identify them with. These boxes stretched a long way, even to the area around Cyprus. On the way to the box, the aircraft would make contact with the relevant Naval vessels with an estimated time of arrival. Then once there, the aircraft would be given its coded exercise. We would be assuming that the Russians would have submarines shadowing a convoy. So the convoy Fleet Commander would come out with a coded number of an exercise,

and we would carry out the exercise. They liked having aircraft around the convoy, to watch for submarines. They called us their eyes in the sky. As aircraft travel at much higher speeds than ships, we would, to put it simply, come back on ourselves in circles, so we would end up in the same position relative to the convoy.

British submarines took part in these exercises, acting as Russian submarines, so we would 'hunt' them, so to speak. Once a submarine was located, we would circle it and drop a smoke float, or flame float at night, at its last known location and then drop sonobuoys to track its movement, around the north, south, east and west of the smoke float, at a distance of a mile, in a circle. (These are portable sonar systems that, when dropped from an aircraft or a ship, can help in detecting submarines.) Each sonobuoy had its own radio frequency and colour, so if the sound of a submarine came up on say, colour red and whatever its frequency was, then the submarine's location would be passed on from the wireless operator to the navigator. From there, the navigator would plot each position and give these positions to the Navy, guiding them to the submarine. The Navy would head towards the last known position of the submarine. Eventually, they would pick up signals from the submarine on their own hydrophones (underwater listening devices).

In this type of exercise, the 'destruction' of the submarine would be left to the Navy.

If the submarine reached the end of the sonobuoy web, then another would be dropped to continue tracking it and so on. I believe we carried eighteen sonobuoys, so could keep this up for quite a while.

During my time in Malta, there must have been six of these big exercises that we did with the Navy, all of them involved convoys and submarines. The American 6th fleet also took part in some of these exercises which could last for several days.

We also had to do exercises to keep our skills up to date. Once a month, we had to practise landing on three engines, which meant stopping one engine. These took place both during the day and night and had nothing to do with Navy; it was all about keeping one's skills up.

I remember that we also went on photography exercises, where we would fly over a site and photograph the area.

I assume that smaller scale exercises took place too?
They were basically scaled down versions of the big exercises, ensuring that our Navy vessels could safely avoid being torpedoed by submarines. They would involve one aircraft, one ship and one submarine.

In fact, it was on one of these small exercises that I helped to save the lives of six men. Prior to the incident, I was in the control tower where I had gone to receive orders for our own exercises which involved doing what was called 'WT homings', WT stood for 'Wireless Transmissions'. Our job was to be way out to sea and to home in to these transmissions. The point of this was that the transmissions would come in from ships so we could navigate ourselves to them and assist if needed. Anyway, while I was in the control tower, another crew was being given similar instructions. Theirs was about homing in on a submarine. Earlier, I mentioned how the sea surrounding Malta was divided up into boxes which had their own letters and numbers. During my briefing, I had heard the box code being given to the other crew.

Our own exercise had taken us way to the south of Malta, and it was on the way back that I was sure I heard the emergency call of 'MAYDAY' on the radio. I asked around my crew but no one else had heard it. I then called control tower and they said the same thing. I asked for orders and I was told to carry on as normal, so I did, but after a few minutes of pondering, I was sure that I had heard that MAYDAY call. So, ignoring orders from my own base, I asked my navigator to set course for the box number that I was sure I had heard being given to the other crew in the control tower. As Captain of the aircraft, I could make this decision, but I would be in serious trouble if I was wrong. I reached the area, and soon enough, spotted a dinghy. It was fortunate that I saw them as the sea was very rough and they were on the top of a wave. Once their dinghy was spotted, I informed the destroyer in the area and the crew was soon picked up. I asked the destroyer how many were on the dinghy and the response came back that there were six crew on the dinghy and that two passengers were missing.

I started circling away from the oil slick, from where their aircraft had crashed, in case there was anyone else in the water. After a while, I saw a body floating, it looked as though it was waving and wearing a Mae West jacket (an inflatable life preserver named after the famous Hollywood star). I informed the destroyer and they put out a long boat to pick up the guy - it was the national serviceman. He was in a really bad state so the destroyer headed for Malta as fast as it could but unfortunately, the lad died on the way. The two who were missing was a Ground Engineer and the other was the national serviceman I have just mentioned. The Ground Engineer was never found. It transpired that the crew I had helped to rescue was the same one I had overheard in the control tower receiving their instructions. It was lucky that I overheard them as when I was mulling over the apparent MAYDAY call, I knew it would most likely be coming from that section of sea. If I had not overheard it, I wouldn't have known where I should have begun my search.

I spoke to the pilot soon after and the reason the Lancaster crashed was because part of the port wing fell off. When the plane hit the water, the Flight Engineer hit the button to release the dinghy, but it wouldn't come out. So, once the crew were in the sea, he had to manually hack it out. The truth is, Lancasters were getting so old by this time that the incident rates were quite high, I had quite a few incidents while flying Lancasters, some of which were quite dangerous. He also told me that the effect of the section of port wing falling off was so violent on the aircraft and controls, that he only managed to press the button which turned on the radio transmitter and shout MAYDAY once, before he had to vacate his seat and get out of the aircraft.

I also met up with the flight engineer from that flight in the mess. He told me that the Lancaster had been flown to Malta from Britain and that when they were in the dinghy, he had said that if 38th squadron were on Air Sea Rescue, they would be in the dinghy 'for bloody days'. He had not long said it, when I showed up.

I also had to speak to the C/O in charge and while I did not face any repercussions for ignoring orders, he told me that if anything like that ever happened again, I had to obey orders. He was the sort of chap who applied the rules to the letter.

While we're on this topic, a non-flying incident comes to mind. A lady who used to wash our dirty laundry was sitting on the wall outside our accommodation when a three-ton lorry came swerving around the corner. The driver, only a young chap on national service, overcompensated for his turn and crashed into the wall. The lady, Elsie was her name, was crushed under the lorry. Those of us who were there tried to lift the lorry off her, but we couldn't move it. She screamed and made a lot of noise but slowly her screams and movements quietened and she died. I watched her die in front of me. It's the sort of thing that sticks in your mind forever.

What were the consequences of this tragedy?
The driver was immediately arrested and taken into the cell we had on site. He was eventually shipped back to the UK, but I'm not sure what happened to him after that.

I imagine that your time on standby for Air Sea Rescue must have been quite active considering the military and non-military activity that was taking place in and around Malta, and the Mediterranean as a whole?
If our squadron was on standby, then an aircraft was always put on readiness. So, if an emergency signal came in, then the engines would be immediately started up to minimise the time needed to get airborne.

The first time was when we had to go and search for a Vampire that had crashed somewhere in the desert. We flew to Tobruk in Libya, as that's where the people in charge of the search were based. We went there to receive instructions and to be told what had actually happened. From there, we went to Benghazi in Libya for the next three days and nights, in order to take part in the search. What's amazing is that from the air, even though the fighting in North Africa had been over for quite a few years, we could still make out the wreckages of burned-out tanks and lorries. Unfortunately, mines from the war were still buried in the sand and camels would occasionally step on them and blow themselves up.

The pilot was eventually found. What happened is that he left the aircraft and was picked up by Bedouins who put him on a camel and took him into the nearest town. He received a strong telling off for abandoning his aircraft.

Shortly after returning to Malta, I took part in a training programme which taught me how to drop a lifeboat from a Lancaster. The height you had to be at depended on the wind direction and the speed of the wind. The lifeboat had to be dropped from a height of four hundred feet at one hundred and twenty miles per hour. The lifeboat had to be dropped upwind from the people in the water so that it would drift towards them. The lifeboat itself could carry eleven people and had enough supplies to last eleven days. When the lifeboat hit the water, floatation lines would shoot out from each side for fifty yards. This was so the people could pull themselves in. The difficulty was that you had to be extremely accurate with your instruments.

Shortly after completing this training, an incident occurred where a Meteor pilot had to bail out off the coast of Tunisia due to engine failure. I was on standby when this occurred, and for the first time, I took off loaded with a lifeboat. When we reached the last known spot of where the plane had crashed, we spent seven hours searching the area. We found no clues and we eventually had to return to Malta where I was ordered to see the Flight Commander. He told me that I was to immediately go to Benghazi as another Vampire had crashed in the desert.

This time I was due to take off without the lifeboat and I objected to having to do this extra search because we had spent seven hours searching. It would have taken two hours to get to Benghazi and then we would immediately be put on to the search. He then turned it into an order and I told the flight commander to put it in the flight log book that I was doing this under duress. We made it to Benghazi and after two days of searching, the pilot was found. He was fine and had stayed with the plane. On returning to Malta, I decided to have it out with the flight commander. First of all, I had to see the adjutant, who asked what it was all about and I told him it was about the entry in the flight log book. He went and got the book and told me that it wasn't entered. I asked to see the flight commander but was informed that he had been given compassionate leave as his father was apparently taken seriously ill. If I had been able to see him, I would have demanded it had been written into squadron records. It was dangerous, how many hours we had to fly, and that we were missing a meal.

Aside from the two I have just mentioned, there was another search off the coast of Sardinia. Another aircraft had gone down but unfortunately, we didn't find anything. The same happened when we had to search for a Meteor pilot off the coast of Cyprus. Strangely enough, it was the same Meteor pilot who had been picked up by the Bedouins in Libya. Unfortunately, on this occasion, he was not found..

Earlier on, you mentioned that the Lancaster that you flew when you helped to rescue the crew, had its port wing fall off. You had quite a few incidents while flying Lancasters. What happened on these occasions?

Well not all of these incidents took place while I was in Malta, but a few did. On one occasion, we were on an exercise and what happened was that a propeller, on number two engine started to increase in revolutions, even though I had pushed the revolutionary control lever straight down. But still, it carried on increasing in speed and it started to come out of its engine mounting. I put the Lancaster into a steep climb with the other three engines pulled right back, so giving minimum power, but the plane stalled. As we were falling, I increased power to the good engines and repeated what I had done before, but this time the climb was steeper. Fortunately, there was a loud noise as the propeller slid back into place. From there, I feathered the engine and flew on the other three. When I asked air traffic control for weather conditions I was told that they were quite stormy and that they couldn't give me permission to land. I was told by the C/O to fly to Libya and land at an airfield named 'Castel Benito', so we changed course and headed for that airfield.

When I was in radio range of Castel Benito, I radioed them and explained what had happened, but unbelievably, they told us that they couldn't help as they were experiencing sandstorms, which we could see from the aircraft. They recommended us to go to an American airfield named Wheelus Field and land there. Also to get there as soon as possible as the sandstorms were forecasted to head in their direction. So I arrived at Wheelus Field and received landing instructions. They had a runway going north to south, I was landing from south to north. The flight engineer looked out the window and saw that there were around six vehicles assembled, prepared for an emergency. I landed, and behind me was a Skymaster with its engine on fire. Behind that, another aircraft came in, an American jet. We arrived at dispersal in front of their control tower. They were surprised that only four of us made up the crew. I repositioned the aircraft so the sandstorm wouldn't enter the air intake. Not long after, the Skymaster landed without problem, but when the American jet came into land but forgot to put down its undercarriage. It landed on its belly and sparks shot out everywhere and it eventually slid to a stop.

We were there for two days waiting for a new unit to be brought out from Malta to fix the engine. But in fact, the Americans actually made one themselves. I'm sure it was on the second night there that a huge meal was put on and it was excellent.

On another occasion, I was going from Malta to join the Mediterranean fleet which was off the coast of Cyprus. It took around four hours to arrive there, and once I was within range, I radioed the fleet commander for instructions and his reply was to tell me that my number four engine was on fire, which it was. There were big flames shooting out of it but luckily, the fire extinguishers that were built into the aircraft worked and the fire was put out; after which we returned to base. We were told that once an engine caught fire, you had thirty seconds to put it out before it reached the fuel tank.

One incident I heard about but didn't see was my instructor who had converted me on to Lancasters was killed. He was captaining a Lancaster when it suddenly exploded on take-off, killing everyone. It was theorised that fuel vapours had leaked into the aircraft and that when the wireless operator flicked a switch, the resulting spark caused the explosion.

I believe that all of my other incidents with Lancasters happened when I was with Coastal Command in the UK.

One non-Lancaster incident: I wasn't there when this happened but was told about it later on. At the southern end of the north south runway, there was a row of Nissen huts but apparently during the Blitz time, a heavy bomb had fallen on the end of the southern end of a runway, leaving a large crater. The crater was filled in with tarmacadam resulting in the bump that I mentioned earlier. But tarmacadam is quite flammable and apparently, someone thought it would be a good idea to set it on fire. But before long the fire had gotten out of control endangering the Nissen huts. The result was that the civil fire crew had to be brought in alongside the fire crew stationed here to help put it out.

Wait, one other incident I had with a Lancaster in Malta was when I removed the end of a five-year-old boy's thumb.

You removed the end of a five-year-old's thumb?
Let me explain. After landing, I was called in to see the C/O and was told that a five-year-old boy had been flying a kite in the overshoot area, which is rough ground beyond the runway that can be used if

you overshoot the runway, as the name implies. The string of the kite was wrapped around his thumb. Apparently, as I was taking off and flew over this overshoot area, the kite became entangled in the aircraft and resulted in the end of his thumb being severed off. From what I later gathered, the boy went to hospital for treatment but I don't know if anything else came of it.

You almost lost your sight on one occasion.
One of my ground duties was to check the fire extinguishers, to make sure that there were not any faults with them. I would take the top off to make sure that there was no leakage. Inside was a small container filled with a chemical which upon contact with water, creates foam. On about the third or fourth extinguisher, the container exploded, resulting in some of the chemical splashing on to my face. I immediately splashed water from the cylinder on to my face to get the chemical off. From there I made a beeline for the sick bay and received treatment. The medical officer told me that by splashing water on my face, I had probably saved my sight

How did you spend your free time?
When the water was warm enough, it was mostly spent swimming. During my entire time in Malta, I leased a car so I or anyone else who wanted to come with me would often drive down to a favourite swimming point, named Delimara Point. One place we often went to was named Ghajn Tuffieha and it was there that a chap we were with died of sunstroke. He was fair haired and light skinned. He was sunbathing which didn't seem abnormal but when someone went over to check on him, he was unconscious. Most of us were in the sea and had not taken any notice of it. We just assumed he was sunbathing and maybe having a nap. So an ambulance was called and he was taken to a naval hospital and from there put on a flight back home and it was during the flight that he died.

Speaking of sunbathing, we had a flat roof on our accommodation block. I used to occasionally sunbathe there with nothing on. One day, one of my crew thought it would be funny to photograph me when I was sunbathing without any clothes on. But the skin that was usually covered by trunks was so white, while the rest of me was so brown, that when the photograph was developed, it looked as though I had swimming trunks on.

I also had a bicycle while in Malta so I would often cycle around the island, taking photographs and enjoying the scenery. Some parts of Malta were really photogenic but it did surprise me how much of the northern half of the island was used for farming.

Speaking about bicycles and myself being so brown. I remember once, it was a hot and beautiful day. I wanted to see more of the northern part of the island; this is when I was doing a lot of photography. Off I went on my bike sometime after I had finished breakfast. First of all, I headed to the beach at Ghajn Tuffieha where the fair haired chap died from sunstroke. I went for a swim and afterwards, I cycled on a bit until I came across a herd of shoats, which is a cross between a sheep and goat, which I photographed. Afterwards I cycled back across the island to a place called St Paul's Bay, which is where St Paul supposedly came ashore after his shipwreck. I had not eaten since breakfast and it was during the afternoon that I wanted to know what the time was. I went into a little town named Paola. There was a policeman standing on a plinth, so I cycled towards him and asked for the time. He looked at me up and down and started talking away in Maltese until I asked him to repeat it in English. 'Oh, you're English,' he said in surprise. I had black hair and was so brown that he thought I was Maltese.

On the west side of the island were some very old ruins named Hagar Quim and near to there was a wonderful place to swim, though you had to be prepared to go down some steep cliffs to reach it. It was due to my time spent there that I became friends with a café owner close to this swimming spot. He was a nice chap but had two rifles in the café. When the café was closed, or he was away, he would rig up the rifles in such a way that if anyone broke into the premises, they would be shot. Behind his café was a wall, around one hundred yards, and he grew grapes along it. I got to know him so well that I became one of the lucky few who could help myself to the grapes whenever I wanted them.

Valletta was quite a busy city, which I liked. It had a nice atmosphere and a good range of shops. In fact, it was in Valletta that I had a chance meeting. My crew and I were walking down the main street when I felt a pat on my back and heard the phrase 'Don't I know you?' I turned around and it was Blackburn. I was surprised but glad to see him. We had a chat and my crew and I drove around with him in his rented car for a while, eventually stopping off at a horseracing track on the outskirts of Valletta. It wasn't a traditional track as the horses pulled carriages. I didn't know it existed until Blackburn showed it to us. For each race, I predicted a winner, and was right for the first five races which caused everyone to put a bet on my recommendation for the sixth race. The horse I chose didn't win so Blackburn and my crew who had bet on my prediction, all lost money. Ironically, the horse I chose came in last.

After watching six races, we all made plans to have an evening meal. By this stage, Blackburn had bought his first yacht and was sailing all over the place. During the meal, he mentioned the letter that he had sent me regarding Marseille and told me that I was a 'bloody fool' for signing on with the RAF and not joining him. Also, I drank cherry brandy for the first time and it went straight to my head. Once the meal was over, we got into Blackburn's car and went down to Delimara Point where I proceeded to strip down and dive into the sea. Most of us swam but Blackburn didn't. After a while, everyone went back to the car, we returned to base and Blackburn to wherever he was staying.

I met him for a second time in Malta. He had given me a telephone number during our first meeting and on one occasion I phoned and asked for 'Wing Commander Blackburn'. He came to the phone and told me not to use his rank anymore as he was just a civilian now. When we met up, we just had a walk along the beach. He told me that he had bought a new boat, a German E-boat from the war. The problem was that both engines weren't working. So, he organised the removal of one engine which was put onto a York aircraft and had it flown to Germany where it was repaired, and then had it flown back and refitted into the boat. Then he had the same done with the other engine. He must have had high ranking contacts to pull that off. I didn't see him again in Malta after that.

It wasn't just Blackburn you met while you were there. You also rubbed shoulders with Royalty.

Yes, briefly. Myself and my crew had gone down to Sliema harbour to see if an air sea rescue boat could be reconditioned to use for pleasure. The next building harboured the yacht of Prince Philip. When we were there, he happened to be there and he wandered over to us to ask what our intentions were. We told him about the boat that we hoped to recondition and had a chat with him, he then told us to come with him. We went to where his yacht was, he opened the doors and we went inside. His yacht was stunning; it was so polished that you could see your reflection in it.

I liked Prince Philip. He was quite chatty and came across as one of the boys, he didn't have a chip on his shoulder or an attitude based on his social standing. That was the first time I met him; it took place early on in my time in Malta. The next time I saw him was after a big Naval exercise that took place off the coast of Gibraltar. Afterwards, by chance, I ended up sitting three or four rows behind him at a bullfight inLa Línea de la Concepción . I didn't speak to him but a photograph was taken of him there and published in a British newspaper. I think it was a Sunday edition and you can see me sitting a few rows behind him.

For what it's worth, I did not enjoy the bullfight at all. To me, it came across as barbaric and the bulls looked drugged to me. I would never go again.

On another occasion, our Queen, at the time Princess Elizabeth, inspected our squadron. All of the aircraft on the squadron and their crews were assembled in dispersal and she came past with her entourage. No words were exchanged or anything like that. In fact, we were told to avoid eye contact with her and to not speak to her unless spoken to.

CHAPTER FOURTEEN

NORTHERN IRELAND, MALTA AND GIBRALTAR

Major exercises and a crew in revolt.
'The Battle of Britain display' and Cyprus.

Not all of your time with 38th squadron was spent in Malta. You were also posted to Northern Ireland, where you spent around eight weeks.
Yes, we were stationed at Ballykelly. We arrived there on the 27th October 1950 for nearly two months. We were there for fairly long exercises involving the Atlantic section of the Royal Navy. Again, it was submarine hunting and protecting convoys. The main difference was that the ranges of these exercises were much longer than those in the Mediterranean. On one occasion, we had to test a new device called the 'Autolycus'. It was believed that by using this device, it was possible to pick up the fumes from a submarine, which were diesel at the time. Then, once the fumes were picked up, the location of the submarine could be located more easily. I only tested it once. I was with the flight commander and we had to ascend to ten thousand feet to start with, on the principle that the fumes would be carried up. We then had to gradually descend, going into the fumes which would then lead us to a submarine. Amazingly, we actually located a submarine which was estimated to be five hundred miles away, which didn't mean much as by the time we got there, the submarine would be long gone. Our trial worked out by sheer luck but due to the fact that it couldn't be relied upon, it was quickly withdrawn.

But looking through my log book, a lot of the flying I did was written in code. I can't remember what they stand for so I can't really say what happened on these flights. I assume that they were exercises of some sort, though only short ones as they are recorded as only lasting two or three hours, all conducted during daylight hours.

Did your flying in Northern Ireland differ from Malta in any way?

No, I can't say that it did. Bear in mind that it was the cold war period so there was a big emphasis on naval defence exercises. The only real difference was that the weather was much worse in Northern Ireland than in Malta.

But one new experience was that I went down in a submarine for the first time. All the squadron, or at least those of us who wanted to go into a submarine, were led by our squadron leader. The theory as far as I know was that because we were working them so much, we should see what it was like on their side. The submarine didn't leave port, but did descend into the water so we got the experience of what that was like, before coming back up.

What was it like being down in the submarine, seeing the inner workings of one?

On this occasion, I didn't get the chance to see how it fully worked as it was docked in port; everything was turned off. We were not in there for long; some of us didn't even have the chance to go in. But I did get a claustrophobic feeling, being stuck inside a metal tube and a feeling of fear and helplessness if anything went wrong. After so many hours flying aircraft, you begin to learn what sort of things go wrong and how to fix them, but in a submarine, I had the impression that if something went wrong, there wasn't much that could be done, the fear of drowning I suppose. I love the open sea and being at sea, but not under it, being under the sea felt unnatural to me.

What did you do during your free time there?

There was only one place of interest to me and that was Londonderry. Its residential area seemed to be built in layers; it struck me as an unusual layout. It was from Londonderry that my navigator at the time and myself took a day trip into The Republic of Ireland. We didn't go far into Ireland, only to the first town over the border. I remember that when were in this town, it was clear that the atmosphere towards us was less than friendly, though to me at least, the same atmosphere existed in Londonderry.

On the 29th December you returned to Malta.
Yes, for the next two months, I was in Malta. The flying was mostly taken up with exercises. I did a few flights from Luqa, in Malta, to Benina in Libya, which tells me that I flew a few Air Sea Rescue flights too, though I don't recall who we were looking for. The exercises during this period included a low-level bombing exercise that took place on the 5th January 1951. Also, there was an instrument flying exercise, which meant that I could fly the aircraft only using the dials in front of me. I wasn't allowed to look out of the windows. All of this prepared me to earn my Master Green Instrument Flying Certificate.

What is a Master Green Instrument Flying Certficate?
Well there were three ratings: White, Green and Master Green. Which ratings one held stated the conditions that they could fly and land in. The reason I had yet to attain a Master Green Test Rating is because during the war, things were completely different and we didn't do tests like that. But once I went back in to the airforce, peacetime rules now applied so I had to take tests, which didn't bother me.

The test itself, I went up with an examiner, who obviously held a Master Green. During the test, I wore a hood which blocked my view out of the windows. They also covered certain dials and instruments, though what they covered up depended on what the examiner was asking you to do. So, if the examiner asked you to do a rate one turn, the instruments which showed how sharp you were turning would be exposed. It was to show that you could perform the exercises without relying on any other instruments. Needless to say, I passed.

I know I have mentioned instrument flying a few times, and while it sounds mad to fly an aircraft without being able to see out of the windows, there are many occasions where it is necessary, like if you are flying at night or through clouds, you can't see your surroundings, so you have to rely on your instruments.

The other exercises that I have in my logbook are coded, though there was a navigational exercise to Benina.

On the 20th of February 1951, 38th squadron flew to Gibraltar to take part in a big exercise that involved the Americans and in which Prince Philip commanded a Frigate.
Yes, the squadron flew to Gibraltar, but before the exercise took place, my crew and I had to take a wing commander to Port Lyautey in Morocco. We had four aircraft at Gibraltar at the time, before the exercise began. But out of the four, three were unserviceable, the fourth one was able to fly but it had no instruments, every single one had been removed. I went and told this and he told me that it would be fine; there were no clouds in the sky so the lack of instruments was not a problem. So, we went there and came back on the same day. It was the only time that I have ever flown without a single instrument. All I know is that the wing commander went to watch a film and I had to stay with the aircraft, so I didn't even get a chance to see Morocco.

Next came the major exercise, in which you flew day and night on four separate days within a week.
The exercise was named 'Straits One' and began on the 26th February 1951. The exercise was to ensure that convoys could safely come in and out of the Mediterranean via the Straits of Gibraltar and to prevent any submarines from torpedoing them.

I remember on the first day of the exercise, I was flying at night. We had been given a patrol to carry out. It could have been a square search, or a north south creeping ahead line. A north south creeping line is when you go from north to south in your zone, then go back on yourself with a slightly different longitude, and cover your area that way. A square search is when you start in the middle of your area and solely expand outwards, covering the area. Those are two example and there are many more.

On the first night, I had a bust up with an American pilot over the radio. He tried to order me to change my height. I remember him coming out with something like, 'Hey buddy, what height are you flying at?' I was at a thousand feet, so that's what I told him. 'I want you to go to two thousand feet,' came his reply. 'Negative,' was my response. He asked me for my rank, I was a flight sergeant at this stage. He told me his rank, which was higher than mine and then ordered me to go to two thousand feet. My reply was that I was captaining my aircraft and that the only person I took orders from was my own commanding officer.

Was this exchange mentioned in the wash up afterwards?
Yes, every captain gave their version of events. Eventually it was my turn to stand up. I proceeded to explain how this American chap had ordered me to change my height which I refused, and I explained why I refused. My wing commander then stood up and said that what I had done was right, that I was the captain of the aircraft and that I had obeyed the orders of my C/O.

Were the next three flights as eventful as the first?
No, the only submarine I came across was on the first night. The submarine was on the surface and its commander was clever and had stopped close to a group of fishing boats, who had their lights on, to attract fish (but who were not supposed to be there). The submarine commander had turned on the submarine's navigation lights to try and blend in, but to me, it didn't look right. So, I came in low without any navigation lights on and circled around so I could confirm it was a submarine. Once I had done so and confirmed that it was, I ascended and came in a second time. This time, instead of dropping sonobuoys around the submarine like I had done with the previous big exercise off the coast of Malta, any submarine I found I had to try and 'kill'. So when I came in on the second approach, I opened the bomb doors and claimed the 'kill'. There were cameras attached to the aircraft too, which captured the whole event.

At the washup, the submarine commander got up and gave his version of events. I then got up and gave my account. Once he realised that it was me who had 'killed him', he came out with the phrase, 'Bloody hell, not you again'. The reason for this, is that I had by pure coincidence, 'killed' his submarine twice in the past.

The first time was going from Malta to an exercise off the south of Cyprus. There was a rule at the time that if you saw a submarine, even between exercises, you could claim it as a 'kill'. On that occasion, it was on the surface heading due east. The second occasion happened when we were on our way to Gibraltar for these exercises. I was south of him, heading due west. I had him on radar but didn't know if it was a submarine as it appeared as just a blip. But it was down to sheer luck that we spotted his submarine. It was on the surface and was lit up by moonlight.

I became friends with this submarine captain and when I was back in Malta, he invited me down into his submarine on an exercise.

But during the exercises, that particular submarine was the only one I found, not much of any note happened on the other three flights.

Wasn't it during this big exercise that your crew revolted?
Yes, during that period, we were doing quite a lot of flying, day and night, as has already been mentioned. Sometime during this exercise, my crew came and told me that they were revolting because of the amount of flying that they were doing. They wanted me to be their spokesperson but I wanted nothing to do with it. In fact, I told them that they would be looking at a court martial if they went ahead. Still, they were undeterred. They went to see the wing commander and told him that they were revolting, but he misheard them and told them that if they were vomiting, they should go to the sickbay as there was nothing that he could do about it. My crew didn't follow it up and just left. They were very lucky that he had misheard them.

Did you come into contact with Prince Philip again during this exercise?
No, not during the exercise. The only time I saw him was during the wash-ups, which were de-briefings. The interesting thing about it was that whenever he got up to speak, whoever was speaking would sit down straight away regardless of their own rank. I don't believe it was a rule, I think it was just courtesy.

After the exercise was over, you had a week in Gibraltar. What was your impression of it?
I really liked Gibraltar and would return during my time with 38th Squadron . The people were very friendly, the food was great, the weather was great and the atmosphere of the place was great. I liked the place so much that I asked a few people I knew if they could purchase property for me, though it never happened.

I actually met Blackburn for the last time in Gibraltar though I can't exactly remember if it was on this occasion or another as I visited Gibraltar a quite a few times. What I do remember is that when I met him, he no longer had the German E-boat. What he told me he was doing was transporting the yachts of rich Americans across the Atlantic and into the Mediterranean. They would fly over and then have a sailing holiday in the Med. After they were finished, they would fly back and he would sail their yacht back across the Atlantic to America. During this meeting, we went to Europa Point, there's a photo of us there somewhere, though I don't know where. But that was the last time I saw him. From what I understand, he ended up settling in Antigua.

Anyway, after the week in Gibraltar following the exercise, we returned to Malta on the 10th March, carrying thirteen passengers who were all ground crew.

After returning from Gibraltar, you had four months in Malta before returning to Northern Ireland for a little over a month. How were those four months spent?
Those four months were mainly spent on exercises, which included things like: coded exercises, navigational exercises, bombing and gunnery practice and exercises with the Navy.

The big Air Sea Rescue flight that we had to carry out was when we were called to search for a Vampire jet that had gone missing off the southern coast of Sardinia on the 5th of May. Despite our best effort, we were not able to find him. I don't believe that he was ever found.

But on our way back, we flew through a big storm, suddenly there was a flash and an instant bang was heard which meant that we had been struck by lightning. We arrived back at base without any issue, but when we landed, one of the other pilots on the squadron saw a huge spark come out of the tail of our Lancaster. The spark showed that the static in the bonding wire had been released. Bonding wire was put in the frame of the aircraft to absorb static electricity. The aircraft had to be taken out of service for a few months to make sure that all the static electricity had come out of the plane and to recalibrate the instruments.

Earlier, you mentioned that you went down in the submarine of the commander who you 'killed' three times and subsequently became friends with.

After the Gibraltar exercise, he and I became quite good friends. Out here at least, there was an agreement that if an airman wanted to go on a naval vessel or if a seaman wanted to go up in the air, it could be arranged so I organised to go down in the submarine that he commanded. Unlike Northern Ireland, this submarine was not stationary. In fact, it went on an exercise. When I entered the submarine, the first thing I noticed was the smell of boiled cabbage. It was a funny feeling when the submarine left port, I was very interested to see how it worked on their side. I noticed that the submarine crew worked like a well-oiled machine to keep the submarine going. What I noticed too was that when a dummy torpedo was fired, the pressure inside the submarine changed immediately.

On July 5th, you travelled to Northern Ireland for your second stint there which lasted just over a month.

The day before we left, I fractured my wrist in a swimming accident. A group of us had gone to Delimara Point for a swim before our departure. As it was July, the weather was wonderful. Everyone else had finished and were heading to the car but I decided to stay in for a few more minutes. One of them called out that they were going to leave without me, so I got out of the water, gathered my things and made a dash for the car. It was then I tripped and the landing resulted in a fractured wrist. It was seen by the medical officer, who bandaged it up. Fortunately, it didn't inhibit my flying of the aircraft, the only thing I couldn't do was apply the brakes, so the co-pilot did that.

Regarding Northern Ireland, it was more exercises, though in my log book, they are written in code, which I no longer remember. Though I only did five flights while I was there. From what I remember, it was quite an uneventful month.

You returned to Malta on the 11th August and would remain there for another four months. What happened during this time?
Well the first month was business as usual with coded exercises, instrument flying, circuits and landings, a night navigation exercise and a low-level bombing exercise. But after those had been completed, I was told that I was going to Gibraltar to take part in a 'Battle of Britain' display.

The C/O called me into his office and told me that he wanted me to take part in the 'Battle of Britain Display'. I assumed it would be in Malta but in fact, it was to be in Gibraltar. I asked him for more information and he told me that I would be flying a Lancaster against a Vampire.

On the way to Gibraltar, I practised my corkscrew flying, as it's the way you throw off a fighter that's trying to shoot you down. I arrived in Gibraltar on the 12th of September. On the 14th, we practised for the display and performed it the next day.

Keep in mind that my crew was with me during this display. Anyway, from five miles out we kept to the line of the runway and began our display, and ended up over the runway. During the display I corkscrewed and tried and make my plane as difficult to get a sight on as possible while the Jet tried to get a sight on me so he could 'shoot me down'. During the actual flying, I couldn't see the Vampire behind me so I just focussed on trying to throw it off. The air traffic controller called up and said it was so impressive and asked if we would do it again, to which we both agreed. The Vampire went out to sea to turn around and I went into a rate four turn which is virtually standing the plane on its side and came back on myself, inside the Rock of Gibraltar. It was a crazy manoeuvre; I would never do that type of turn again. Looking back I still sometimes can't believe I did it because that turn was done within the limits of the runway and the Rock itself.

Once we were at the starting point, we both repeated what we had done but afterwards, we both went out to Algeciras Bay. I can't speak for the Vampire but I circled out around for about an hour until the display was over, this was because other aircraft were taking part. After the display was all over and I had landed, the group captain in charge of RAF Gibraltar told me that when I performed the rate four turn, he could see the top of my cockpit. In fact, he seemed quite annoyed about it. The Vampire pilot told me that he was unable to get a sight on me and would most likely have been unable to shoot me down.

By the way, both my Lancaster and the Vampire had cameras fitted to film it. It was also filmed from the ground, so footage of this must exist somewhere.

After I returned to Malta on the 17th, I only flew once more in September; a coded exercise on the 26th. Even when we weren't flying, there were still duties to do. I already mentioned one with the fire extinguisher where I nearly lost my eyesight; other duties included things like assisting the officers on their rounds. Any days where no duties had to be complete, we were free to leave the airfield, as long as we had permission from the C/O.

How did October compare?

I flew seven times in September, and seven in October. In fact, October 4th was when the prop started to come out which resulted in me diverting to Wheelus Field, the American air base. On the 8th, we had to do a simulated lifeboat drop exercise. We didn't actually drop the lifeboat, we just had to practise maintaining the correct height and speed. The rest of the month was more exercises and one

Air Sea Rescue call out.

November carried on in a similar vein. The problem with November is that by then, it was much colder and the sea was too cold to swim in so it limited the things that one could do. I started playing a lot of squash, as RAF Luqa had its own squash court.

One noteworthy event that happened in November was that a disagreement that I had been having with my C/O regarding my rank also concluded. For a few months prior, he had been pressuring me into becoming a commissioned officer again. He claimed that it was part of the outlook of the RAF, who wanted all aircraft captains to be commissioned officers. But I had no interest in becoming a commissioned officer. Remember, I had been one before and didn't have any interest in becoming one again. The reason for this is because life as a commissioned officer was more formal, rigid, and expensive. Expensive in the sense that you had to pay for things like mess fees, garden fees, C/O's charity, formal occasions and things like that, while if you were non-commissioned you didn't have to pay for any of that. This dispute lasted several weeks until it came to the surface when he called me into his office and told that it was now official RAF policy that all pilots had to be commissioned, so I relented and agreed to become a commissioned officer for the second time.

A special plane, a twin engine Valetta, was put on to take me to Fayid airfield in Egypt on the 19th November 1951. I underwent an interview and a full medical before returning to Luqa on the 24th. I passed, the results were sent to my C/O and I became a commissioned officer for the second time, with the rank of Flying officer, skipping the rank of Pilot officer. The reason for this was that the pay of a pilot officer, which is the lowest commissioned rank, was lower than that of a flight sergeant.

December was more eventful. The first few days were spent in Tunisia, flying to Bizerte and El Aouina. On the night of December 3rd, the engine caught fire not far off the coast of Cyprus, just as we were going to join the Mediterranean fleet. When I told you about this event earlier, I forgot to mention that I was not even the pilot on that occasion. The C/O told me that my co-pilot should act as pilot to 'gain further experience'. So that's what happened. He took off and flew to Cyprus. Just before the engine caught fire, he went to use the lavatory, so I sat in the pilot's seat while he was away. While I was in the seat, the engine caught fire, which turned out to be fortunate as my co-pilot told me that he would not have known what to do if he was in the pilot's seat when it occurred. He landed the aircraft upon our return to Malta. Afterwards, the C/O told me that in the flight log book, I should write that I was the captain as opposed to the co-pilot as it would look ridiculous that a captain had only a hundred hours or so of flying and the co-pilot had well over a thousand hours of flying. I agreed with him that it looked ridiculous, but I refused to enter it into the flight log book as he wished which resulted in quite a dispute. I faced no punishment for it.

The first few days of 1952 were spent in Cyprus?
Yes, we flew to Cyprus on December the 31st and were there for about four days. We had a set number of exercises to complete and a set amount of time to complete them in. The first exercise was air to air firing. Another aircraft would tow a torque quite a way behind it which was the target, and using live ammunition, we would have to get ourselves into range for the gunners to hit it. Then we would swap roles, my aircraft towing the torque and the other aircraft firing. The exercise on the second day was bombing and the third day was a repeat of the first. We then flew back to Malta on the 4th January.

The 1950s were an interesting time in the history of Cyprus. Though the beginning of the 'Cyprus crisis' was still three years away, the majority Greek-Cypriot population of Cyprus had made their feelings known, they wanted a union with Greece. Though your time there was limited, what impressions, if any, were left on you?
Right, I can only speak for myself but fortunately I can't say I experienced any direct anti-British feelings; in fact, I enjoyed my time there. We would go to places like cafes where locals would

be and they seemed friendly enough. I remember that I used to go swimming in Morphou Bay. Hard to believe how things would change just a few years later.

By this stage, you were coming up to two months as a commissioned officer, how had life changed for you?
It became more rigid and formal; there were more duties to complete and responsibilities to take on. I just had to adapt from being a non-commissioned ranking to a commissioned officer. It was not as hard as it was the first time.

Also, I had so much leave saved up that between January 10th and March 13th, I only flew three times. Upon my return to Malta, my first flight was a coded exercise on March 14th. On March 18th I flew twice in one day. The first was a simulated sonobuoy exercise, homing in on smoke floats acting as sonobuoys and the second exercise was the same as before but with radar homing added in.

My last exercise was a circuits and landing exercise with three landings which took place on March the 21st and my last flight with 38th squadron was a coded exercise on the 22nd March 1952. I was posted back to the UK on the 29th March and then went on leave until the 15th May.

Was Malta a country that you have a positive opinion of?
Well I liked Malta, it was a nice place to be, there were interesting places to see and the people were generally friendly. My main attractions with Malta was flying when on duty and swimming when not on duty.

Valletta itself was nice, it had great cafes, there was a relaxed atmosphere and it was quite a visually pleasing city. But the problem for me was that the posting of two and half years was too much for a country of its size. Within time, I felt as though I had seen everything, so I wasn't sad to leave.

CHAPTER FIFTEEN

ON THE STAFF AT THE SCHOOL OF MARITIME RECONNAISSANCE

Aging Lancaster bombers, witnessing the Farnborough Air Show disaster, 228 squadron, the Comet, a stay in hospital and role in The Suez Crisis.

On the 15th May 1952, you were posted to the 'School of Maritime Reconnaissance' in St. Mawgan, Cornwall.
Yes, I was posted there to become a member of staff. To that school came qualified aircrew, but the idea of going through the school was to learn the Naval side, in regards to combined operations. So, whoever was heading the Naval side would contact the aircraft and explain what they wanted each aircraft to do. So for example it could involve checking areas ahead of the fleet or areas either side of the fleet, or even areas behind the fleet to check if they were being shadowed. But of course there were many other different exercises that the aircraft could be required to do. All of these exercises were coded by the Navy, but each aircraft navigator had a copy.

All the staff member would do is fly the plane, the trainee pilot was already a qualified pilot so he didn't need to learn how to fly the aircraft. He would be learning the naval side of the patrols so he could eventually go and join a squadron. The other trainees would practise their trade. Any mistakes that they made would be corrected afterwards by the chief navigator or chief of whatever skill they were covering. Staff pilots had to keep their flying skills up, so had to complete a minimum of thirty hours a month of flying. I usually did a lot more.

Generally, how did the students do?
Quite well I would say. They had already learnt their respective roles, otherwise they would not have been at St. Mawgan. The reason they were there was so they could learn how to work with

the Navy. Though there was a time when a student navigator got it completely wrong. We were flying in cloud at one thousand feet, which was the standard height for flying over the sea. We suddenly experienced turbulence but I knew from experience that we were over land. There are different types of turbulence depending if you are over land or over the sea. I quickly realised that we were flying over Ireland and due to the direction we were travelling in, I put the aircraft into a rapid climb to ten thousand feet as I knew that we would fly into the Wicklow mountains if I did not and also, so I could send a transmission to St Mawgan. I asked the student navigator where he thought we were and his reply was that we have to be over Bristol. I then told him to give me a course to get back to Saint Mawgan and his response was to plot a south westerly course. So, I informed him that if we did that, we would finish up ditching in the sea. The staff navigator took over and plotted a course to base. Later on, I spoke to the trainee navigator and it transpired that what he had done wrong was he completely misjudged the wind, calculating that it was coming from the north when it was actually coming from the south. It doesn't sound like much, but for example say the speed is twenty knots from the north and a navigator works out his course assuming that the wind is twenty knots from the south. Then in total, that's forty knots. The chief navigator also went over the charts with the student, and showed him where he had gone wrong.

Another story that comes to mind. A navigational exercise that we used to do with student navigators would be to take off from St Mawgan, head one thousand miles due west, then turn to a south easterly direction, heading for a turning point that we used to use north of Spain. Once there, we would turn north and fly back to base. The exercise was a big triangle. But on this occasion, the Lancaster completely missed this turning point north of Spain and ended up crashing into mountains in northern Spain, killing everyone on board. The mystery is why the staff navigator didn't take over from the student navigator.

On another occasion, I was captaining a Lancaster with a student pilot and a student navigator on board, learning sample exercises of how to cooperate with the Navy. I had to go to the Elsen (which was the lavatory facility in the aircraft) and handed the controls to the flight engineer while I was gone. When I returned, I heard the student navigator having words with the flight engineer. He was complaining to him about not keeping straight and level while I was gone. I pointed out that a slight deviation was acceptable when the flight engineer was at the controls. He was silent for a few minutes but then he started up again, arguing about the flight engineer. I ordered him to put down his equipment, that I was going to navigate for the rest of the way and to consider himself arrested. Once in range, I contacted the control tower and asked for the C/O to be available. He was waiting for us when we arrived. I explained the situation to him and left it in his hands. The punishment handed out, as I later learnt, was that the C/O gave the student navigator a strict talking to and confined him to his room for the rest of the week.

What range did the navigation exercises take place in?
They solely took place in the Atlantic, mostly down to the coast of northern Spain and back. Though sometimes we would take weekend trips down to Gibraltar which were always a nice break, but they were counted as an official exercise. Sometimes, groups of RAF passengers went along and a lot of the time, the main reason they wanted to go there was to buy thousands of cigarettes. Apparently, they were much cheaper in Gibraltar. Now, none of this happened on any of my flights to Gibraltar but I remember hearing that another aircraft had landed back in the UK after a trip to Gibraltar only to be met by customs officials. So, it was something that was known to the authorities.

As a senior staff member, how did life differ there compared to the squadrons you were on?
Yes, there was a difference, but it wasn't so much where I was as what I was. The difference was that on 159 and 38th squadrons, I wasn't a commissioned officer, aside from the last month or so in Malta, while during my time in Cornwall and Costal Command, I was. But we have already spoken about the differences that being commissioned brought on.

As a senior staff member, what duties did you have to complete?
Things weren't that different from that of my commissioned duties. But on one occasion, the flight commander was posted away, so I took over his role on a temporary basis until someone else came and took over. The first thing I did was to order a tool inspection which I and four other officers would conduct. The objective of this was to see if any tools were missing and if so, why. Upon inspection, several tools were missing. One corporal alone was missing around five or six items. Some of the excuses were laughable. The main one was to claim that they had loaned it to someone else. The ground crew were divided into three flights: A, B and C and they would claim that they had loaned it to someone on another flight and had not received it back. All I could do was write a report to the C/O who had the power to charge them for the missing items, but I don't know what came of it. The main objective from my opinion was to keep the ground crew on their toes. If no one checked on them, they would have taken advantage of it indefinitely.

Aside from exercises with the students, did you have to complete any exercises yourself?
Yes, when checks on the staff were done by the C/O or flight commander on a regular basis, to make sure that one was up to standard. The exercises weren't basic circuits and landings, they were more extreme. Things like stalling, sharp turns and asymmetric landings. Every month, we had to practise landing on three engines. Also, once a year, staff pilots were tested by an examiner from the Central Flying School, which was the highest level. With them, we had to do more extreme exercises. On one of these examinations, one of the staff pilots was grounded as an examiner from the Central Flying School was not happy with his performance. He ended up being posted away to a squadron.

Even though I was on the staff at this school for three years, it was quite repetitive in the sense that the exercises were the same and the objective was to get the students to be able to perform to the same standard as the ones who came through before. There was a lot of repetition.

When we were talking about your time in Malta, you mentioned that the Lancaster Bombers being flown were suffering a high incident rate due to their age, and that you experienced this for yourself during your time with Coastal Command in both Malta and Britain. What incidents occurred during this period?
The first incident that comes to mind is that a new pilot joined the staff. On one of his first flights, he had the misfortune of suffering a double engine failure. As he was making his final approach to land, he completely misjudged the strength of the wind and as a result, crashed about half a mile short of the runway. Fortunately, everyone survived, though there were some bad injuries. The Lancaster they were in was completely written off.

On the 15th December 1954, I was due to fly on an exercise with students, but I just had a bad feeling telling me not to fly, it was a very strong feeling. On that night, nothing would have got me up in the air. So, with the Lancaster I was due to fly, I found a fault with it, and then did the same with the Lancaster in reserve. I was on 'B' flight and I then repeated it with two Lancasters from 'A' flight. Eventually, the C/O called the exercise off. The next day, on December the 16th, an incident did happen. I was with students in one Lancaster, and the flight commander of 'B' flight, also with students in another Lancaster. We were on a night time exercise. We were to go out to the Atlantic, turn and go down to the Spanish coast, then turn around and come back to St Mawgan via the Scilly isles. It was the same triangle exercise that I have already mentioned. Anyway, everything was going well until our approach to base, when the flight commander, who was about half an hour ahead of me, called the control tower for landing instructions. Then no further transmissions were heard from him. I called for landing instructions which they gave, and they asked if I had heard from the other Lancaster, which I had not. I landed, then went for a post flight meal, and afterwards I went to bed. I could only have been there for an hour or so when I was woken up and told that I had to take the lifeboat Lancaster to St.Evel. I went and was put on standby as nothing had been heard from the other Lancaster. We had been there two or three hours when message came through that a trawler had spotted wreckage and had picked up a body floating in the water.

In the wreckage, it was found that one wheel had come to the surface complete with its oleo leg, which is the piston that connected the wheel to the undercarriage. The body of the flight engineer with his head caved in was also floating on the surface. What the authorities theorised is that the flight commander must have left his seat and handed the controls to the flight engineer who probably stepped on the undercarriage lever. Once the undercarriage was down, drag on the aircraft would have increased, causing the nose to lower and the speed to increase. It was worked out that they must have been doing around one hundred and eighty miles per hour when they hit the water. Everyone on board was killed. Though there was a bolt that locked the undercarriage lever in place to stop anyone accidently stepping on it and lowering it, Lancasters were getting so old that it was believed that the bolt was probably worn down and had snapped.

Somebody in Air Ministry had decided that co-pilots were no longer essential as the flight engineer would have enough experience to fly the plane straight and level. What was overlooked was that it was true during the day, but not during the night as during night time flying, one is completely reliant on instruments, which a flight engineer would not have known how to read.

The feeling that told you not to fly on that occasion, could you describe it? Was it a religious feeling?
To me, it wasn't a religious feeling, it was an instinct telling me that if I went up in the air, something would go dangerously wrong. Yet the next day, I didn't have that feeling at all, everything felt fine.

Let's go back to the incidents that happened to many of the Lancasters.
There was a case of a young chap on another squadron, who forgot to put his undercarriage down and just slid along the runway with sparks and flames shooting out. I know this because I saw the whole thing.

On one occasion, I lost both inboard engines due to a lack of oil pressure. I was around fifty miles away from base when I called up control tower to tell them that number two engine had failed due to a lack of oil pressure. After I had received new instructions and feathered number two engine, number three engine failed for the same reason, which I also then feathered. So, I was now coming in on two engines, which I told control tower. I maintained height and was told by control tower that the circuit was clear of other aircraft, so I carried out a normal circuit at a reduced height and landed safely, but there were ambulances and fire engines waiting for me. After I landed and got off the runway, I radioed control tower and the C/O who was there told me that I had done a good job. I then replied that my next trick would be to land backwards, which was met with a dry 'Ha ha'.

What differences occur when you land on two engines as opposed to four?
Well you only have half the power so you have to increase the power on the good engines. Fortunately, we were close to base, only around twenty minutes of flying left when my two engines failed, so I was able to do a low-level circuit and land. If two engines fail on the same side, you have to increase power but you also have to put on a lot of trim and rudder to compensate on the side where both engines aren't working.

While we are back on the topic of the problems that many Lancasters experienced and the awful consequences that often resulted from them, you were in the crowd for the Farnborough air show disaster, one of the worst in British history. What do you remember about that tragic event?
Just to be clear, this didn't take place in the Farnborough I grew up in, but in Farnborough, Hampshire.

What I remember is that I had not long joined the School of Maritime Reconnaissance. A fellow officer, named Alex, asked if I was going to the Farnborough Air Show, and if so, could I give him a lift, to which I agreed. On arrival there, we were able to park quite close to the main runway which was fenced off from the public by a post and wire boundary. Alex noticed after a few minutes of standing there that there was a small mound about a hundred yards away that would give us a better view. However, it was already quite crowded so we decided to stay put on the grass verge that ran parallel to the runway. There were quite a lot of people where we were, the crowd was quite deep too.

The high point of the display that day was going to be a display by a De Havilland 110 aircraft, piloted by a chap named John Derry, who was a test pilot for De Haviland, the aircraft manufacturers. It wasn't long before we heard his aircraft arriving. He flew up the runway at about five hundred feet, and at least five hundred miles per hour. He then went into a steep climb, to what I estimate was about two thousand feet. He then flew away from the crowd, then turned opposite the way he had come. He then turned again, which put him directly facing the crowd. It was then that the aircraft broke up into numerous pieces. Unfortunately, the main part that broke away was an engine, which was bouncing along the ground, heading towards the mound that Alex and I had almost joined, but had decided against. The engine went into the crowd and we later learnt that twenty-nine people had been killed and many more injured. The cockpit was heading straight towards the crowd that we were in, bouncing along the ground. Fortunately, it eventually stopped, about one hundred yards away. We could plainly see John Derry and his flight observer inside the cockpit.

In no time, rescue vehicles were racing towards the cockpit and the mound. Alex and myself decided that it would be best for us to leave, to avoid all the rescue activities that were taking place.

What impact did it have on you considering all your years piloting aircraft and the risky manoeuvres you had performed yourself?
Well the impact, to use your word, was so strong that I clearly remember all the details of it, even all these years later. It's the kind of memory that can never go away.

It was without a doubt the worst crash I have seen in my life.

Let's go back to what we were discussing prior to talking about the incidents befalling many Lancasters. After three years at the School of Maritime Reconnaissance, you left.
Yes, I left the school on the 3rd April 1955. The next day, I was posted to a separate unit next to the school. It was an experimental unit where new technologies were tested. I was posted there as an adjutant, but I had learnt my lesson from Norfolk so I started complaining straight away. As a result, I was only in that role for around three months which is fortunate as I wasn't very good at it. On one occasion, a squadronleader came in and asked me where the C/O was. My reply was something like, 'How am I supposed to know?' 'Ask a silly question,' was his response, and he stormed off in a huff. I was fortunate as he could have put me in serious trouble for that remark. But, the role was the same as in Norfolk, basically acting as the secretary of the C/O and without any flying at all from March until August.

The Lancaster was the plane you flew more than any other, two thousand one hundred and seventy - two hours according to your log book. What are your thoughts on the Lancaster?
Lovely plane, my favourite out of every one I flew. It was highly manoeuverable and handled very well. I can't fault it. It was an excellent plane. The cockpit had a great layout and the bomb bay and doors were huge, really big. The only problem with them is that by the time I flew Lancasters, they were getting old. The joke at the time was that they were kept together by string and chewing gum.

The next step for you was being posted to 228 squadron, and on to a new aircraft, the Shackelton.
On the 27th July 1955, I was posted to 228 squadron where I spent three weeks in St. Eval not doing a lot, just waiting to be posted to Kinloss in Scotland to be converted on to Shackletons. In the time I was there, I only went up in the air three times, as co-pilot, all in Shackletons.

I drove up to Kinloss in my Austin 10, arriving on the 22nd August and had to wait two weeks for the course to begin. In that time I would drive the twelve miles or whatever it was to Elgin on most days to go shopping, swimming, to the cinema or to have a meal. I really liked Elgin, the pattern of the town and the friendliness of the people. But I have always found the Scots to be friendly, generous people, I like Scotland. Even today, when looking through the football scores, I always look out for Elgin City.

Eventually the course began, I was in detachment unit 236. The process of learning to fly a Shackleton was basically the same as it was when I learnt to fly all the previous aircraft: learning what effects the controls had, taxiing, straight and level flying, then climbing and descending, stalling the engines while flying and recovering from it, turns, turning while gliding and climbing, taking off into the wind, approaching and landings. There were no written exams.

Like with the Lancaster, I also had to fly over the sea, coming down to low levels and performing manoeuvres. The Shackleton really was different to the Lancaster. It was a heavier aircraft which affected the handling and manoeuvrability. The electronic systems were different too, among other things, all of which had to be learnt. The Mark I Shackleton had a short nose and a short tail while the Mark II had a longer nose and longer tail, which effects manoeuvrability and balance. The Mark III introduced a nose wheel, as opposed to a tail wheel which the Mark I and II had, so when I eventually flew the Mark III Shackleton, I had to adjust to that, which took me back to Liberator days as they had a nose wheel too.

After I had completed my training in Kinloss, I was posted back to St.Eval and returned on the 5th December 1955.

I believe that around this time, you were promoted to the rank of flight lieutenant.

One of the reasons I applied to sit the exams was increased pay, alongside it being a stepping stone in case I wanted to advance further in the RAF. At this stage, I wasn't sure what I was going to do going forward, so I wanted to keep my options open, and that included the possibility of staying in the RAF.

As I mentioned, I applied to sit the exams and was approved. I had to sit exams on five subjects, only one of which was aeronautical. The five subjects were: Airmanship, Air Force Law, Administration, Queens Regulations and General Knowledge. Before the exams, I tried to get a copy of Air Force Law, but so many people were taking exams that there wasn't a copy available, not to mention that I took the exams only the day after returning from Gibraltar, from a navigational exercise.

The rules were that if you failed on one subject but passed the other four, you could retake that one subject six months later, but if you failed on more than one subject, you had to retake all the subjects. I passed four out of the five subjects, failing on Air Force Law, but passed on the second attempt. I then became a flight lieutenant.

I remember you once telling me that during your time at Kinloss, you had the opportunity to be posted back to the Far East.
Yes, during the course in Kinloss, vacancies in Hong Kong, Singapore, Malta and St Eval came up. The idea of going back to the Far East really appealed to me, especially to Hong Kong. Hong Kong was a new place, somewhere I had never been before. I applied for Hong Kong and finished up with St Evel. This is because two officers with senior ranks to myself, took Singapore and Hong Kong. I had been in Malta for two and a half years so it didn't particularly interest me. So, the only place available was St Eval, back in Cornwall, which didn't really bother me as I liked Cornwall.

Judging by your location, I imagine that 228 squadron spent a lot of time over the sea. Was the role of 228 squadron similar to 38 squadron?
Yes, for the most part, we did the same duties as we did in 38 squadron. The clue is in the name 'Coastal Command', which both 228 and 38 squadron came under. In the case of 228, we would usually be detached to Malta for special exercises which involved

the navy. We also acted as troop carriers as unlike a Lancaster, Shackletons could carry troops. A Shackleton could carry a platoon of troops, which I believe is about twenty-five, with all their kit and equipment in the bomb bay.

It's hard to remember much about the specific exercises we did because a lot of them are coded and from February until October 1956, when the Suez Crisis started, I was only flying three or four times a month.

On May 28th, a high-ranking government official, someone to do with Air Ministry came out on an exercise to see first-hand what it was like to do a long-distance patrol. This was on the understanding that after it was all over, we would drop him off at London Airport.

On June 8th, I flew to Malta with my crew to join in with a Mediterranean exercise that involved the Royal Navy. The exercise involved acting as convoy escort lookouts, we were the Royal Navy's eye in the sky, that was the nickname they gave us. Once the exercise was over, we spent another month in Malta, where I only flew three times, June the 11th 21st and 25th. But between June 25th and July 10th, when I returned from Malta, I suffered quite a bad injury to my neck.

What happened?

Malta was going through an unusual period of heavy storms and rough seas, ruling out swimming as a possible activity and I knew that we were flying back to the UK the next day. Four of us went to Sliema, to a place that resembled Delimara Point and sunbathed. I hadn't swum once during my time there and I'd had enough of not being able to swim. So despite warnings that the sea was still rough and that the red flags were flying declaring that swimming was not allowed, I decided to go for a dip. One of our party warned me about the red flags and I came out with something like, 'You know where you can stick your red flag'. I timed my dive to hit the peak of a wave, but I missed it and fell into the trough behind, which meant that the next high wave came crashing down on to my head at an angle that injured my neck. I was pulled out of the sea by the other three, unable to move or even support my neck. We went back to where we were billeted, my head being supported the entire way, and then an ambulance was called. From there, I was taken to Bighi Naval Hospital. I was taken to a small room offset from the main ward and I was laid on boards with my head held, clamped either side so I couldn't move my neck at all. The assumption by the doctor was a broken neck. In time, he returned to say that an x-ray had revealed that as a child, I had broken my neck, but that the present injury was strained ligaments. The childhood injury that resulted in a broken neck was the incident I mentioned when we were talking about my childhood, when I fell backwards banging my head, which resulted in the injury which was missed by our elderly family doctor.

I was in the hospital, in this room for two weeks. There were two of us, myself and a naval officer. The two of us got on very well. On the first night there, we were telling each other jokes that had us in fits of laughter. Eventually we were told off by a nurse as we were making too much noise. After two weeks there, I was discharged and I returned to St Mawgan on July 10th, the day before my birthday.

In August and September, I only flew six times, three times in each month. These flights were basic exercises and circuits and landings. Nothing else of any note happened during this period.

On the 9th October 1956, not long before the Suez crisis, I gained my private flying licence, in an Anson, a twin-engine aircraft which was large enough to carry twelve passengers. Also, I didn't have to do any written exams, I went up with the instructor and did a circuit and landing. The instructor told me to go up on my own and to keep in sight of the airfield, so I did, for thirty minutes. That's how I got my Private pilots licence. It's funny really; it took me a year of hard work in Rhodesia to get my wings but only thirty minutes to get my private pilot's licence.

Weren't you a passenger on a Comet around this time?

Yes. As part of getting troops to Nicosia quickly as a result of the

Suez Crisis heating up, we of 228 squadron, then based at St Evel, were taken to Lynham, where on October 31st 1956, we boarded a Comet that took us to Luqa, in Malta, so we could transport troops from Malta to Cyprus. At one point, I asked one of the crew at what height we were flying and he told us that we were flying at forty-four thousand feet, which amazed me; I had gone From Orphan to Highflyer.

Wasn't the Comet facing structural problems at that time which had caused a few to break up in the air?
Well it had been through that phase, yes. It was public knowledge during this period that a few had disappeared so there was a degree of apprehension among us while we were in the aircraft. At one point during the flight, there was a bump as we went through an air pocket, which caused apprehension for a while, though the crew told us that it was quite common to experience things like that at such a high altitude.

Though you were only a passenger, what was your impression of the Comet?
It's a difficult one. For one, it was much faster; it got us to Malta in little over three hours whereas a Shackleton would take us six to seven hours to reach Malta. I also formed the impression that it was an aircraft that was well ahead of its time.

Tell me about your role in the Suez Crisis.
It was quite minimal really. I flew a Shackleton taking troops out to Cyprus on November 2nd 1956 and in December, I was bringing them back. How it worked is that the troops would be flown from St.Eval to Luqa, in Malta, and then from Luqa to Nicosia. I didn't fly over Egypt or conduct any raids or anything like that. All I did was transport troops from Luqa to Cyprus and back. Our first time carrying troops was to Nicosia in Cyprus. It was strange in the sense that when we got to Nicosia, air traffic control would not allow us to land as there was ice on the runway. So, we had to circle north of the island, aroundKyrenia, until it had been cleared. We eventually landed at around four in the morning.

After dropping off the troops, we flew back to Malta and stayed there for a few days. Whilst we were there, we saw one of the V-bombers take off, the noise was tremendous. Their target, as we later learnt was the main airfield at Cairo.

One thing we did hear is that apparently, there was a bomber pilot who refused to take off to bomb a target on religious grounds. I don't know what the target was but I would guess that it was Alexandria or the Port of Suez itself. Following his refusal, he was warned that he would either be court-martialed or he could resign his commission, in other words, to leave the RAF, which he decided to do.

During the crisis itself, did you stay in Malta in case things escalated?

No, after we returned to Malta after dropping off the troops in Cyprus, we returned to St. Eval the next day, on the 3rd November. In regards to flying, the rest of the month was taken up with instrument flying and exercises.

Though on December 11th, we flew back to Luqa, then from Luqa to Nicosia on the 13th to pick up troops again.

But one amazing coincidence happened when we flew the troops back to Lynham via Malta. Billy, my younger foster brother had been called up for national service in late 1946, then afterwards signed on. He had remained in the army during the 1950s, and during the Suez Crisis, he was posted out there. What we both didn't realise until the Christmas of 1957, when we compared notes, is that I was flying the Shackleton that he came back on, an amazing coincidence.

The next two months I don't remember too much of, there was no flying during this time, but I am sure that alongside ground duties, I had leave saved up. I flew twice in February and my last ever flight was on March 5th, taking up ATC cadets. It's quite symbolic to me. That my first time going up in an aircraft was as a cadet and my last flight was as a pilot taking up cadets.

In the weeks and months prior to your last flight, what were your plans going forward? You must have known that your time in the RAF was coming to an end.
Originally, I planned to go into air traffic control. In my mind; it was a way to get back overseas and the RAF did a course on it, which I applied for. Unfortunately, I was turned down on the basis that once I qualified, I would just leave the RAF and go overseas, which was true. There was a big demand for air traffic controllers overseas, especially in Africa.

After I was turned down, I was offered a 'Permanent Commission' which would have been a twenty-two-year contract once my current contract had ended. But I turned it down. I had met the woman who would later become my wife, and in my mind, I had to choose one or the other, so I chose her. But I did receive a letter from Air Ministry telling me that I could keep my rank of flight lieutenant.

Did you know that March 5th flight taking up cadets would be your last?
Yes, but I didn't really have any feelings at all about it. To me, it was just like any other flight.

What was your opinion of the Shackleton?
The Shackleton was an aircraft that I never took a liking to. It was big, noisy and tended to vibrate. It didn't have the manoeuvrability that the Lancaster had. The turn I did in Gibraltar, during the 'Battle of Britain' display. I could never have done it in a Shackleton.

It was a powerful plane with a dual purpose. One was as a maritime reconnaissance aircraft and the other was as a troop carrier. It could also be used as a bomber if a war was going on. It was an ideal plane for long range patrols over the oceans because it could stay in the air for anything up to twenty hours with an overload tank without refuelling, which was ideal for the Navy.

The one good thing that I can say about it is that it was a lot more stable in stormy weather than a Lancaster, which I believe was due to the increased power of the Shackleton, it could just bulldoze its way through.

CHAPTER SIXTEEN

COMING OUT OF THE RAF

Working in a children's home, a chilling discovery, running a car business and life as a civilian.

March 5th 1957 was your last flight and you began terminal leave over a month later, on the 22nd April. Did you have any idea what your next step would be?
Yes. I had an idea to set up a car delivery-collection service based in Falmouth, which is where myself and my lady, Ruby lived at the time. So it wasn't as though I was lost in regards to what I would do with myself as a civilian. However, I was persuaded to go into youth work.

In my last few months with 228 squadron, I had become a PETLO, which stands for Pre-Entry Training Liaison officer. The previous chap had been posted to Gibraltar and the C/O wanted me to take on his role. This position was basically the link between the Air Training Corps and the RAF. When the cadets from the ATC came to St Mawgen, it was my job to organise their accommodation, schedule, the contents of their lectures and other activities. They would occasionally have the opportunity to go up in an aircraft, and it was my job to organise that. In fact, as I have already mentioned, my last flight was taking up a group of cadets.

The senior officers at St Mawgen believed that I was good at PETLO duties, so they recommended that I made it a career. The education officer arranged two interviews for me, one was for a juvenile prison type of place in Surrey, and the other was a place named 'Lambeth Children's Reception Centre', in London. The main problem with the first place was the atmosphere, it was horrible. On top of this, there was a handbook filled with things that I would not be allowed to do. There was a lot of them, there was a lot of restrictions there. When I went in for the interview, I sat in a chair and in front of me was close to fifteen people sitting in a semi-circle before me: doctors, social workers, staff from the facility and a nurse too. After the interview and a tour of the facility, I was asked if I could return for another interview but I just told them that I was not interested at all. Their response was to ask me if I would be interested in an interview for the place in Lambeth, which I agreed to. It was completely different to the first, with a much better atmosphere, but the main difference was there seemed to be a greater sense of freedom. So I agreed to try the position for a month.

If we include your four years in the reserves, you were in the RAF for nineteen years, with only a gap of a year and a half after you had finished your time in Norfolk. Was it hard for you to adjust back to civilian life?
Not at first because I immediately went into youth work, and it was something that I enjoyed.

Tell me about the youth work.
The children themselves could be there for a number of reasons. The courts would send us children who the education system couldn't cope with or various other reasons. There were cases of parents going through a divorce and whoever had custody of the child or children couldn't cope with that situation. Sometimes, one parent would just vanish, abandoning the home in the middle of the night leaving the other parent unable to cope, things like that.

Under the structure of the superintendent in charge, there were two senior boys' houses, for boys who were thirteen or older. Then there was one junior boys' house which were for boys from age five to thirteen. The junior house had a house father and house mother. The two houses for senior boys had a house father and house mother and two part time house mothers. Each house had a cleaner too. The role of the house mother and house father was to be like surrogate parents to the boys. There was also a girls' house on the same site, but separated from the boy' houses. The girls' house took in all ages and just had a house mother in charge and an assistant house mother. There was also a nursery type set-up for boys and girls below the age of five, which a nurse oversaw.

There was also a school on site with its own staff. It had been created by converting what had been a junior boys' house into classrooms. The whole site of the homes was quite large in that it had its own admin block, a huge meeting hall attached to which was a large kitchen. It had a gymnasium, its own swimming pool and another hall that would fit in every child for special occasions, like for example, Christmas. At other times, every child ate in their own houses, with meals being prepared in the main kitchen and transported to each house via trolleys which the houses provided.

Every Friday, I as a house father for one of the houses for the senior boys, a house mother who worked until 8pm and a psychiatrist, would write reports on every boy and how they interacted with everyone, their general behaviour, and things like that. Those reports would then be passed on to the superintendent.

Considering that you spent around four years in an orphanage, what was it like for you to be back in a similar environment, except this time in a position of authority?
Overall, I found it an interesting job. I definitely had a great deal of empathy towards the children and their situation, of which my experience during growing up must have had a great influence.

The first thing I did was to appoint prefects in each dormitory. I did it to lessen the load on my behalf and to keep the boys well behaved. Everyone had to be up at half past seven. It was then up to them if they wanted a shower or strip wash, which the prefects dealt with. Afterwards, it was breakfast which would be brought from the main kitchen on trolleys. After breakfast, I would choose two boys to take them back. Then they went to school, which started at nine. From there, the school took control of them, they had lunch in the main hall. At around five, they would come back to my supervision and have a light meal. During this meal, I would tell them what activities would be available afterwards, things like table tennis, snooker, football, volleyball, to keep them entertained. One thing I introduced was that every Friday, I introduced something called 'mad hour'. I told them that they were allowed to use the gymnasium and all its equipment and make as much noise as they like. If they wanted to fight each other, I would let them do so, as long as it was done with boxing gloves on and under the condition that I would supervise them. There were wrestling mats that they could use too.

How did you keep these boys disciplined? There must have times where one or two would try and push their luck.
I found that the best solution to that problem was to interview every boy there and any new ones who came in. It was something that we were meant to do anyway. During this interview, I would ask them what their favourite pastime was, then if they misbehaved, I would curtail that activity. So if they liked football, I would take the opportunity to take it away from them. I also had a reward system in place. For example, for the boys who were best behaved, I would organise trips into London or to the countryside. I would only take a small group that I could keep a watch over myself. This resulted in the boys behaving well in the hope that they would be chosen to go on one of these trips. Some of the boys, who were from London, had never seen the countryside before, and they were amazed when they saw fields and farmyard animals. However, the most successful reward system I had in place was to organise a dance with the girls' house also invited.

How did the dance come to be?
I decided that it would be good for the boys to mix with girls as they would have if they were living under normal circumstances. So I asked the superintendent who agreed and then went to speak to the house mother about it and she agreed. But I said that I would need at least one house mother there, preferably two. That was agreed to.

Honestly, the first dance was an experiment, I had no idea how it would all work out. I decided to keep it a secret until the last second, so I told the boys that an official from the Home Office was coming so they had to dress in their best clothes and make the place look spotless so they would make a good impression. When I eventually told the boys what was going to happen, I can tell you, I had never seen them in such an excited state. They were all trying to get into the showers, all putting on their best clothes, doing their hair, trying to make themselves look as nice as possible for the girls. I told the boys that they could bring any records that that they wanted to dance to.

Did it prove to be successful?
Very much so, it was something that I repeated, and enjoyed doing so. The boys really enjoyed it and the house mother in charge of the girls told me that the girls really enjoyed it too. Even the Superintendent came along with his wife and congratulated me on my idea. It was nice for me to see these boys and girls, with less than ideal backgrounds, enjoying themselves so much.

It seems like you had a good relationship with the boys under your supervision.
Yes, we were a happy house on the whole. I never smacked any of them, hitting them was banned anyway. I only had a few bad incidents while I was there. The only one that comes to mind is when one of the boys called one of the house mothers a 'stupid cow'. That really angered me. I called him in to see me with her present and asked him if he wanted to apologise. His response was something like, 'No, she is a stupid cow'. In a flash of anger, I slapped him on the back of the thighs, which caused him to leave the room crying. It was something I have always regretted doing. He apologised to her the next day and incidentally, those two became the best of friends.

It seemed like a job you enjoyed, why did you leave?
I had been considering moving back to Cornwall and setting up a car collection and delivery business that I had in the back of my mind since my last year in the RAF. But one incident made me decide to leave. I was doing some work in the office when one of the boys came in and told me that one of the boys from my house was having a serious confrontation with another boy who wasn't in the home, who had come from the outside. This other boy was a known troublemaker and would often come into the grounds for whatever reason. Anyway, I went outside to find them squaring off against each other. The boy from my house was holding a cricket stump

while the other boy was holding a piece of wood. I got between them and just shoved the other boy out of the way. I told the boy from my house to get back inside and the other boy scampered off. I thought that was the end of it but once he got home, he told his mother who contacted the police saying that I had smacked her child. The policeman came to interview me, to hear my side of the story. After I had finished recounting what had happened, the policeman went to speak to the mother and boy. Eventually he came back and told me that after speaking to them, it was the mother who had smacked her son for misbehaving, causing him pain in his ear, and it resulted in them trying to put the blame on me. Fortunately, the police officer had found this all out while speaking to them, so I was told that the matter was closed and nothing else would come of it.

But what really made me decide to leave was that we now had a change of superintendent who was not as helpful to staff as the first one had been. He called me into his office and told me that if an incident like that happened again and it went to court, I would have to deal with it myself, I wouldn't have the support of the home. It was then that I decided to leave and move to Cornwall with Ruby to set up the car collection and delivery service.

When I told the superintendent of my intention to leave, he told me not to tell the boys until the last possible moment as it would upset them. When I eventually told them, the reaction was awful, half of them were in tears, it really tore at my heart. Honestly, I would be lying if I said that I didn't reconsider leaving. It was horrible to see them in such a state, but I had decided to move back to Cornwall and set up the car collection business.

I later found out that the chap who took over from me was unable to control the boys, that they had run riot and he had to be moved to the junior house, who he also failed to control, resulting in him being asked to find another job.

But there's something else I must tell you about this children's home.

What is it?
Well after I left, I kept in touch with one of the staff members there. After Ruby and I had moved back to London, I would go and visit him in his office at the children's homes to catch up and have a game of cards or something. He had been promoted to superintendent by this point. Anyway, on one occasion he told me that he was short of staff, so asked me if I would be willing to look after the boys in the junior house for a few hours as a one-off as the House fatherhouse father had an appointment he was at and the house mother was away on holiday.

Anyway, I agreed to help. However, during my time there, I had never even stepped foot in the block where the junior house was before. To get there, I had to walk through the dining hall and kitchen area, and something felt strange, but I just couldn't place my finger on what it was. So I arrived there, and the chap who usually looked after the boys would read them a story, so that's what I did. They were very well behaved and quickly went to sleep. Once they were asleep, I went for a wander around the block and found myself in the upstairs dormitory. It no longer housed children so it was used as a storage room. When I entered the room, I switched on the light, which emitted a slight blue hue, and that's when memories started to flood back. I remembered where my bed would have been located so I began to search for my initials that I knew I had carved into the wall, but I wasn't able to find them. I then remembered that I would have been half the height at the time so crouched down, and there it was, carved into the paint:'DK', which stood for Denis Kimber, my name at the time. That's when I fully realised, that I was in the orphanage that I entered at around the age of three and a half. It was then that other memories started to flood back, like the area where my own mother came to visit me on the few occasions that she did. At this point, I basically froze, I could feel all the blood rushing out of my face. I quickly left the room and went back to see my friend. He asked me if I was OK as in his words, it looked as though I had seen a ghost. I told him that I had to go, making up a reason why I had to. After I left, I never went back.

What a harrowing story, and to think that you worked there for a good period of time without realising it was where you spent so much time as a child.
Well it was a different part of the set-up. I was with the seniors and never went anyway near the junior block. But it's a horrible event for me to recall, truly awful.

Why do you think that in your time working there, you never realised that it was the site of your orphanage?
Well during my time working there, I never went to the part of the grounds where the juniors were housed, or in my case, where I was housed when I was there. Also, I was a small boy when I was living there, so I had no reason to go to the senior side of the grounds. One must remember that the site itself was very big. Because I was a small boy when I was there, I guess that I just forgot and blocked out a lot of it.

Going back a bit, tell me about the car business.
Setting up the business took longer than anticipated though, mainly due to the difficulty in getting insurance for any vehicle and acquiring trade plates for the vehicles that I would be driving. This is because the council wouldn't release the trade plates until I had insurance and the insurance company wouldn't insure me until I had the trade plates. Eventually, the council gave in.

It started off as purely collecting new cars from Rootes Group in Birmingham or Morris's from Oxford and then driving them back to Cornwall. It would take quite a while as there was a strict running-in speed of thirty miles an hour for the first thousand miles, which was meant to run the engine in.

Eventually, I got to know a chap who transported second hand cars from the South West to Southampton and Brighton, so I started driving second hand cars to those places for him. I would then travel to Birmingham or Oxford and would drive a new car back. There were two main garages in Falmouth, one dealt with Hillmans and the other with Austins, and I dealt with them both, alongside others.

How it worked is that someone would make an order for a new car with the garage in Cornwall. Then I would take their old car to whoever was buying it up country then drive a new car back to Cornwall, to a buyer or a garage. I scheduled it so more often than not I would drive a car there and back.

What sort of cars were you driving?
I was mainly delivering Morris's and Austins. I once delivered a Ford Zephyr which was owned by an American chap who wanted it taken from Cornwall to London to a place where it could be shipped to America. It was a left-hand drive which made it somewhat difficult for me. It was quite a powerful car, big too; it could seat six and had a bench seat at the front.

I remember that I eventually had the brainwave that some holiday makers must get ill while on holiday and would need their car driven back. So, I registered with The AA so that I would be able to drive back anyone who was unable to drive back themselves. On one occasion, a family had been on holiday in Looe when the father had a heart attack, leaving his wife and two children stranded while he was being treated in hospital. I was contacted by The AA regarding driving the family back to Hull while the father remained in hospital.

I inspected their car and discovered that the windscreen wipers didn't work. They had to be fixed before we could depart. Both her and her husband ran an insurance company with a few staff members so it was essential that they got back to Hull. The windscreen wipers were repaired that day and we set off for Hull. I pointed out that it would be dark for most of the way. She had never been in a car at night, nor had the children, so they were all fascinated with the different lights and signals that they were seeing. We stopped at a café called the 'Black Horse' in Exeter to have a light meal and let everyone use the lavatory, otherwise, my only other stops were for petrol. We arrived on the outskirts of Hull at half past six in the morning. The lady was fast asleep so I had to wake her up so she could navigate me to her house. She later phoned to say that her husband had made a full recovery. That journey must have been in 1958.

How long did the business last for?
Just under two years. Everything was going well but I then made a mistake, I took on a partner. He turned out to be a liability to the business.

By the way, it was during this time that my foster mother passed away. I had received a phone call from her biological son to say that she was in hospital and didn't have long left and that if I didn't come now, I wouldn't have any chance of seeing her again. So I drove back to Kent that same day. She had suffered a stroke, but when I arrived at the hospital and saw her, she was able to talk and communicate. After my visit, myself and her son went back to her home, which was no longer in Gladstone Road, but in Borkwood Way, which is in Orpington, so not far. She had moved while I was in Malta. It wasn't long after we arrived back that a colleague of her son, who worked at the hospital, came by and told us that she had passed away.

I stayed in Kent for around five days, helping to organise the funeral and everything else that had to be dealt with. After all of that had been sorted, I went back to Cornwall.

Upon my return, I discovered that while I was in Kent, a garage owner had an urgent request for a car that had to be sorted out that day. The garage owner phoned my partner who said that he could not do the job as he had a wedding to attend. The result of this is that the garage owner lost the sale and told me that he never wanted to see my partner again.

Though things like that didn't help, what really killed the business was Falmouth Docks going on strike. The result of this was that people stopped buying new cars and as a result, were no longer selling their old ones. As a result of all this, the car business quickly dried up.

So what did you do?
I managed to find a job as a 'Second Salesman' in a men's outfitter

which I held for just over two years. During my time there I was called in for two weeks RAF reserve service in Plymouth in July 1959. There was no flying; it was all ground work, things like going over the theory of exercises with the Navy.

During my time with the outfitters, I had married Ruby, this was in 1962. Though I had been with her during my time in the RAF, I had not wanted to get married while I was serving or in the reserves. I had seen quite a few pilots enter marriage then get killed a short while later. I had no interest in testing fate, so I waited until I was no longer flying to get married. We were never blessed with any children due to a medical issue that Ruby had. Though Ruby suggested that we foster children, I was against it due to my experience as a foster child. To me, fostering a child would have constantly brought my childhood to the forefront of my mind, and it wasn't something I wanted to go through.

But the biggest mystery is that not long after our wedding, I received a letter of congratulations from Blackburn.

From Blackburn? How did he find out that you were married?
To this day, I have no idea how he found out. He was a wing commander which is quite a high rank, and the story I told you about having the engines re-fitted on his German E-Boat suggests that he had contacts in high places, so I am sure he could have pulled a few strings to find out my address considering that my wife and I lived in the same house as we did during my time in the RAF reserves. But I wasn't even in the reserves when I got married, so my marriage can't have been in RAF records, so how did he find out about it? Also, he must have kept tabs on me for quite a while. I can't imagine that the first time he checks up on me just so happens to be when I got married. It's an amazing coincidence if it was the first time. Assuming he did check up on me over the years, why did he do it? To this day I can't answer these questions.

Unfortunately, your job with the outfitters wasn't to last.
The job itself was steady, but during my second summer there, it

seemed to rain non-stop. This caused the boss to cut staff numbers, and he did it on a principle of last in, first out. I was the last staff member to join so I was the first one out. He was kind enough to give me a suit as a farewell gift. This was in October 1962.

Fortunately, during my time at the outfitters, I had passed a three-month telephone operators course and had got a job as a telephone operator part time, so I was still employed.

What was your next step? Being a part time phone operator can't have been a long-term solution.
At the end of 1962, we moved to Saltash which isn't far from Plymouth. There, I got a job with the Co-op, in their accounts department. I was there for just over a year before a high number of staff were let go, including myself. Unfortunately, I wasn't entitled to redundancy as I had not been with them for two years, which was the minimum required time to be entitled to it.

What came next?
Due to the lack of employment opportunities in Cornwall, we decided to move back to London, where there were many more jobs available. This was in the latter half of 1964.

Looking back, did you enjoy living in Cornwall?
Oh yes, it's a nice county to live in. Living in Falmouth, there were plenty of swimming opportunities. But the people were very clannish. Ruby had a friend who came down and stayed from London and once when we were in a shop, she openly started saying how she was from London, like it was a badge of honour, something to be proud of. The result was that she was cold shouldered and I told her it was the worst thing she could say.

Another example is a chap I worked with in the Co-op, he was ex Navy. On one occasion, he told me that a friend was coming to visit him from London. When I enquired which part, he told me that he was coming from Peterborough, which is a different city all together. 'It's all London on the other side of the Tamar,' was his response, half joking, half serious.

I don't know if the attitude is the same now, maybe it's changed. Still, it was a nice county to live in.

London was next for you.
I had gone up ahead of Ruby to London, by this time the house in Saltash was put up for sale. I got a bed and breakfast room in Bromley in Kent and from the local newspaper I applied for a position of housekeeper on Ruby's behalf in a Roman Catholic family helping to look after their house and children. In return, on top of pay, they provided rent free accommodation without bills. During this time, I had gained a job with ESSO petroleum company, near Victoria station, London, in their accounts department. I was only with ESSO for less than a year. What happened is that I had gotten the job through an agent. This chap had set up a firm putting people in work. But how it worked was that the company that his client worked for would give the workers' wages to him, who would then give it to the worker but not before taking a cut. Once I found out about this, I promptly quit with ESSO and cut all ties with this agent, who ended up being murdered.

Murdered?
Yes, someone walked into his office and shot him. As my name was on his books, I was questioned by the police regarding the shooting, but only the once.

Where did you go from there?
I went to work for a firm called 'Ultra Electronics', in the accounts department. Ruby had only lasted three weeks or so with the Roman Catholic family before finding another job that she enjoyed, which was helping to look after a young man with Downs Syndrome. We had also found another flat in West Ealing, which was very nice.

I was with Ultra Electronics for about four years. They made electrical equipment, things like irons, radios and televisions. They also had a government contract for sonobuoys which was ironic as I was dropping them a few years earlier.

After four years with them, I applied for a job with the accounts department of a company named 'Metal Box'. This was around 1969-1970. The reason is that the terms and pay at Metal Box were better than those at Ultra Electronics.

Metal box produced cans of various sizes. Including the overseas factories, they had fifty one in total, eleven of which were known as 'open top'. They were known by this name because they turned flat metal into cans without the top on. It was done his way so Heinz or whoever, could fill each can with whatever they wanted. However, Metal Box did produce the tops for the cans but they were sent separately. The other factories produced a variety of products. Some produced 'flat sheet products', like trays, biscuit tins, things like that. Others produced paper items, cheque books being a prime example, though I was only concerned with the open top.

Was it a good place to work?

It was a very good place to work, we had our own accounts office and I worked with a good team and we all got on well. It also had its own sports and social club; it also had its own canteen. All of this led to a good working atmosphere.

After a few years of working there, I was promoted to 'Stock records controller'. In this new position, I had to cost every material coming into the factory and the bits and pieces that would go with it. There would be the calculations of the cost of converting the flatplate to cans and the overall production cost, to give to the factory manager who held a daily meeting with myself and the upper tier of the factory regarding all of this information. In these meeting, I would provide the estimations of the cost of all the materials and everything else that would be required for the following day's production.

During this time, Ruby was still working with the Down Syndrome boy.

Everything went well for the next few years until around 1978, when labour disputes caused my factory, in Acton, London, to close, alongside the open top factories in Glasgow and Liverpool. I was asked to stay on until April of the following year, to provide final financial figures.

Towards the end of that year, the mother of the Downs Syndrome boy retired and they moved to Devon. His mother had a sister already living there who agreed to be his housekeeper, so that put Ruby out of a job.

With both yourself and Ruby facing unemployment, what did you decide to do?
Fortunately, Ruby and I had bought the house in Waterloo Road, Norwich, in 1974 as an investment. So in 1978, when we both lost our jobs, we decided to move into it.

Tell me about your time living in Norwich.
I heard that Norwich Union were looking for two commissionaires, which is a person in uniform who directs people to the relevant department that they are looking for alongside keeping out troublemakers. Their response was to inform me that both positions had been filled but that in light of my accounting experience, they could offer me a position in their accounts department, which I took up.

Fortunately, they were a good company to work for. Unfortunately, I was there for just under five years which ruled me out of their pension scheme.

The reason I left Norwich Union is because they had a policy that everyone, regardless of position, had to retire at the age of sixty. So when July 1984 came along and I turned sixty, it was my turn to retire.

My opinion on Norwich was still the same as it had been when I visited there during my time at Swannington, that it was a great place. The people were friendly, it had a great atmosphere, great market and wonderful shops.

What came after Norwich?
After my job with Norwich Union ended, we sold the house in Norwich and moved to Dereham, a small town in Norfolk. Personally, I could never take to Dereham. There was nothing of interest there. When we first arrived there, the surrounding area was nice but within time it was all built on. There used to be two lovely strawberry fields that I enjoyed walking the dogs through, but one became an industrial estate and the other had houses built on it. When we first moved there, I took a year out from working and in 1986, went back to work as a carer for the elderly.

It was quite a lengthy career for you.
Yes, it was something I did for around ten years and as a result met some interesting people along the way. I was fortunate with my first client because we got on very well. I was with him for three years until he died. He came from quite an affluent background but was a genuinely nice man.

The rest of the clients I had over the years were a mixed bunch, some I liked more than others. In fact, one had a brother who was a Japanese prisoner of war; he was put to work on the Burma railway, though he never spoke about it.

In 1994 you moved to Suffolk.
A few years prior, Ruby had passed away, she was the victim of a very severe stroke. She was taken to a hospital in Dereham which specialised with stroke victims. Unfortunately, while she was there, she suffered another stroke, which sadly proved to be the end.

Afterwards, I decided to move, but it took two years to sell the house. During this time, I was in residence with a client. After the house was sold, I moved to a town in Cambridgeshire, to a converted slaughterhouse, but I didn't like the place at all. The first house I found was in eastern Suffolk, so I moved there. By the time I made the move, I had decided to fully retire but the care agency managed to convince me to take on one more client who I was with for six months at the most before he died from stomach cancer.

Was it hard to adjust living on your own in a new area after so long?
No, because I had two dogs who needed to be taken out and a good-sized garden to attended to. I have always been quite comfortable in my own company and I had good neighbours, so it wasn't really difficult or anything like that.

How long were you there for?
I was there for twenty-four years, from the age of seventy to ninety-four, from 1994 until 2018. In those years a lot changed. For the majority of my time there, until my late eighties, I was quite active, walking dogs, gardening, going into town and meeting with friends. But eventually I started to slow down, as happens to everyone. In 2005 I sold my last car; I sold it to your mother, which is how you and I first met.

Even without a car, I still kept active, especially with the garden. I would walk into town and get the bus back, go to the beach to swim, walk in the countryside, socialise with friends.

By the early 2010's, you, your mother and myself had become quite good friends and we would go shopping together, socialise and have days out, which we still do. It was around this time that you started to help me with my garden.

But in April 2018, after a few days of bad health, I had a serious fall which resulted in me being trapped on the floor for twenty-eight hours unable to move. During this time, you and your mother became concerned and phoned the police and paramedics who broke in and released me. During a lengthy hospital stay you helped organise new accommodation for me which is where I am now, and from where we are now working on this book.

CHAPTER SEVENTEEN

REFLECTIONS ON AN UNBELIEVABLE LIFE

You have lived an extraordinary life. You have experienced and witnessed things, both horrific and magnificent that most people will find very difficult to comprehend. What thoughts come to mind when you look back on your life?
What really comes to mind are memories of my mother from when I was around three years old, such as when I was out walking with her, and an older girl, a half-sister, and my half-brother. I was pulling a toy horse on a lead and as the toy moved, the head bobbed up and down. Another memory that comes to mind is the statue of Queen Victoria outside of Croydon town hall. I was upset and stomping my feet that the pigeons were landing on everyone else's hands except mine and my mother telling me that if I stood still, they would come and land on me. On this occasion, both my half-sister and half-brother were there.

Considering your childhood, it's impressive that you went on to achieve everything that you did.
I would say it's astonishing how things turned out. Growing up, I always lacked confidence compared to boys my own age and it wasn't until I joined the ATC that I began to realise that the results I was achieving were just as good as everyone else, both physically and mentally.

There's no doubt in my mind that World War Two was a positive event for me personally and in some respects, was for my generation. In a way, it gave us freedom from the old stiff rules of British society and gave us opportunities that would never have been available otherwise. Even before going overseas, when I was in the ATC, I learnt so much and picked up so many skills.

What positive effects did the ATC have on you?
It made me more confident in myself, in my ability to achieve things. I also met new people and made new friends, there was a good sense of camaraderie among us. On Saturdays, we had a social event put on which also included civilian girls. This camaraderie I mentioned was also reflected in society. People were more open and friendly towards each other, there was this sense that everyone was in it together, fighting for the common good. The ATC was something I really looked forward to, even the lectures. It became the most important part of my life. Acquiring these skills, and the increase in confidence lead me to look forward to what the future had in store for the first time in my life.

Not only was the ATC enriching my life, but in my day job, in the showroom, so many of the staff had been called up that I quickly advanced within the business. When I first started, I simply swept the floor, but by the time I was called up, I was an assistant cashier and was in charge of the storeroom where things like plugs, fuses and cables were stored. I really enjoyed the responsibility I had. I flourished in these new roles, and I actually enjoyed going to work. I looked forward to the next day, to work and the ATC. It was an interesting time. More than once I would be cycling home with the sound of German aircraft overhead, alongside the sound of anti-aircraft fire and the sight of searchlights.

All of the things I have spoken about would never have happened if it wasn't for the war.

To go from working in a showroom to being stationed on the African continent in less than a year was a huge step, a change in every way. How do you look back on that time now?
I look back upon it with the feeling that I had then. I went from feeling that I had not achieved anything to feeling that I was achieving so much. During my time on the African continent, I saw, experienced and achieved so many things. There was a constant sense of eagerness for what lay ahead. Everything in Africa was such a novelty to me, it was completely different to Britain in every

single way. I remember being in school listening to the Geography Master talk about his travels to Egypt and seeing things like the Sphinx and a few years later, I was standing in front of it, seeing it and taking photographs of it. Amazing.

But the crowning achievement for me during that period was earning my Wings. So much went into it that to earn them was a spectacular achievement. It was something that in my earlier years of little self-confidence, I never thought I would reach.

After going solo for the first time in the Tiger Moth, I felt more mature and confident in myself. There was a brief period that I even slipped into overconfidence. I was up in an Oxford and was preparing to land at Kumalo, near Bulawayo, and I looked out of the port window and thought to myself that I was the only person on board who could land this aircraft. I then performed a terrible landing which taught me a lesson about overconfidence.

Looking back, Africa was an interesting continent. I grew to like Rhodesia; it was my favourite country on the continent, even though I only really saw one city there, Bulawayo.

Is Palestine, as it was called then, somewhere you look back on fondly?

Yes, being in such a historically rich area really made me feel that I was a part of history which has proven interesting considering that many people now study the period of time that I was there. Jerusalem was such an interesting city to me. To read about places in the Bible and to then visit them, and see them with my own eyes was extraordinary. It's a place that I would have liked more time and more money to explore.

How do you look back on India?

On the whole I liked India, I liked the people. It's hard to describe, but as busy as the cities were, there seemed to be a relaxed feeling at the same time. It's a country I could quite happily visit again. It was in vast contrast to Malaya where there was definite tension in the air. Look at it this way, in India I could walk around any city by myself without any worries, but in Malaya, we were told to never go out alone and were even issued with side arms during our time there. Fortunately, they never had to be used, but when we first arrived in Malaya, my crew and I were billeted in an old Nissen hut. We used to take turns turning out the light at night. On one occasion I told my co-pilot that it was his turn to turn off the light. He just grabbed his pistol and shot out the bulb. So at least they were used for something.

Looking back on my time in India, I don't recall seeing huge feelings of animosity from the populace towards the British, especially when you compare it how other peoples felt towards their occupying power. It's amazing how things changed so drastically a few years later.

It's quite extraordinary to think that at the age of twenty, you were captaining Liberator aircraft and flying operations.
During that time, my age didn't really come into my mind. It wasn't until after I had finished the tour that I thought about it and realised that I had completed a full tour and I wasn't even twenty one. To put it into context, the average age of a Liberator captain on our squadron was twenty-four.

To me, it's extraordinary that in under three years, I had gone from working in a showroom to captaining bomber aircraft. When I look back on those years, from call-up to operational flying, I feel that in that time, I reached the maturity of manhood.

It can be argued that your age helped you. You have already spoken about not fully appreciating danger at that age, and that must have helped you during your operational flying.
It certainly did. I couldn't see or appreciate the danger that the more mature captains could. For the most part, each operation was an adventure to me. I had no real fear of going on them. I think I have already mentioned it, but there was the occasion that one of my engines wouldn't start so I couldn't go with the rest of the squadron

and I was given until one in the afternoon to take off. I kept nagging the ground crew to get my plane airworthy so I could join everyone else. Most pilots would have been happy that they didn't have to take the risks that came with bombing a target, but I was desperate to get up in the air. I just wasn't scared.

I can't say I ever really did develop that sense of danger. I think a big part of it is the fact that I just love flying so much, all I wanted to do was to get up in the air, and that love of flying overshadowed any fear I might have had.

But looking back, some of the things I did were mad, sometimes I can't believe I did them. Like the journey to meet Laurie, when I put the Dakota on autopilot and played cards with the crew in the back. No one was keeping a lookout in the cockpit, all of us were in the back. The only reason I went into the cockpit every so often was to check on an oil leak. But someone, preferably me, should have remained there, keeping a lookout for things like other aircraft and making sure that everything was working. Other mad things like beating up airfields and coming in so low to land and hopping over trees at the last second, it's hard to believe I did those things. I'm certain that it was because of my age and not appreciating the danger element that I even did those things. Happy days!

Looking back on them, what are your thoughts on the operations themselves?
The tour of operations itself turned out a lot easier than I expected, with one or two exceptions. Going in to the tour, I expected to come under a lot more anti-aircraft during our flights. But of course by that time, the focus of the Japanese was heavily focused towards the Pacific region. This resulted in Japanese troops and equipment being pulled out of Burma and being sent to the Pacific.

Having said all this, we lost eight aircraft during my tour, which was half of the aircraft on the squadron, of which I saw three shot down myself. Another three, which I didn't see, were shot down and two just disappeared, it was theorised that they collided into each other.

So the danger that the Japanese posed was certainly there. But it's a miracle that we didn't suffer more collisions as on occasion; the entire squadron was attacking a single target.

But completing a tour made me feel that I had achieved what I had been trained for, what I had spent years working towards.
Flying my own Liberator at the age of twenty, I can't get over that.

Which operations are you most proud of?
The three raids on Penang harbour are achievements I am really proud of. This is largely because everyone believed that it wasn't possible and we proved them all wrong. Also, at least on the first occasion, we took the Japanese by complete surprise; they were not expecting it at all, resulting in the operation being a complete success. It's amazing that we flew for nineteen hours non-stop.

The occasion that we dropped Napalm bombs leaves me with a sense of achievement because it resulted in us completely wiping out an essential Japanese supply depot which depleted their ability to continue fighting the British army. Also, it took a week of training to prepare for that one raid because the target was in quite a concentrated area and the Napalm bomb and incendiary bombs had to be dropped in a specific way. It was also the only occasion that I dropped bombs myself, so that sticks out in my mind because it was the navigator who usually dropped the bombs or mines.

Your operations seem to have generally been a resounding success, with 159 squadron working like a well-oiled machine. How much of this do you think was down to Blackburn, the C/O?
Blackburn had an uncanny way of organising quite unusual raids, The Penang raid and the Napalm raid as examples, would never have happened without him. I found that if I was flying my own plane to a target and I knew that he was also flying to the same target, it made me feel safe, that everything was going to be OK. What it boiled down to was that he inspired confidence in people. As I have already mentioned, when I met up with him later on, he

admitted that he made a mistake in allowing me to go to the target when I met the one in the afternoon deadline after one of my engines wouldn't start. He claimed that not only was he worried about me, but that if anything happened to me, the obvious question in the enquiry would be what was he doing allowing a twenty-year-old to carry out an operation entirely on his own.

I was fortunate to have him as my C/O, especially at that time in my life and under those circumstances. During my career with the RAF I had a good number of C/Os, but he was by far the most competent; he was excellent.

How did the war change you?
It made me mature more quickly. When war was declared, I had not long left school, but with all the men I was working with soon being called up, I had to take their place and take on their responsibility, adolescents had to grow up fast. In a short time I had gone from sweeping the showroom floors to taking on jobs that came with real responsibility and that was before the RAF came into the picture.

The training itself was excellent. You can't dispute the standard of training that the RAF provided and because of it, I learnt so many new things that I never would have learnt otherwise.

Fortunately, my new found confidence and acceptance of responsibility served me well in that I quickly adjusted to the fact as captain of an aircraft; I had a lot of responsibility. I was responsible for not only my life, but the lives of my crew too in the sense that I was flying the aircraft and had to keep it in the air. As captain, I was also in the position to give orders. It's quite a lot to take in, especially when you are only twenty years old.

Since you were a boy, key decisions have altered the course of your life. For example, whether to go into the Air Training Corps or the Sea Cadets, or whether to re-enlist with the RAF. With all this in mind, do you have any regrets?
Only one outstanding one. I wish it had been possible for me to

go into the Sea Cadets. I love the sea, I really do. For example, the troop ship we were on for five weeks, most of the others were bored and sick of it. But I loved every minute of it, I really did. I looked forward to every day and spent as much time out on the upper deck as possible. I believe I would have been well suited to the Navy. I remember that when I was twelve, we went on a choir outing to Chatham in Kent, where we went on board the King George V Battleship. I soon separated from the group and was exploring everything, the gangways, going up and down steps and just taking it all in. I was eventually found, but even then, I loved it.

What about Blackburn's offer to meet him in Marseille?
Yes, looking back I regret signing on with RAF because if I hadn't, Blackburn's letter still would have come but I would have been able to take him up on his offer. I certainly regret not being in a position to take him up on that offer though it wasn't so much Blackburn as it was the pulling power of the sea. The idea of being out at sea on a yacht for extended periods of time really appealed to me. If the two options of signing on with the RAF or taking him up on that offer had both arisen at the same time, I would have been off to Marseille in a flash, no doubt about it.

Is there anything you regret not doing?
That's a tricky one. I suppose it goes back to not being able to go into the Sea Cadets and then the Navy. I also regret not being able to go to Hong Kong when the opportunity arose when I was on 228 Squadron . I liked the idea of going somewhere new and was looking forward to the opportunity to fly the Sunderland Flying Boat. But these things are sometimes taken out of your hands.

What are your total flying hours?
Let me look at my log book. I flew 3543 hours as a pilot or co-pilot. However, I'm certain that it's actually more as I know that I flew on a few occasions but didn't enter it into my logbooks. Out of the 3543 hours, 2172 were on Lancasters and 362 on Liberators and the rest were on various other aircraft. I was also a passenger for 450 hours.

So according to my logbooks, I have spent 3993 hours in the air.

How many different aircraft did you fly in total?
About fifteen in total, a list of which is in the addendum after this chapter.

Out of all the aircraft you flew, which one did you like the most?
The Lancaster, because it was so highly manoeuvrable as I demonstrated against the Vampire jet in the 'Battle of Britain Display' in Gibraltar.

However, the Liberator was certainly more advanced than the Lancaster. For example, many things within the cockpit of a Lancaster are operated by levers which could be a job to operate, while the Liberator has switches which one just flicks. Also, in typical American style, the Liberator was built for comfort, with padded seats and the like, there was even armoured plating behind the pilot's seat to protect him from the back. Blackburn had this removed for the Penang raids to help achieve the range needed to reach the target, which there and back totalled around three thousand miles and nineteen hours spent in the air non-stop. Even though the Lancaster had cushions instead of padded seats and was not as advanced as a Liberator in many ways, it was still my favourite aircraft.

The flying you did involved many risks, especially on operations. What you went through, did it have any effect on your religious views?
I have always believed in God, right from early childhood. I told you how my second foster father had died on the same day as I received my wings, well I believed that he had passed on in order to become my guardian angel, to keep me safe, a conviction I still hold to this day.

Also, while I was stationed at St Mawgam, I became friendly with the Methodist minister of the area and went to the service every Sunday, if flying duties permitted. To this day, I still say my prayers every night before going to sleep.

What are your thoughts when you look back and see how much Britain has changed in your lifetime?
One immediate thought is that British society has lost its authoritarian side and what is left of it is virtually non-existent. The respect that figures like policeman and teachers used to have has fallen a lot. Figures like the ones I have mentioned used to receive automatic respect whereas now, people snub their noses at them, for lack of a better saying. In short, authority is losing its grip. Before the war, gun and knife crime hardly existed, unlike now where it is so often in the news.

I'm sure that when you stepped foot on to the SS Rangitiki you had all these hopes and dreams for what the future held. Did you achieve your dreams?
For the most part yes, I thoroughly enjoyed all the different adventures I experienced and all the travelling that came with it. I visited all the places I had read about, especially India. I was especially attracted to India. I remember being in school and the Geography Master asking me to trace the flow of the river Ganges, and there I was years later, flying over it. Achieving my wings and flying were other dreams that came about.

Not being awarded the DFC, an award that Blackburn recommended that Frizzy and I both have, an award that I had been told about so many times, all because of a change of C/O is very unfortunate.

Is there anything else that you would like to add?
Looking back, I was rather surprised how quickly the time went by, bearing in mind that I was in the ATC and RAF from 1941 up until 1961.

Thank you for your time Denis.
Thank you for your time.

ADDENDUM

AIRCRAFT THAT I FLEW

Aircraft type	Hours flown
Tiger Moth (single engine)	77
Comments: It was an excellent training plane, easy to fly. I learnt to preform many acrobatics in it. The one weakness was that if one performed a three point landing, the skid risked breaking.	
Air Speed Oxford (Twin Engine)	157
Comments: It wasn't an aircraft I particularly liked, but at the same time I didn't dislike it. It wasn't difficult to handle but one had to be careful when landing so as not to land nose first as the propellers would make contact with the ground.	
Vickers Wellington (Twin Engine Bomber)	107
Comments: Wonderful plane, my first feeling of real power. It seemed to easily push its way through the air. A wonderful plane to handle.	
Liberator (Four Engine American Heavy Bomber)	362
Comments: A truly lovely plane, it handled very well. The crew positions were well thought out. The pilot seat was luxurious, it even had armrests. It was great to handle and the autopilot was very good which helped on long distance operations.	

<table>
<tr><th>Aircraft type</th><th>Hours flown</th></tr>
<tr><td>Vickers Warwick
(Twin Engine Passenger)</td><td>96</td></tr>
<tr><td colspan="2">Comments: A plane I didn't like. After the Liberator, the Warwick seemed rather cumbersome.
Handling wise, it was average.</td></tr>
<tr><td>Dakota
(American Twin Engine Passenger)</td><td>224</td></tr>
<tr><td colspan="2">Comments: The Dakota was a marvellous plane, well ahead of its time. It was claimed that it could still fly on one engine with a five thousand pound load.
I have never heard one word said against the Dakota, it handled very well and was a joy to fly.</td></tr>
<tr><td>Sentinel
(Single Engine Passenger)</td><td>37</td></tr>
<tr><td colspan="2">Comments: A light single engine aircraft that I found easy to fly with all the experience I had built up by the time I flew it.
It's claim to fame was that it could land in very small spaces.
It was easy to handle</td></tr>
<tr><td>Argus 1 & 2 (Single Engine Passenger)</td><td>5</td></tr>
<tr><td colspan="2">Comments: Like the Sentinel, it was easy to handle. To me, it was quite similar to the Sentinel.</td></tr>
<tr><td>Proctor
(Single Engine Passenger</td><td>1</td></tr>
<tr><td colspan="2">Comments: There isn't much I can say about the Proctor as I just borrowed it to get up in the air, only flying it for a single hour.</td></tr>
</table>

<table>
<tr><th>Aircraft type</th><th>Hours flown</th></tr>
<tr><td>Avro Lancaster (Four Engine British Heavy Bomber)</td><td>2172</td></tr>
<tr><td colspan="2">Comments: My favourite plane, it handled so well. It had comfortable seating and didn’t provide me with any problems with taking off, handling or landing. It was highly manoeuvrable too.</td></tr>
<tr><td>Chipmunk
(Single Engine Passenger)</td><td>6</td></tr>
<tr><td colspan="2">Comments: The only comment I can make about the Chipmunk was that it was a little difficult for me to adjust to it after so many hours flying Lancasters.
Once I had adjusted to it, it was easy to handle. I sometimes performed aerobatics when I was flying it.</td></tr>
<tr><td>Anson
(Twin Engine Passenger)</td><td>2</td></tr>
<tr><td colspan="2">Comments: I only flew it once, for two hours, so like with the Proctor, it’s difficult for me to comment on it.
The plane I was tested on for my private pilots license.</td></tr>
<tr><td>Avro Shackleton (Four Engine British Heavy Bomber</td><td>297</td></tr>
<tr><td colspan="2">Comments: It was the plane I liked the least out of all those that I flew.
Though it was a powerful aircraft, it was very noisy, it vibrated.
In my opinion, its handling didn’t match that of the Lancaster.</td></tr>
</table>

Aircraft in as passenger	Total hours
Tiger Moth Blenheim Short Sunderland Beechcraft Expeditor Dakota Valetta Anson Comet Hastings Lancaster Bomber	450

Printed in Great Britain
by Amazon

41249189R00161